IMAGES
of America

FORGOTTEN BATON ROUGE

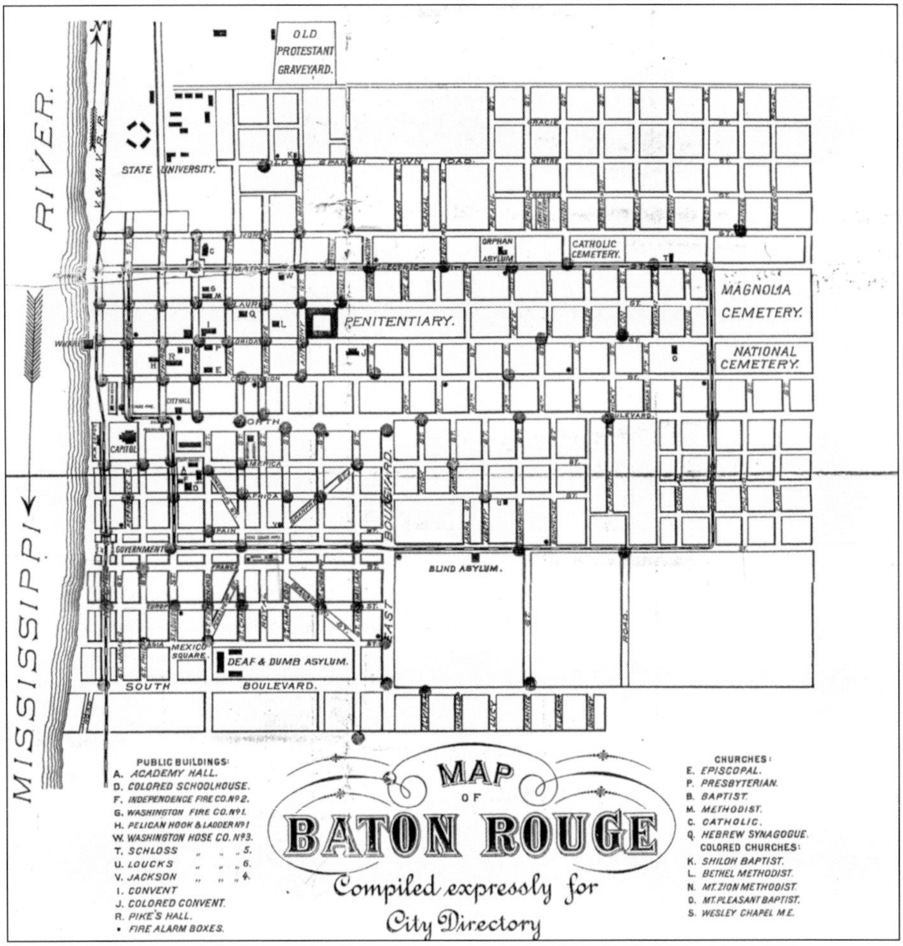

In the 1890s, the incorporated area of Baton Rouge was approximately 240 squares (city blocks) and was composed mainly of residential structures. The city was roughly 1.5 square miles of developed land with a few large tracts comprised of farmland. The city limits reached as far north as Bayou Gracie, University Lake, today Capital Lake, and the US Government Grounds. The city limits extended no farther eastward than Duggan Street, today Twenty-second Street, and the east side of Magnolia and National Cemeteries. The southern city limit boundary ran along an east-west line between South Boulevard and Railroad Avenue, today Myrtle Avenue. A few of the oldest subdivisions were called towns, such as Spanish Town, Beauregard Town, Aubert Town, Grass Town, Tivolier Town, Devall Town, Hickey, Duncan and Mather Town, and some exceptions went by different nomenclature like Suburb Swart. (Courtesy of the East Baton Rouge Parish Library.)

On the Cover: In this photograph, the front of city hall on North Boulevard provides a backdrop for Chief Justice Breaux of the Supreme Court of Louisiana as he administers the oath of office to Gov. Jared Y. Sanders. For the May 18, 1908, inaugural occasion, a large crowd of supporters gathered along the parade route decorated with strings of incandescent lights that crisscrossed Third Street at 100-foot intervals from North Boulevard to the Pavilion on the university campus. The parade featured marching bands and clubs from schools around the state, and the evening concluded with fireworks on the university campus and an inaugural ball held in the Pavilion. (Courtesy of the State Library of Louisiana.)

IMAGES
of America

FORGOTTEN BATON ROUGE

Douglas L. Villien Sr.
Foreword by Davis S. Rhorer

ARCADIA
PUBLISHING

ISBN 978-1-4671-1477-6

Published by Arcadia Publishing
Charleston, South Carolina

Printed in the United States of America

Library of Congress Control Number: 2015945449

For all general information, please contact Arcadia Publishing:
Telephone 843-853-2070
Fax 843-853-0044
E-mail sales@arcadiapublishing.com
For customer service and orders:
Toll-Free 1-888-313-2665

Visit us on the Internet at www.arcadiapublishing.com

To Maude G. Villien, who never forgot Baton Rouge

CONTENTS

Foreword

I first met Doug over 30 years ago when we worked together at the East Baton Rouge Planning Commission. As Baton Rouge grows, it is here that the delicate balance must be struck between preserving the legacy of one of Louisiana's strategic river towns and promoting smart growth and development of the next great American city.

Since our time at the planning commission, I have worked to revive the bustling heart of the city as Baton Rouge's first director of downtown development. This has included renovating and restoring to the public sites of critical historical significance, including revitalization of the two oldest neighborhoods in Baton Rouge: Spanish Town and Beauregard Town.

Like many cities across the United States, Baton Rouge underwent a period of rapid and at times unchecked modernization and suburbanization during the latter half of the 20th century. This period witnessed the destruction of far too many landmarks and historic structures in the name of progress. Much as some of the grandeur and personality of New York vanished with the demolition of Pennsylvania Station in 1963, so too was a part of Baton Rouge irreparably lost when the theater that once crowned the city's civic life and architectural persona, the Paramount, was razed and replaced with a parking lot in 1979.

In spite of this loss, Baton Rouge has witnessed nothing short of an urban renaissance in the restoration of its oldest residential districts, riverfront, historic train station, and most prominent of all the Gothic-inspired Old State Capitol. The shadows of the past, embedded in the facades of its Jazz Age skyscrapers like the old Heidelberg Hotel and Louisiana National Bank Building, are no longer expunged but rather embraced by new investment seeking to capitalize on all that makes Baton Rouge unique. And while the paddle-wheel riverboats of Mark Twain no longer serve as the region's lifeline to the outside world, these Mississippi River icons are once again docking in Baton Rouge with increasing frequency, disembarking tourists from around the world.

As our community continues to develop and progress, *Forgotten Baton Rouge* reminds us not just where we come from but who we are as a citizenry. It is in recognizing our heritage that new development best serves the community. Doug Villien's latest book is more than a rote archive of Louisiana's capital city; rather, it is a reminder of our academic, economic, civic, and political heritage.

—Davis S. Rhorer
Executive Director
Downtown Development District

ACKNOWLEDGMENTS

This work could not have been possible without the help of very knowledgeable librarians Jessica Lacher-Feldman and Judy Bolton of the LSU Libraries, Special Collections; Charlene Bonnette, head of Louisiana Department, State of Louisiana Library; and Melissa Eastin, archivist, East Baton Rouge Parish Library. I am grateful to Douglas Perret Starr, Phd, retired professor emeritus of journalism at Texas A&M University, for the cache of information he provided from his research and archives. I offer many thanks to Thomas Edward Hart, son of photographer William B. Hart, Ernest Ritchie of Rembrandt Studio of Baton Rouge, and Malcolm P. Ewing Jr. of Jasper Ewing and Sons, Inc.

I would like to express sincere appreciation to Faye Phillips, retired associate dean of the LSU Libraries, for giving me support and encouragement during this writing.

I gratefully acknowledge and extend my appreciation to Randy Bringhurst for his technical knowledge and advice on graphics and imagery.

Thanks to Florent Hardy, Phd, and Bill Stafford of the Louisiana State Archives for their assistance and access to records. Also, I owe great appreciation to Wendell Huffman, curator of history at Nevada State Railroad Museum, and to John Sykes, Magnolia Mound Plantation manager.

I sincerely thank Heather and Jeff Frantz for editing and technical assistance. I wish to thank my editors at Arcadia Publishing, Lydia Rollins, Maggie Bullwinkel, and Jesse Darland, for their encouragement and technical advice in moving this project forward.

Finally, I express my deepest appreciation to my wife, Karen, for her patience and understanding through the duration of this work.

In an effort to improve the flow of the text and increase the size of the photographs, a key to courtesy abbreviations is listed below:

CBR—City of Baton Rouge, Planning Commission
CHM—Chicago History Museum, DN-0008646
DLV—Douglas L. Villien Sr.
POVPC—Dr. Paul O. Villien Sr., private collection
ESBR—Elk's Souvenir of Baton Rouge
EBRPL—East Baton Rouge Parish Library
JES—Jasper Ewing & Sons, Inc.
LSS—Louisiana Secretary of State
LSUSC—LSU Libraries, Louisiana State University, Special Collections
NSRM—Nevada State Railroad Museum
SLL—State Library of Louisiana
TABR—*The Advocate*, Baton Rouge

Introduction

A hard look at this city reveals a great American story. This settlement dates back to 1699, when a tall reddish pole on the bluff of the Mississippi River, placed there by Native Americans, was only a waymark called Baton Rouge by French explorers. The settlement's growth was very gradual for nearly 180 years. A number of flags flew over this city until the Stars and Stripes was raised here in 1810. In 1846, the seat of state government was moved from New Orleans to Baton Rouge. During the Reconstruction era following the Civil War, the population grew, in part, due to the migration of African Americans leaving rural plantations for jobs in the city. When the US Army departed its stronghold on the Mississippi River and closed its military outpost, David F. Boyd, professor at the Seminary of Learning of the State of Louisiana, pursued an opportunity to move the university from Pineville to Baton Rouge. When the state obtained a lease on the vacated Army post and transformed it into a home for Louisiana State University, Baton Rouge's economic growth was profoundly changed.

Between the 1890s and 1930s, Louisiana was still rebuilding after the Civil War and moving toward a fast-paced age. This period was politically called the Progressive era, which had deep-seated effects on almost every aspect of society, including economic, political, social, educational, and moral reforms. The nation as a whole was experiencing a new beginning with a proliferation of inventions that flooded the marketplace, and all were influenced by Progressivism.

As the 19th century closed, Baton Rouge came of age to the new urban industrial and corporate lifestyle that was part of the new America. The city became less reliant on the business of farms and plantations. Reformers of the Progressive period worked to make changes in education, labor, suffrage, philosophy, and political platforms. Success of Progressive programs came in the form of Prohibition, boards regulating public health, child-labor laws, women's suffrage, and a good roads program. The city's rate of growth was astounding under forward-thinking leaders. One of the most aggressive politicians of local government was Robert A. Hart, who served as mayor from 1898 to 1902. His push for issuing bonds for infrastructure improvements was historical. The bonds financed new schools for whites and blacks, drainage, sewerage, and paving of streets.

By 1912, Louisiana reached a milestone and celebrated its first 100 years as a state. The city of Baton Rouge was witnessing significant commercial and residential growth spurred by improvements in transportation, communication, and industry. Congress enacted legislation making Baton Rouge a port of entry for foreign trade, and Standard Oil of New Jersey established a refinery and deepwater port. The refinery developed into one of the largest oil refineries in America. The sleepy little river town was changed forever.

In a short span of time, the city and parish began to experience changes in wealth and prosperity not experienced since before the Civil War. Improvements in transportation led to increased river and rail activity. Larger ships visited the deepwater port of the oil refinery, and railroads connected to cities in all directions. Railroad companies such as the Louisiana Railway & Navigation Company, Yazoo and Mississippi Valley Railroad, Louisiana and Arkansas Railway, Illinois Central Railroad, and Texas and Pacific Railway were a few of the routine lines to Baton Rouge. Passenger and freight transportation gave cause for establishment of Baton Rouge's own board of trade, which influenced railroad rates significantly. In addition, the Yazoo and Mississippi Valley Railroad built a large brick depot on Natchez Street across the street from the Old State Capitol.

Employment in Baton Rouge soared with the arrival of the new refinery. The devastating flood of 1912 sent thousands of refugees from outlying towns and villages to the city searching for employment as well. Many of them remained in Baton Rouge after the floodwaters receded. In a short span of time, the landscape had changed with dozens of new residential subdivisions built to accommodate the growing number of citizens. Between 1910 and 1920, the population nearly doubled.

By the 1920s, Louisiana State University had grown to its geographic limits. The campus was hemmed in, with no available acreage for growth. The university acquired a 2,000-acre tract called Gartness Plantation, located south of Baton Rouge, through a purchase by friends of the university in 1918. The university hired the notable Olmstead Brothers to plan the campus. By 1921, a plan for a new campus was complete, and construction started in 1922. From that year, the landscape south of Baton Rouge began an immense transformation, with numerous buildings designed by Theodore C. Link, an architect from St. Louis, Missouri. The new campus was dedicated on April 30, 1926.

Baton Rougeans also witnessed a surge in construction of modern buildings downtown during the 1920s and 1930s. Presented in this work are images captured by well-known photographers of the high-rise buildings that changed the skyline of the city. Most of the high-rises ranged from four to eight stories in height, and the first skyscraper, Louisiana National Bank, reached a height of 12 stories. In 1932, Baton Rouge's tallest building, the new Louisiana State Capitol, was completed in the Art Deco style and reached a towering 450 feet in height with a total of 34 floors.

In 1918, another forward-thinking politician came to Baton Rouge and left an indelible mark on state politics and eventually changed the landscape of the city. Huey P. Long was first elected member of the state railroad commission and quickly fell out of favor with utilities companies, railroads, and Standard Oil Company. When Long became governor in 1928, he made enormous increases in expenditures for public education and particularly LSU. While the new campus was in its early stages of construction, Governor Long assured LSU that its building program was to have the finest facilities, faculty, and winning football team. By 1930, the third-rate institution had risen to the 11th largest in the nation.

Governor Long continued to change the landscape around Baton Rouge through the 1930s by initiating an aggressive road- and bridge-construction program. He created a modern highway system by paving thousands of miles of roads throughout the state. He pressed and achieved, not only a new state capitol constructed of stone and steel but also a new governor's mansion modeled after the White House.

This Forgotten Images volume from Arcadia Publishing presents a visual history of Baton Rouge as it appeared during a period of its most significant rate of growth. Changes were happening as fast as the shutter speed of the cameras. The images chronicled in this book were assimilated from a few of the well-known photographic collections on Baton Rouge during that period, as well as a newly unveiled private collection photographed by William B. Hart. All of the images in this presentation contributed to the visual history of this city, a place with a great American story.

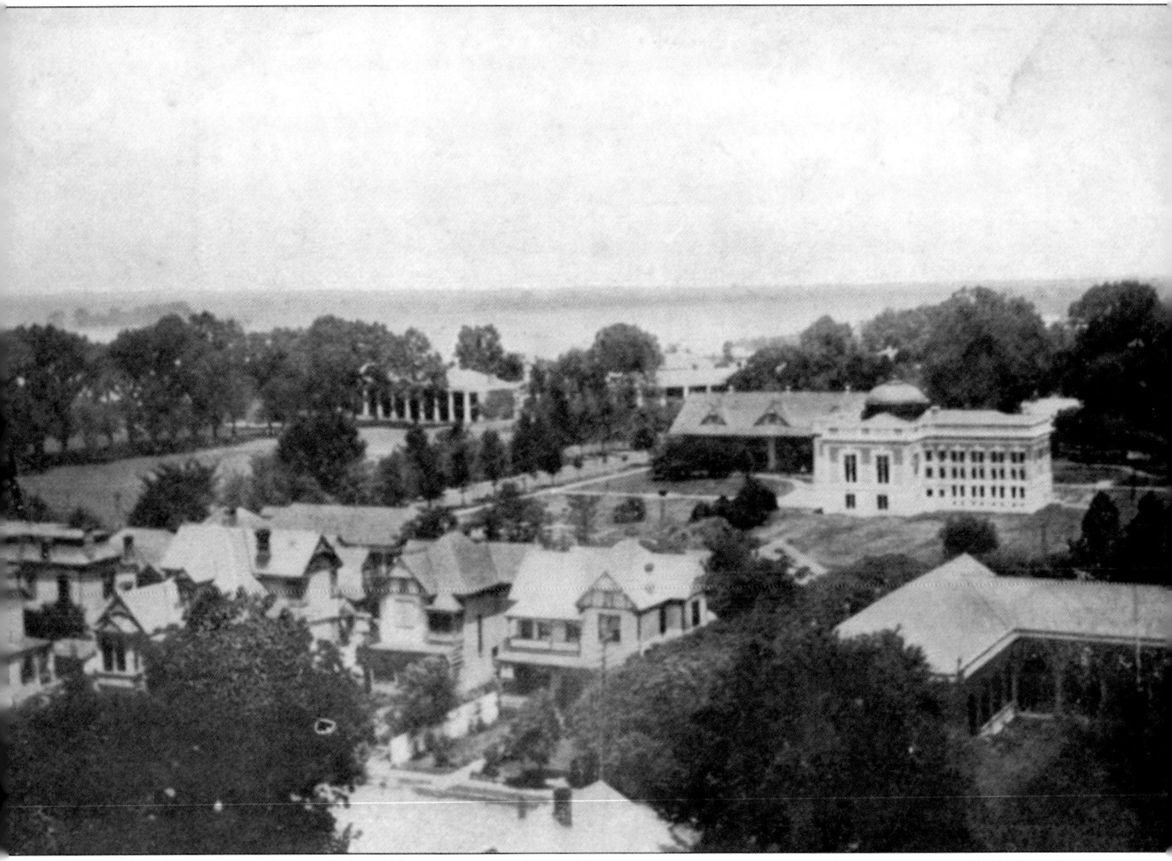

This bird's-eye view of the old Louisiana State University campus was taken around 1900. Looking northwest, it depicts Hill Memorial Library (domed building) on the right and Garig Hall and the Pentagon Barracks in the upper center. This photograph predates Alumni Hall, which broke ground in 1903. (LSUSC.)

One

Louisiana State University

The founding of Louisiana State University predates the Civil War. Its establishment and site selection for a permanent campus were equally uncertain, as were the political discussions for a name change. The arduous task began with the first campus site in Pineville, Louisiana, in 1852. The school was called the Seminary of Learning of the State of Louisiana. The school opened in January 1860, with 19 students under the guidance of William T. Sherman, superintendent. Other faculty included David F. Boyd (professor), Francis Smith (professor and commandant of cadets), Anthony Vallas (professor), and E. Berté St. Ange (professor). Events relating to the future of the university in the ensuing years were fraught with pressure from secession, a war between the states, military politics, and catastrophe. Despite all adversity, the seminary survived the war, but in 1869 it was without a building or classrooms, which were lost in a disastrous fire. David Boyd, seminary superintendent, made arrangements for the school to move into a wing of the Institute for the Deaf and Dumb in Baton Rouge only a few days after the fire. The temporary relocation from Rapides Parish to East Baton Rouge Parish became permanent.

In a short span of time, Boyd was able to persuade the state to purchase the 200-acre army arsenal north of town as Louisiana State University's new permanent campus. Though the campus was in great disrepair, its size sufficiently met the needs for university horticultural gardens, the Pentagon Barracks filled the requirements for dormitory and classrooms, and a couple dozen other buildings on the former military post were easily transformed for university use.

By 1918, the university decided that the campus on the north side of Baton Rouge was hemmed in with nowhere to expand. A new site was selected and purchased south of Baton Rouge. Nine friends purchased Gartness Plantation, and by 1925 enrollment began with 1,712 students.

Images in this section highlight buildings, relics, and events of both the old and new Louisiana State University campuses from about 1890 to 1930. During this period, university football, among other programs, gained prominence among the nation's colleges. The school's impact on Baton Rouge had an important influence on the city's development.

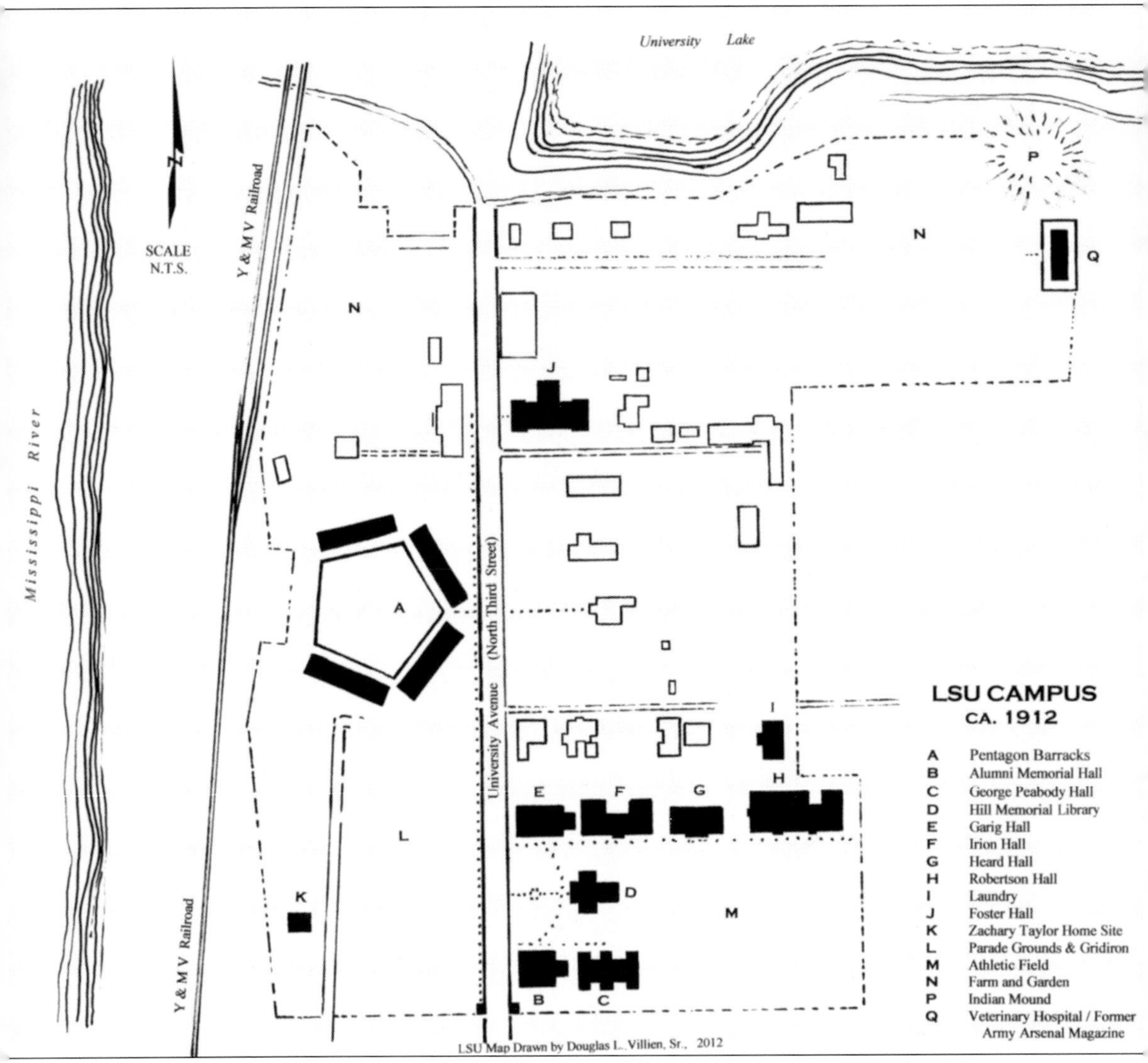

The Pentagon Barracks, Zachary Taylor's home, and the magazine were among the oldest existing relics from when this site was an Army arsenal and before it was transformed into the Louisiana State University campus. Affectionately known as the "Ole War Skule" because it was founded as a military academy, it was easily adapted to a military-style school. The buildings shown on this map depict how the campus was laid out in 1912. A decade later, the university began its transition to a new campus south of Baton Rouge. (DLV.)

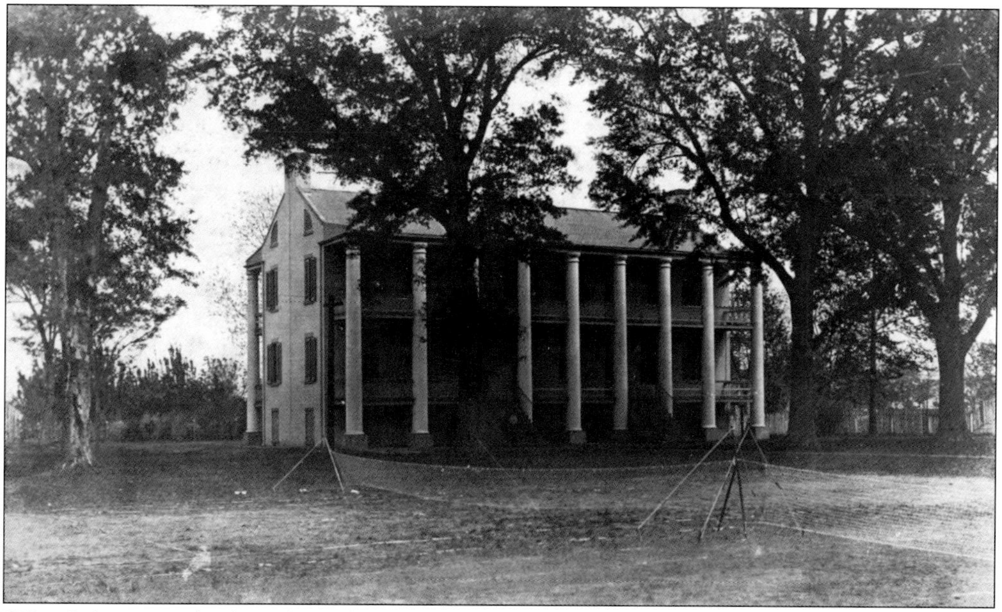

"The Colony" was built in the early 1800s when the site was a US Army post. When LSU moved its campus here, the building was initially used as living quarters for the mechanics professor and the university treasurer. The two-story building was converted to a student dormitory around 1905. (LSUSC.)

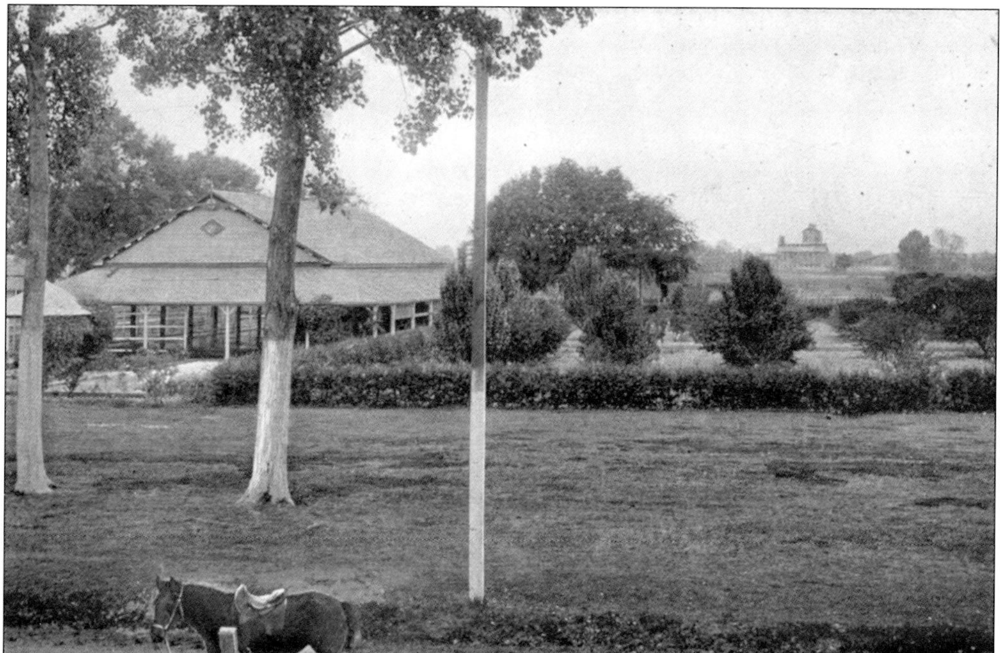

The building on the left was known as the Pavilion on LSU's old campus. It was located along University Avenue north of Foster Hall. The old sugar factory can be seen in the far right background of this c. 1900 photograph. The building was regularly used for university activities and social events. Gov. Jared Y. Sanders, among others, held inaugural balls in this building. (LSUSC.)

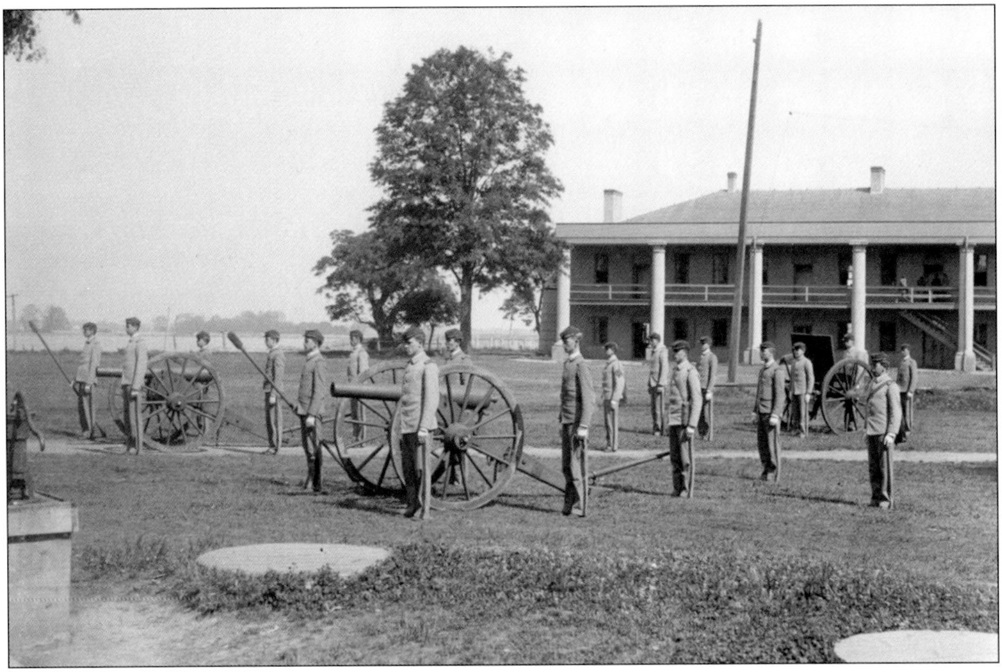

Cadets repeatedly trained in a variety of military skills. On the grounds of LSU's campus, cadets became acquainted with the theory and practice of the artillery art, including how to disassemble, clean, and assemble every weapon assigned to their unit. Here, cadets and instructors, in routine practice, prepare to fire cannon toward the river. (LSUSC.)

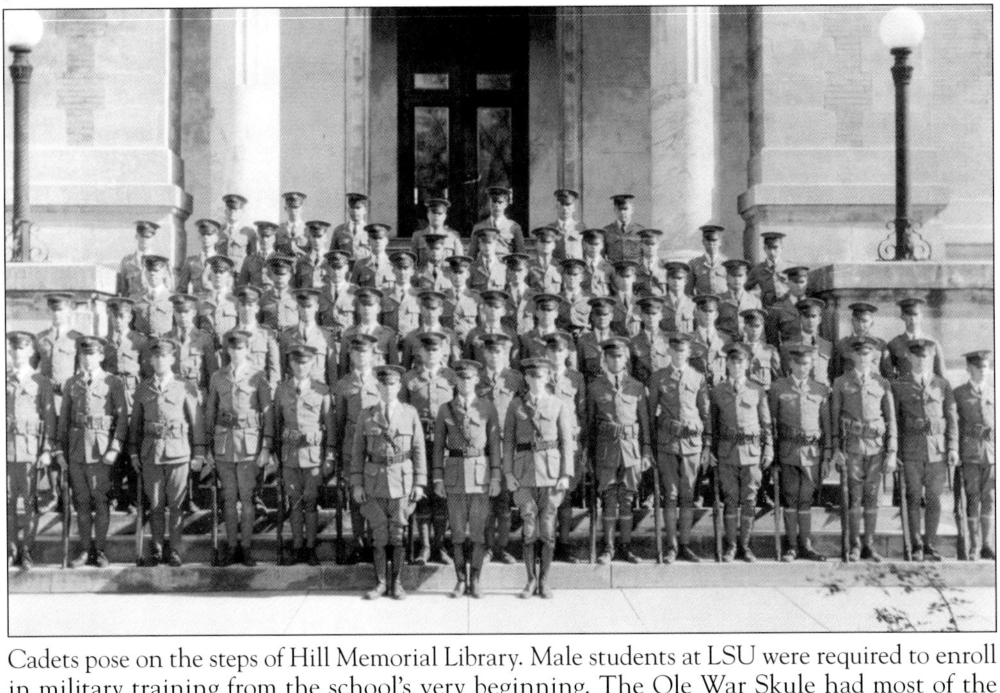

Cadets pose on the steps of Hill Memorial Library. Male students at LSU were required to enroll in military training from the school's very beginning. The Ole War Skule had most of the components of a US military post. In 1921, the battalion consisted of Companies A through D, a motor-transport corps, and a machine-gun company. (LSUSC.)

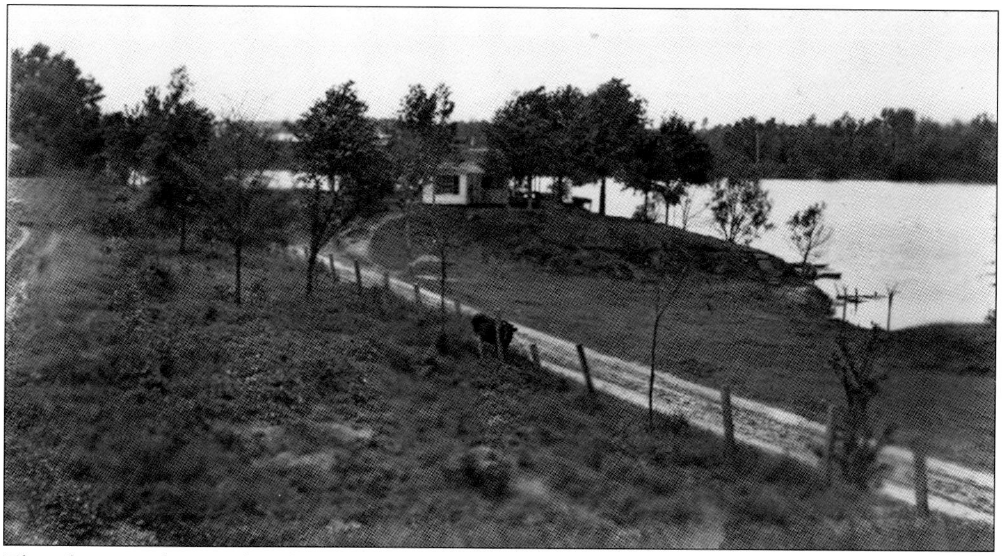

This photograph was taken from atop an Indian mound located on the university's old downtown campus. The vantage point of this mound overlooks University Lake (today Capitol Lake). Archeological digs estimated the age of the Indian mound to be approximately 5,000 years. The site surrounding the mound was one of three agricultural stations in the state, used by the School of Agriculture for experimental gardening and later as the site for the new state capitol, which was completed in 1932. The campus was located between the northern limits of the city and this man-made lake that was formed by damming Bayou Grassie, a natural tributary of the Mississippi River. (POVPC.)

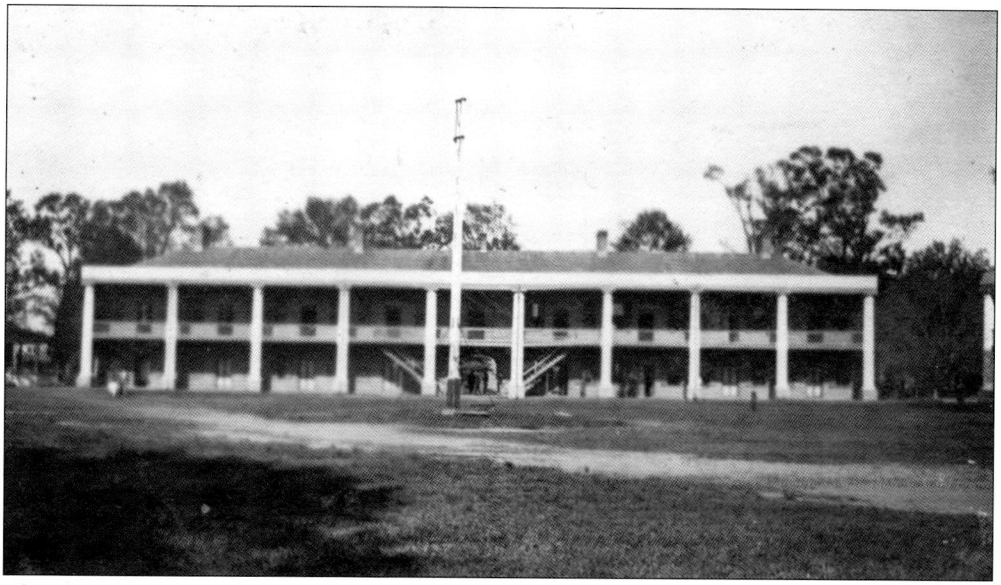

The plans for the Pentagon buildings were completed 1818, but construction began in June 1819. The Classical Revival military barracks were completed in 1824 under the direction of Capt. James Gadson and Joel Hill. The buildings were used as living quarters by US Army soldiers, Confederate army soldiers, and Louisiana State University cadets. After LSU moved to the new campus located south of Baton Rouge, the State of Louisiana converted the buildings into legislative apartments and offices. (POVPC.)

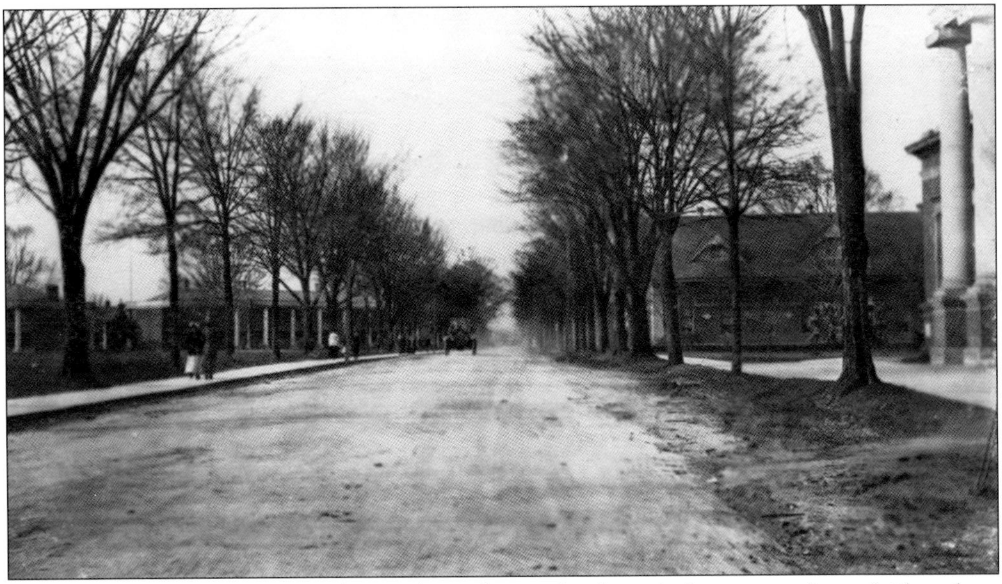

In 1912, University Avenue was the north-south corridor through the campus. It was laid out long before the university arrived in Baton Rouge and moved onto the old Army post. The avenue was an extension of Third Street, which radiated northward from the heart of downtown. After LSU relocated to its new campus south of Baton Rouge, the street was renamed North Third Street. In this image, the Pentagon Barracks are visible on the far left, with Garig Hall and a portion of Alumni Hall visible on the right. (POVPC.)

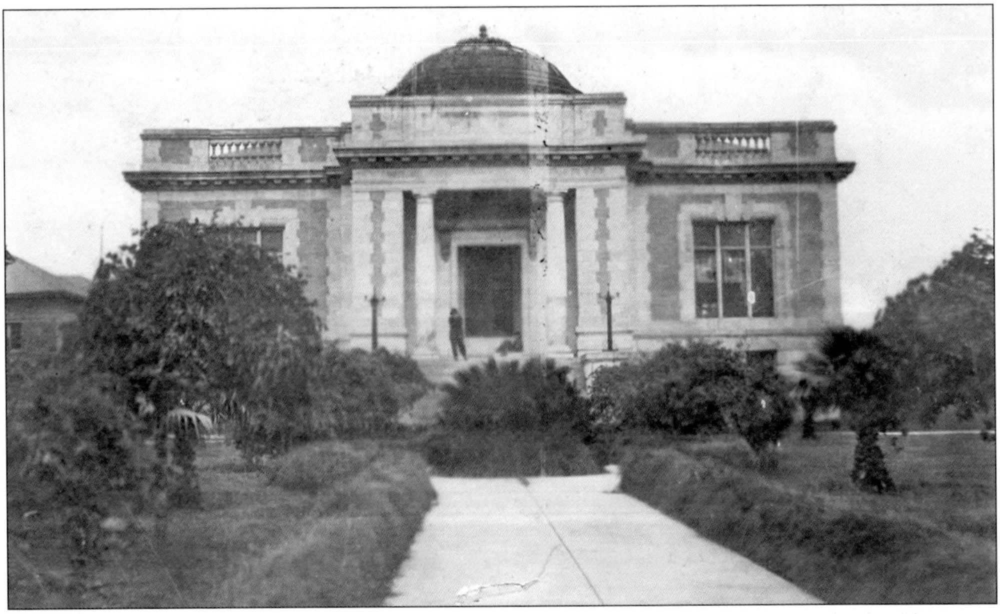

Hill Memorial Library was one of LSU's most prominent buildings in 1903. The building was named in honor of its benefactor, John Hill Sr., who provided funding in memory of his son John Jr. In 1907, the library was designated a Federal Depository Library, one of 43 in the United States. By 1908, the law school was established, and its home was in Hill Memorial Library. The law school consisted of one room for its library, two lecture rooms, and two offices for professors. (POVPC.)

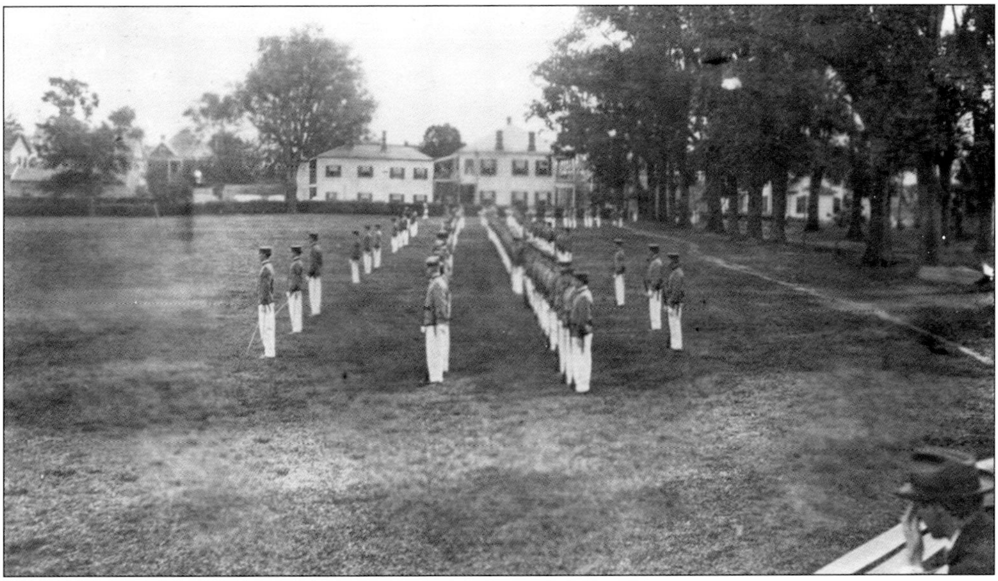

Cadets shown here are at attention in regular marching and drill practice on this campus field. The football field was referred to as "the gridiron," a descriptive term introduced around 1880 in modern American football. The field was commonly used for exhibitions, parades, and a variety of athletic events. The avenue of oaks shown on the right side of the photograph was also known as Lafayette Avenue, which bordered the west side. The gridiron spanned from near North Street to Barracks A of the Pentagon, the length of the file of cadets seen here. Beyond the oak trees on the right was the home of Zachary Taylor before he became president of the United States. (POVPC.)

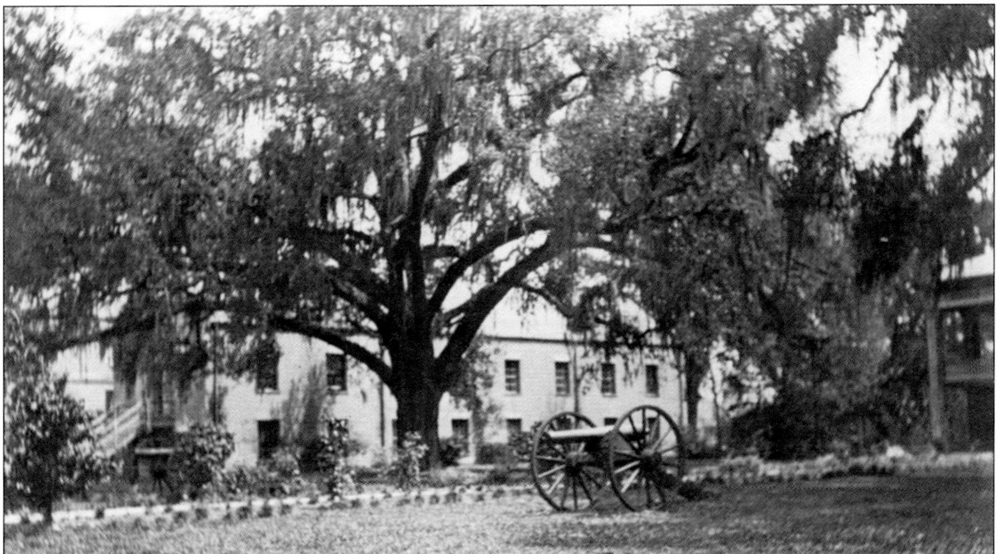

Photographer William B. Hart was greatly impressed with the historic significance and legend of the twin cannons that were said to have fired the first volley of shots on Fort Sumter on April 12, 1861. Gen. W.T. Sherman arranged for the procurement of the two brass cannons from historic Fort Sumter, South Carolina. The cannons were gifted to LSU from General Sherman. Here, the cannons appear to guard the entrance to Col. Thomas Duckett Boyd's residence, visible on the right. (POVPC.)

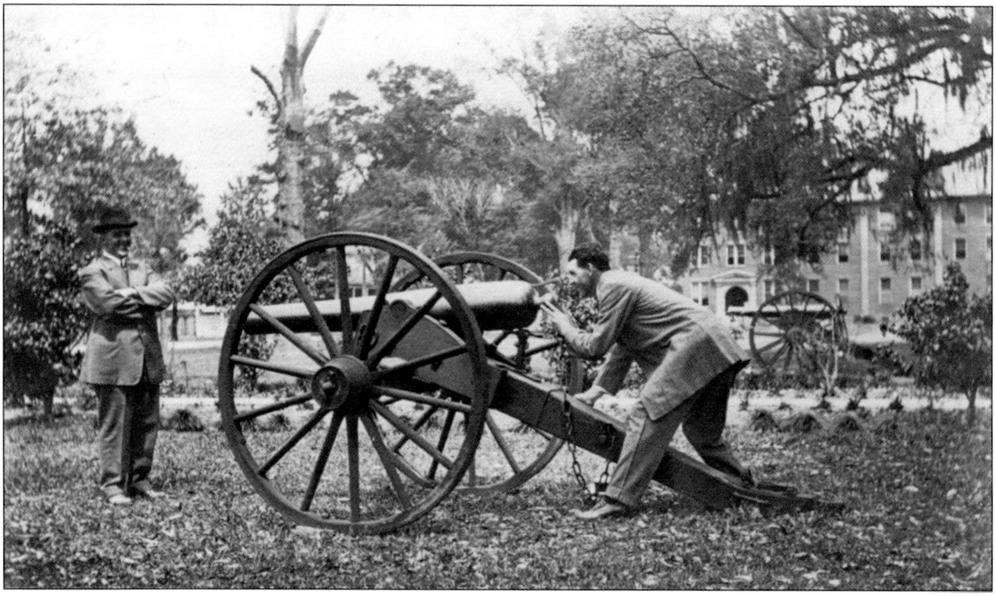

The two brass cannons in this photograph are displayed at the entrance to Col. Thomas D. Boyd's residence. The cannons were placed there to honor the university's military history and its contribution to the US government, giving rise to the school's nickname the Ole War Skule. (POVPC.)

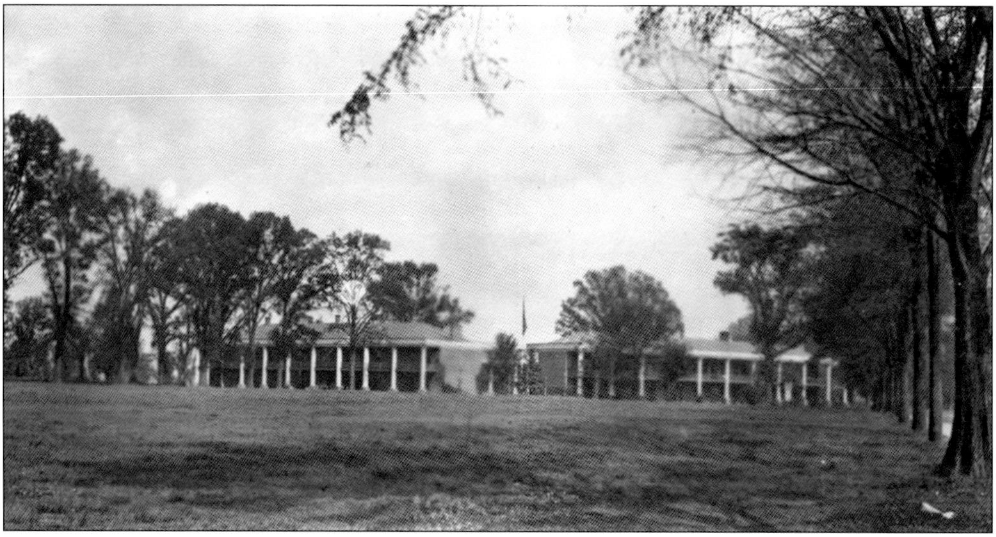

The Pentagon Barracks overlooked the Mississippi River and were constructed of red brick with hipped roofs and broad galleries across the front and rear of each building. Four of the five buildings survive to this date. The fifth building was situated on the west side, open toward the Mississippi River. Rooms on the upper floors were cadet living quarters, and ground floors were used as classrooms, offices, reading rooms, and armories. The field in the foreground of this photograph is the gridiron and parade grounds. An impressive short list of individuals who visited the barracks includes Marquis de Lafayette, Gen. James Wilkinson, Jefferson Davis, Abraham Lincoln, Robert E. Lee, John C. Calhoun, Henry Clay, Gen. George A. Custer, Gen. James Longstreet, Gen. Nathan Bedford Forrest, Gen. Thomas J. "Stonewall" Jackson, and Gen. William T. Sherman. (POVPC.)

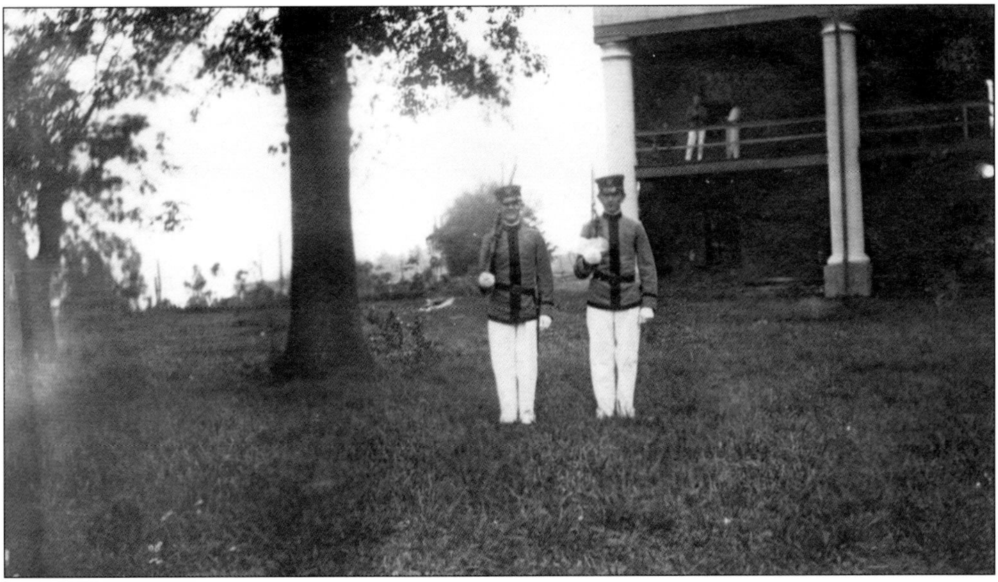

Jesse Afton Hart (left), younger brother of photographer William B. Hart, attended Louisiana State University. Here, he poses in full dress uniform for a photograph with fellow cadet G. Hasting. Jesse enrolled at the university in 1910 and graduated with a bachelor of science degree in 1915. (POVPC.)

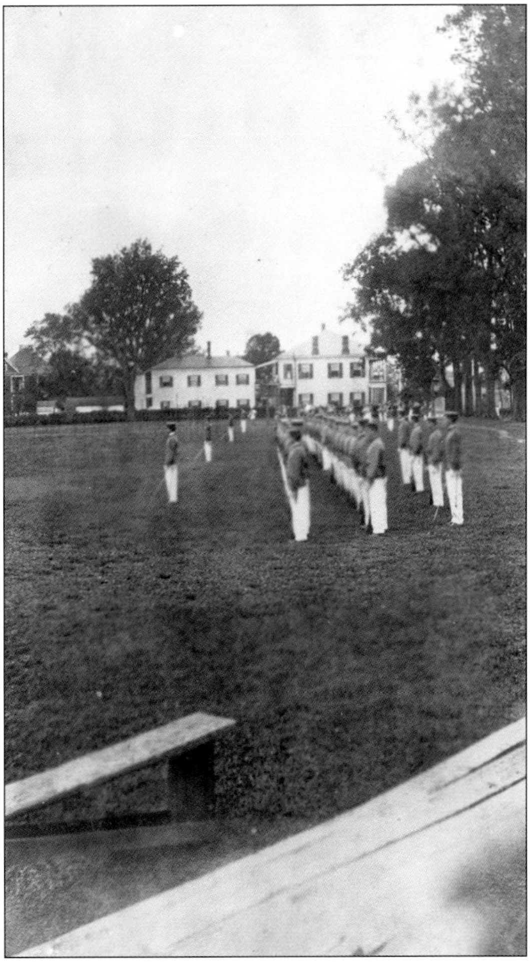

Since LSU's beginning, the Ole War Skule fostered military training. Initially, Louisiana State University was a compulsory training school for male students entering the military. Drill, as seen here, provided a foundation of teamwork, discipline, and self-control. (POVPC.)

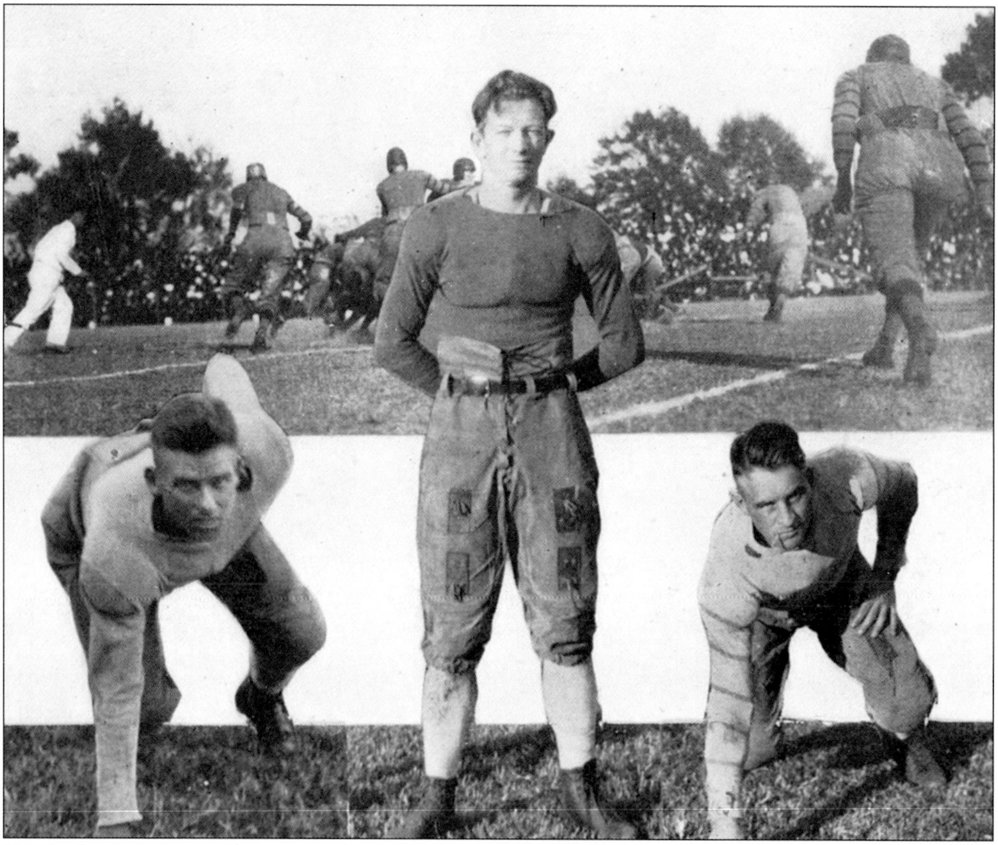

Football was very popular at LSU but was almost banned because of injuries and deaths. Uniforms were fitted with thin leather pads tucked under the jerseys, and pants providing little protection. Around 1910, helmets were still optional. A few years later, players who earned their letter playing football were called L Men. The three players in this photograph belonged to the elite L Club: halfback Perry Hague (left), right end Johnny Lewis (center), and fullback Tub Ewen. Lewis played first for Southwestern Louisiana Institute (later called University of Louisiana at Lafayette), and in 1917 he scored that school's first touchdown against LSU. (LSUSC.)

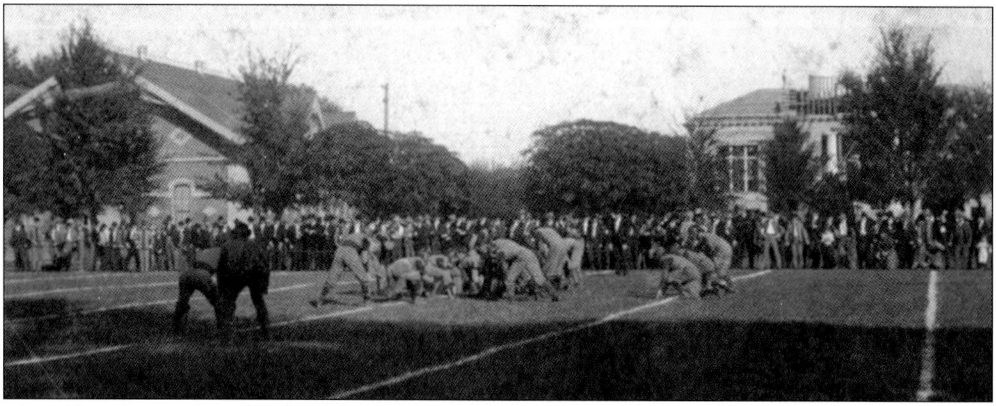

The old gridiron is lined with spectators in this 1902 football contest at LSU. The building on the left behind the crowd is Garig Hall, and on the right beyond the trees is Hill Memorial Library, under construction. (LSUSC.)

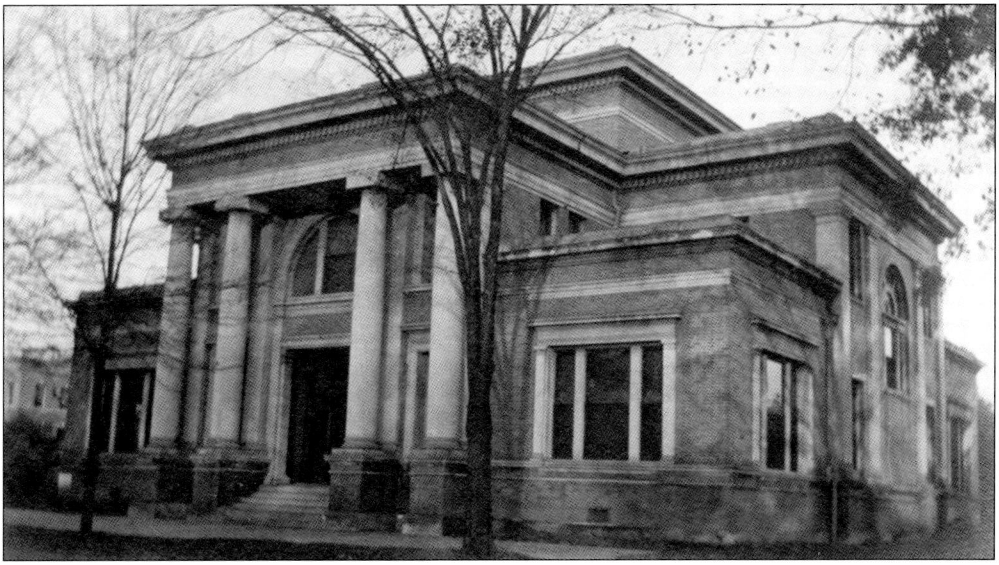

University president David F. Boyd initiated the ground-breaking for Alumni Hall in 1904. The Palladian-style building consisting of a center rotunda was designed by New Orleans architects Favrot and Livaudais. The building housed offices for the Society of the Alumni, the president, and treasurer of the university. After the new LSU campus was opened, this building became offices for the extension service, then the state tax collector, and lastly a cultural school for children. In 1934, the building was dismantled, and much of it was moved to the new Louisiana State University campus and rebuilt, an identical replica of the original structure. This photograph was taken around 1914. (EBRPL.)

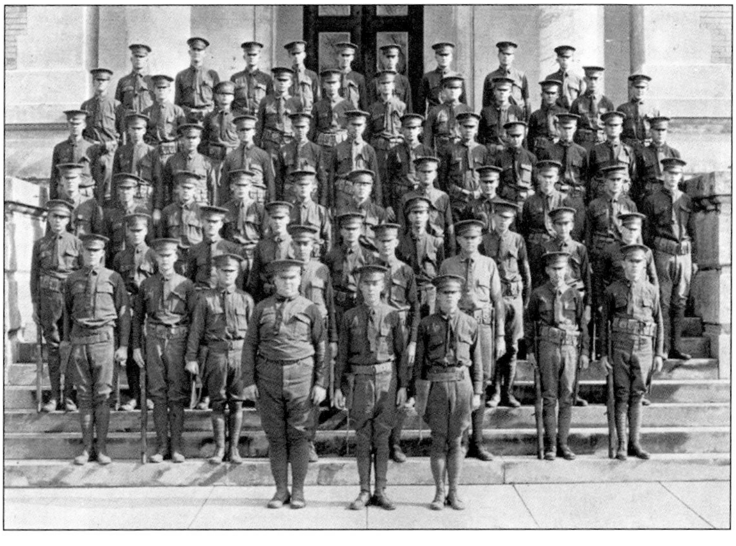

Cadets pose on the steps of Hill Memorial Library. They were assigned to the Motor Transport Corps. Part of their military training in this division was to maintain and operate all of the military vehicles. The Motor Transport Corps was one of several companies in the battalion at Louisiana State University. (LSUSC.)

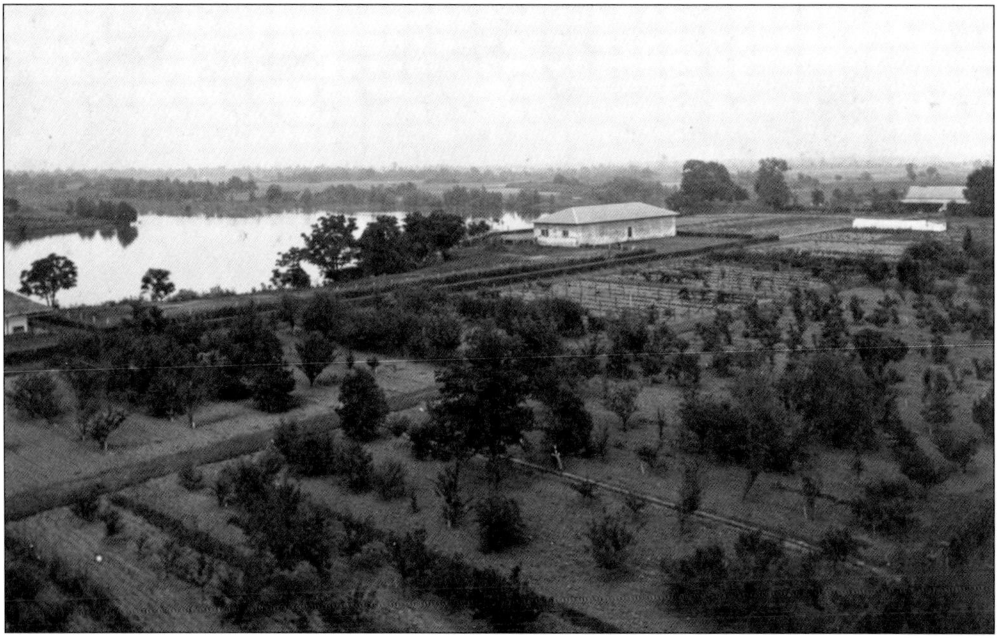

This early-1900s view of the university's horticultural experiment station and gardens also captures a distant look of University Lake, now Capitol Lake, the Indian mound in the upper right, and the old arsenal powder magazine on the far right, which was used as an LSU veterinary hospital. The center is where the Louisiana state capitol stands today. (LSUSC.)

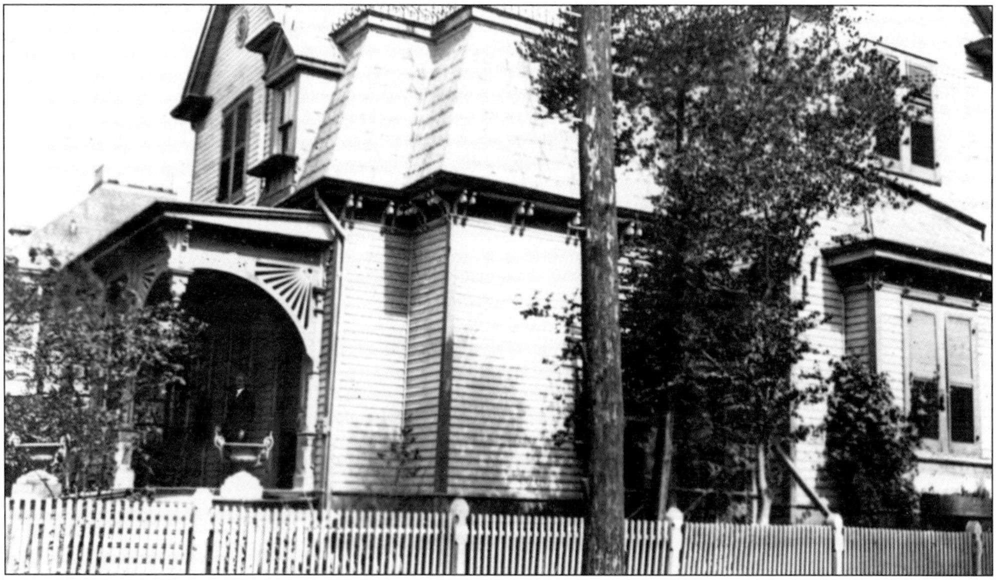

During the 1910s, LSU experienced exponential growth under President Boyd's direction. The number of buildings nearly doubled in less than a decade. In 1906, there were 17 women enrolled at LSU. By 1912, Louisiana State University was faced with a housing shortage for a student population of nearly 700. The campus was hemmed in by the limits of Baton Rouge, and the prospect of additional classroom buildings and living quarters on campus was out of the question. Homes like this one on North Street and throughout the downtown area were being transformed into boardinghouses. (POVPC.)

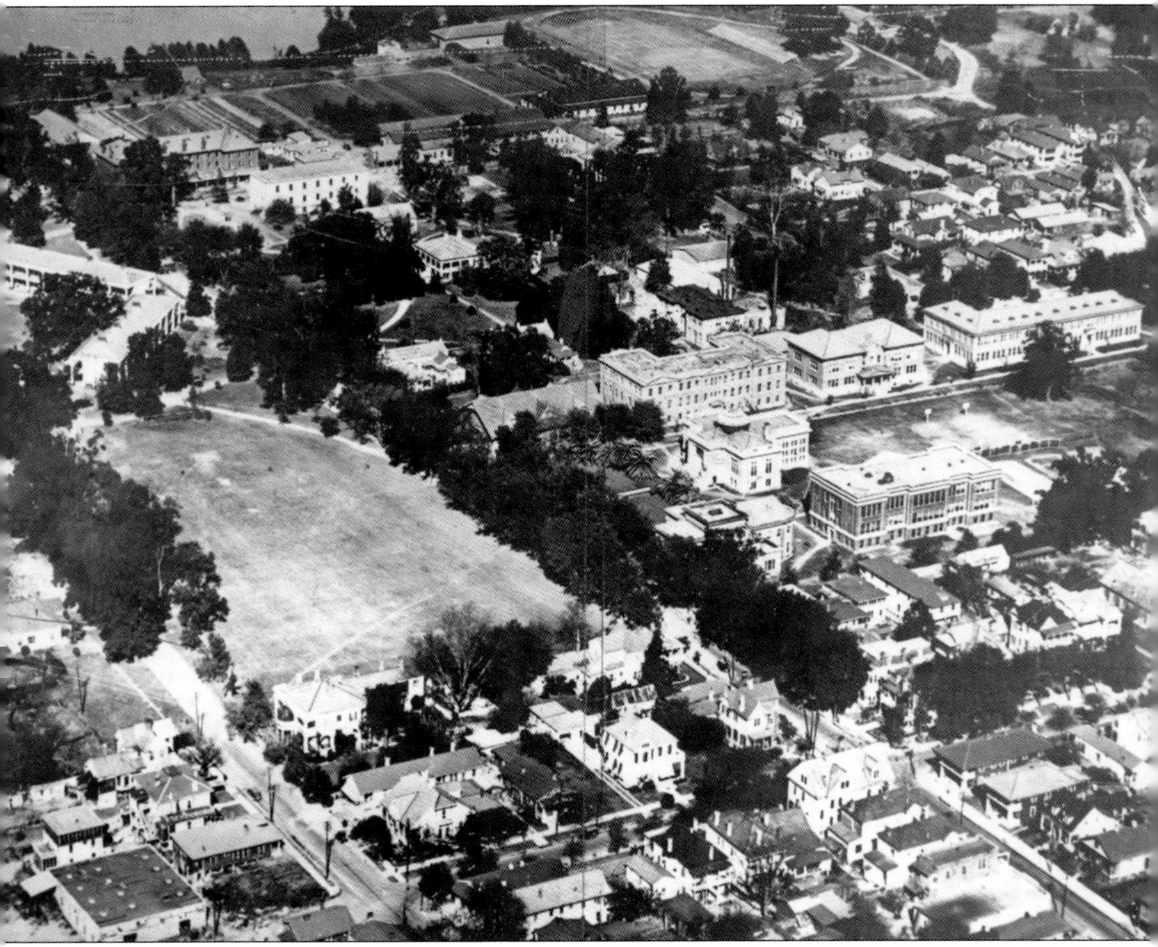

This aerial photograph from the mid-1920s provides a view of the downtown campus in its final days. Familiar open areas are the parade ground, which also served as the original gridiron and the horticultural gardens, seen at the top. A feature that has largely been forgotten is the location of the football field that was home for the Tigers immediately before relocating to the new south campus in 1925. The field, pictured here, was situated between the magazine and the horticultural gardens. Some of the familiar buildings are Garig Hall, Irion Hall, Heard Hall, Robertson Hall, Hill Memorial Library, Alumni Hall, and Peabody Hall. The new university campus located south of Baton Rouge had begun enrollment about the time this photograph was taken, and the downtown campus was slowly phased out for university use. (LSUSC.)

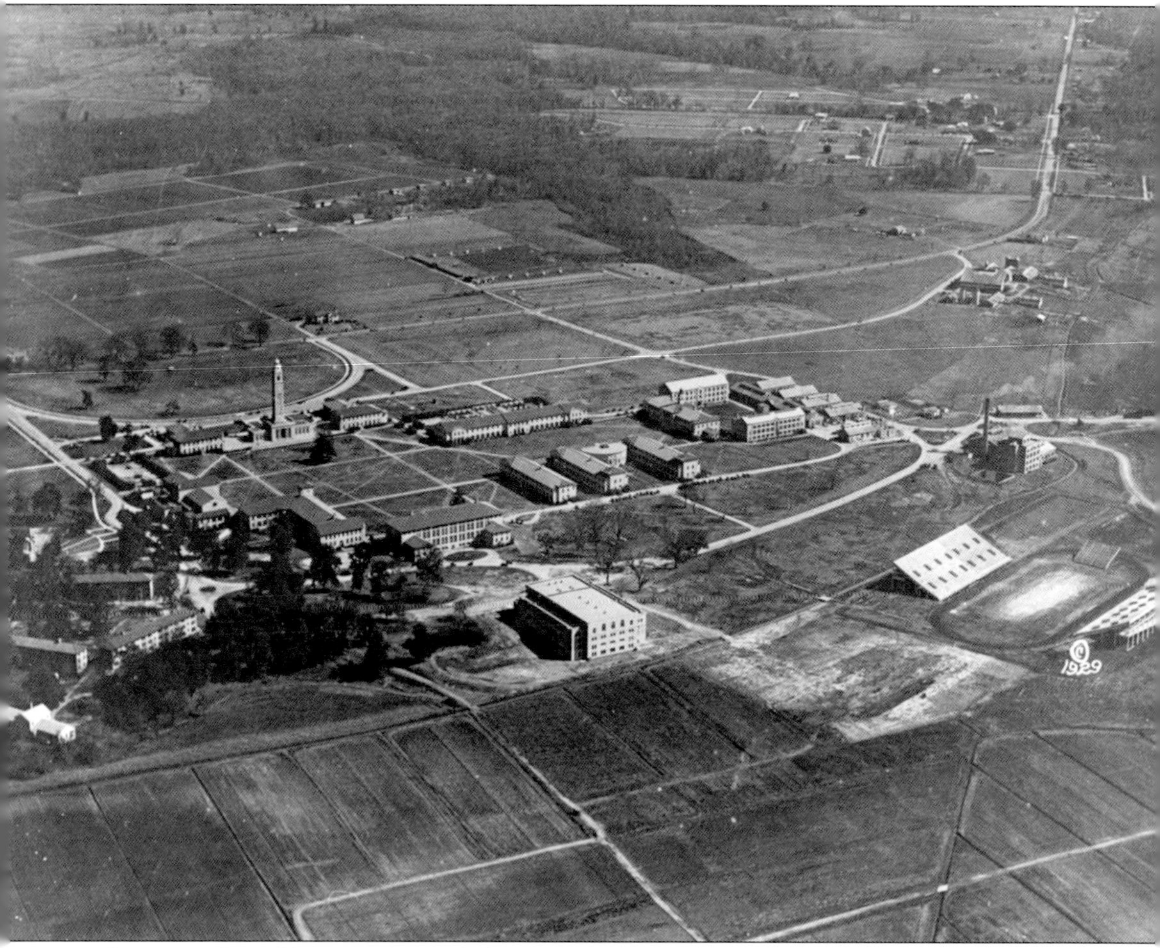

Louisiana State University opened the new campus amidst the cotton and cane fields south of Baton Rouge in 1925. Highland Road was the main route to the new campus. In this 1929 aerial, a substantial amount of construction had taken place in less than a decade. Here, the 15,000-seat football stadium and the sugar house (above the stadium) are visible on the southwest side of the campus. Memorial Tower is visible left of center. (EBRPL.)

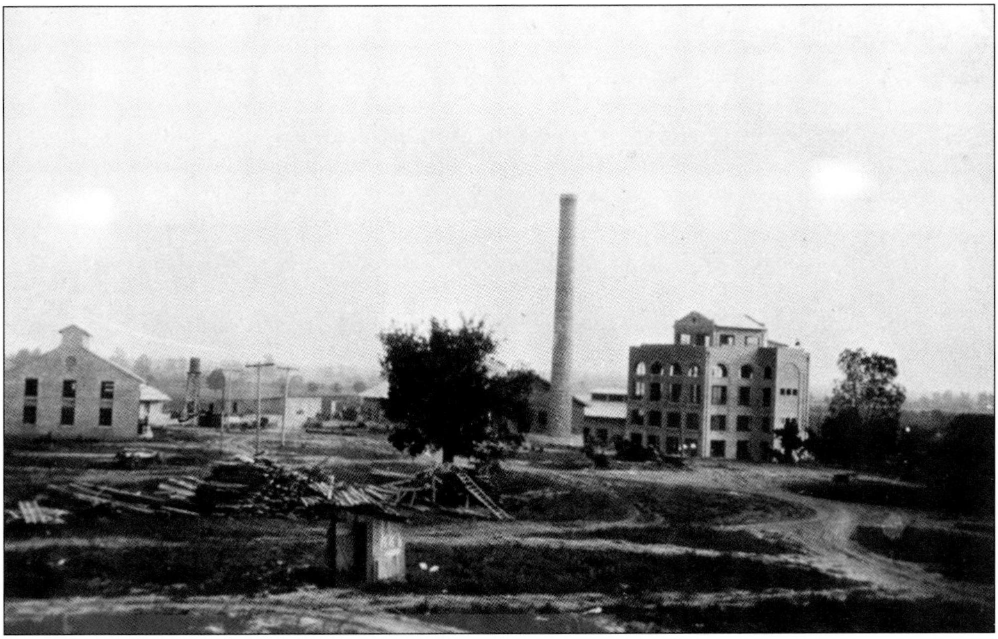

Louisiana State University invested heavily in sugar research. The sugar house was constructed around 1924–1925. It was one of the school's first buildings on the new campus and a major investment for the university's agriculture department. (EBRPL.)

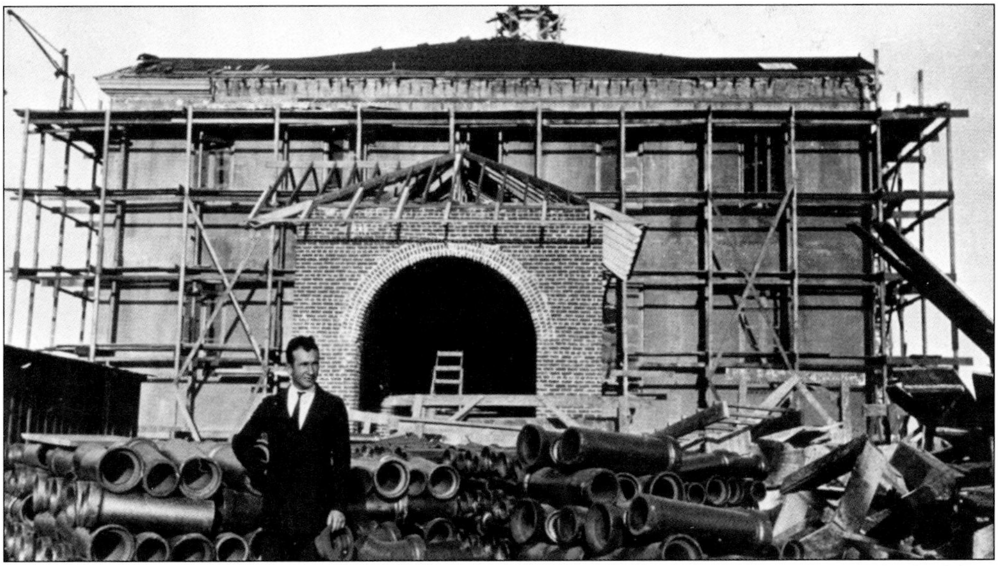

In 1925, the agriculture building was under construction on the new university campus. This building was one of dozens erected in the mid-1920s. Because Louisiana State University was an agricultural and mechanical college, it was to become a showcased structure on campus. (EBRPL.)

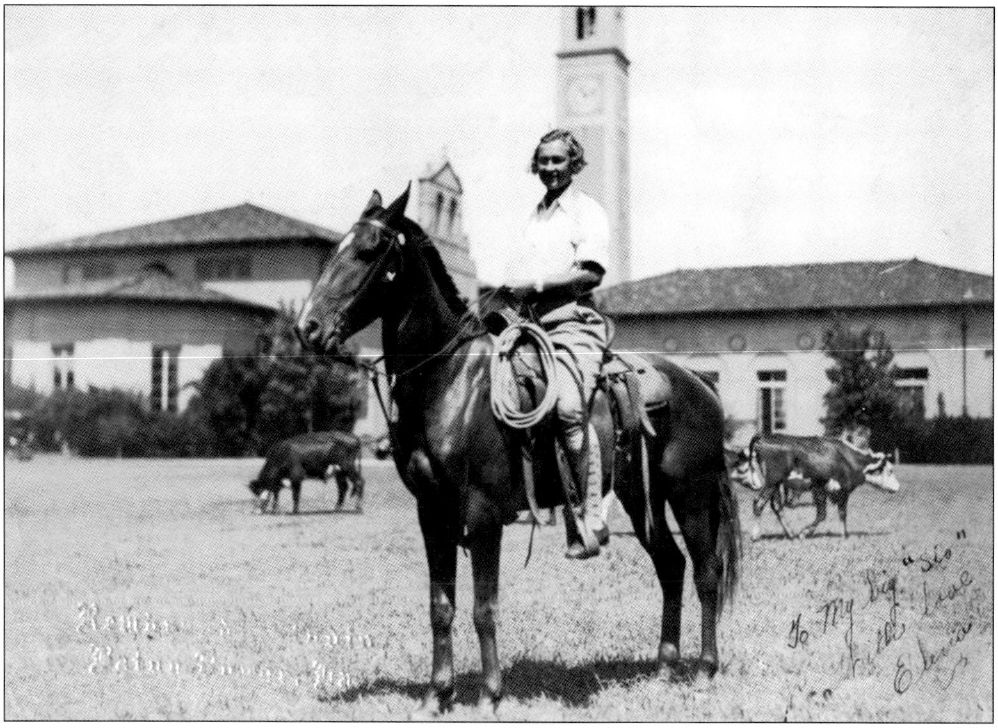

Elena Carter Percy of West Feliciana Parish was intent on enrolling at Louisiana State University in 1932. Elena drove nine cattle nearly 40 miles from her home north of Baton Rouge to the campus in exchange for room and board. University president J.M. Smith personally accepted the cattle when Percy arrived. (EBRPL.)

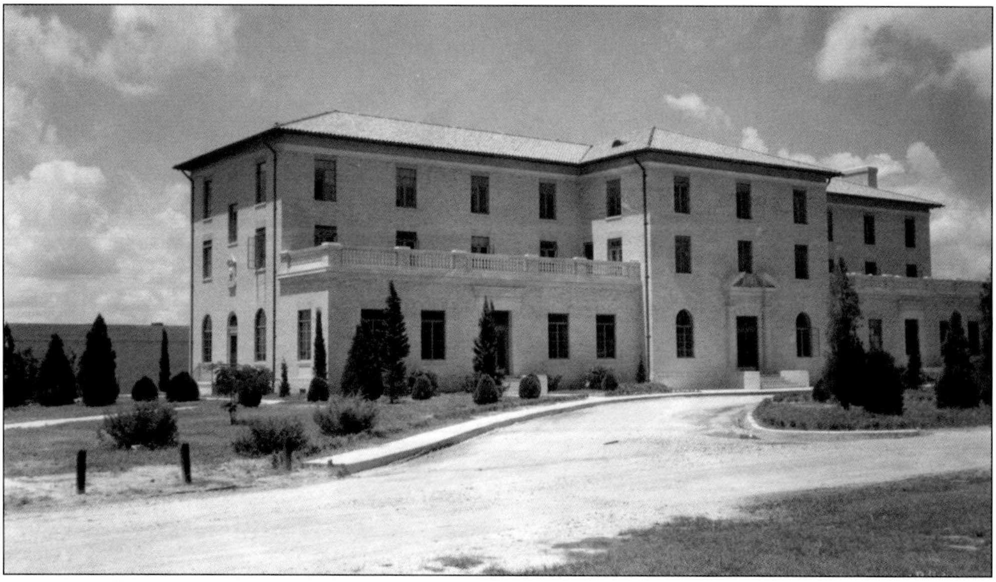
Louisiana State University's Huey P. Long Field House was completed in 1932. Governor Long wanted the Olympic-size pool to be the biggest in the state. He was passionate about the state's flagship university and particularly its sports. The field house was meant to be a first-class facility that would attract aspiring athletic students. (EBRPL.)

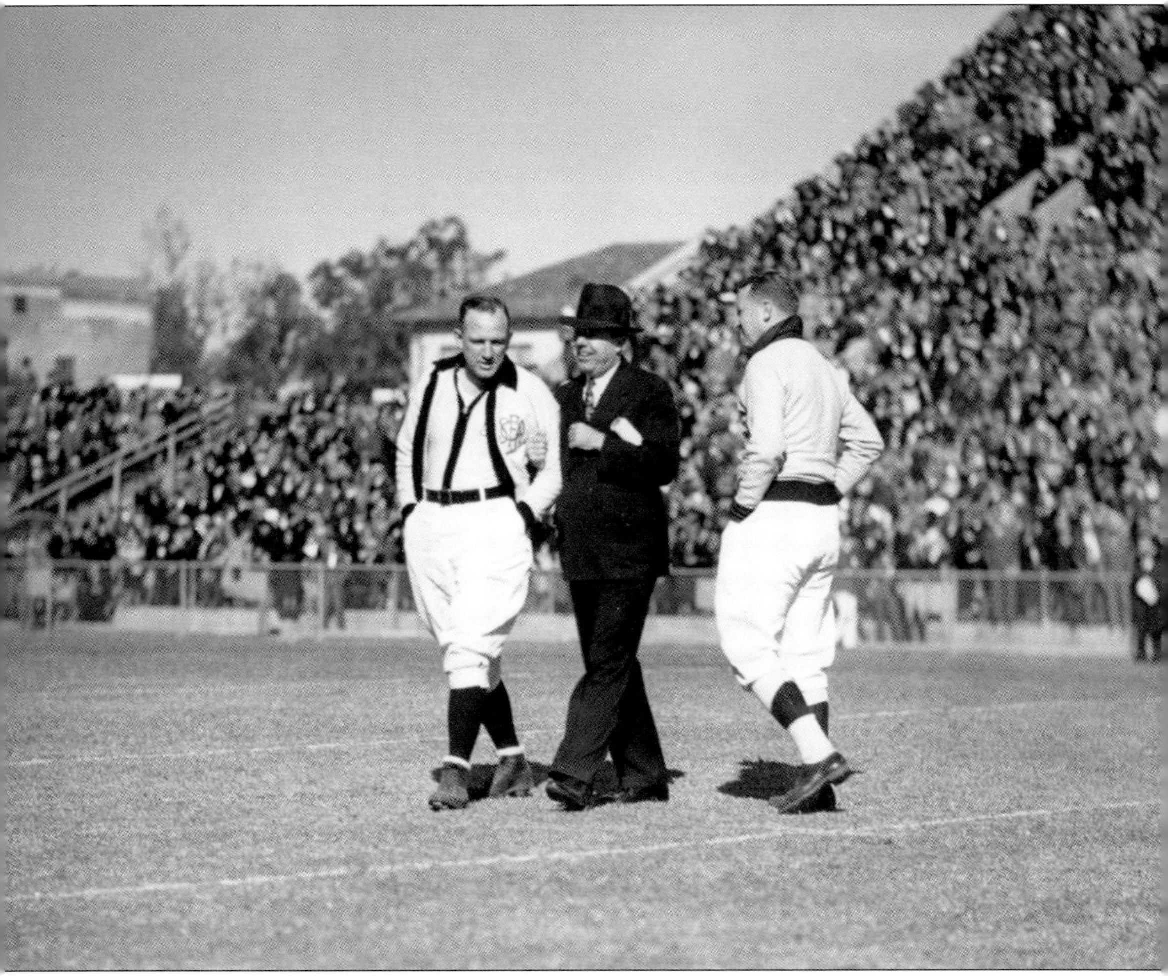

In 1930, a photographer captured this image of Gov. Huey P. Long conferring with football referees. Governor Long was known for locker room pep talks to university players and giving advice to coaches. He often led the Tiger marching band onto the field at halftime. It was Governor Long who collaborated with Tiger marching band director Castro Carazo on writing the fight song, "Touchdown for LSU." (LSUSC.)

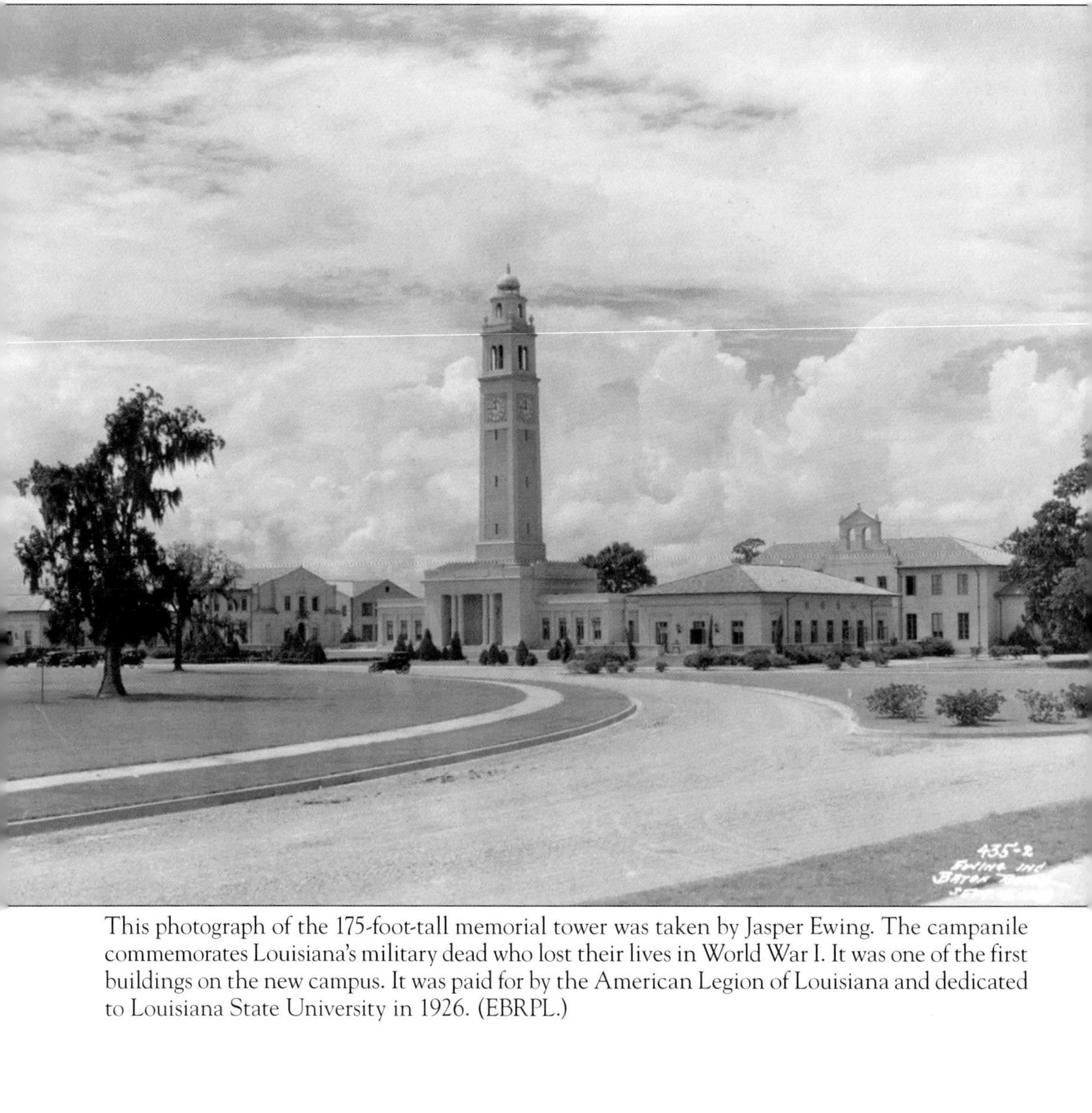

This photograph of the 175-foot-tall memorial tower was taken by Jasper Ewing. The campanile commemorates Louisiana's military dead who lost their lives in World War I. It was one of the first buildings on the new campus. It was paid for by the American Legion of Louisiana and dedicated to Louisiana State University in 1926. (EBRPL.)

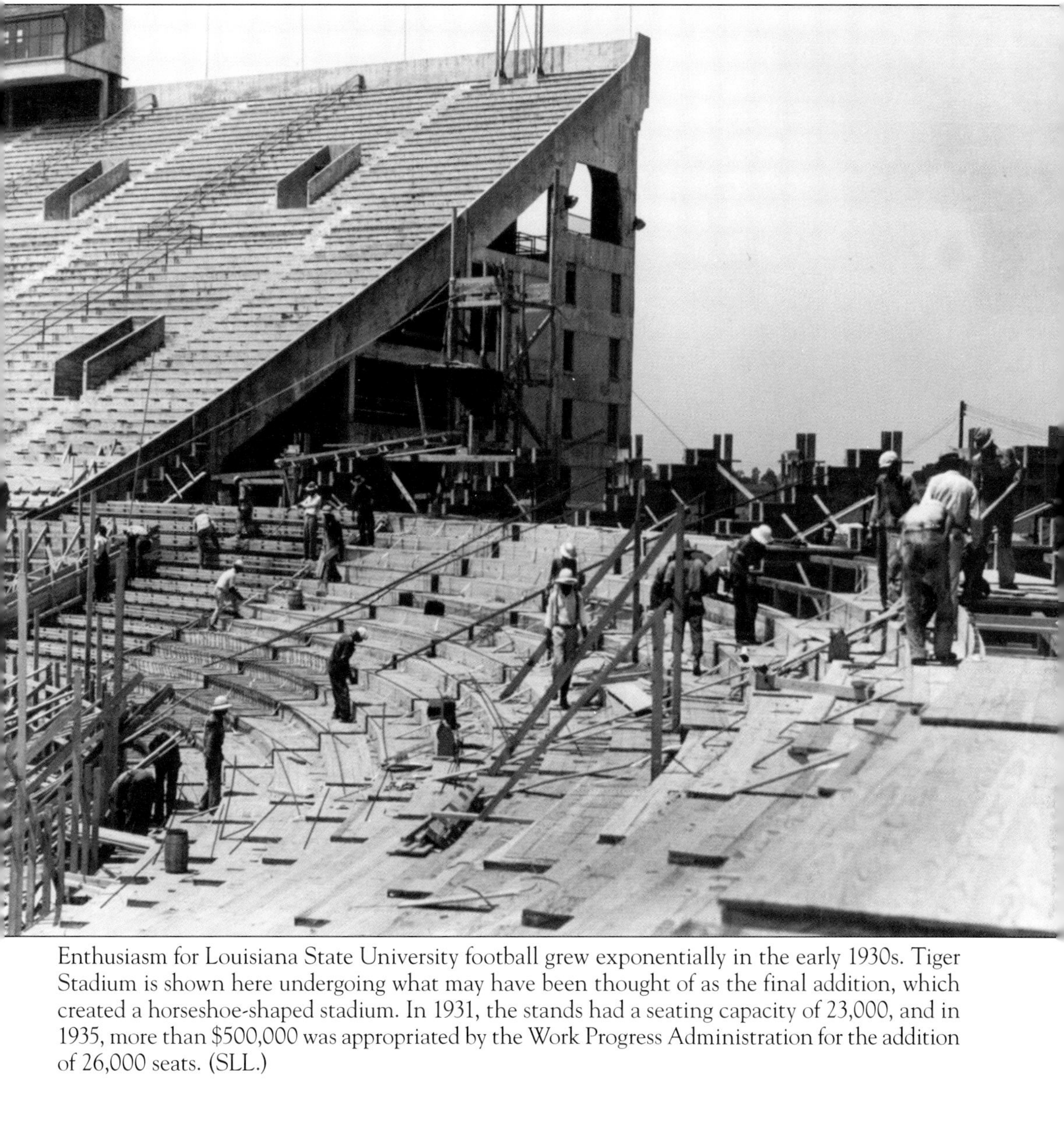

Enthusiasm for Louisiana State University football grew exponentially in the early 1930s. Tiger Stadium is shown here undergoing what may have been thought of as the final addition, which created a horseshoe-shaped stadium. In 1931, the stands had a seating capacity of 23,000, and in 1935, more than $500,000 was appropriated by the Work Progress Administration for the addition of 26,000 seats. (SLL.)

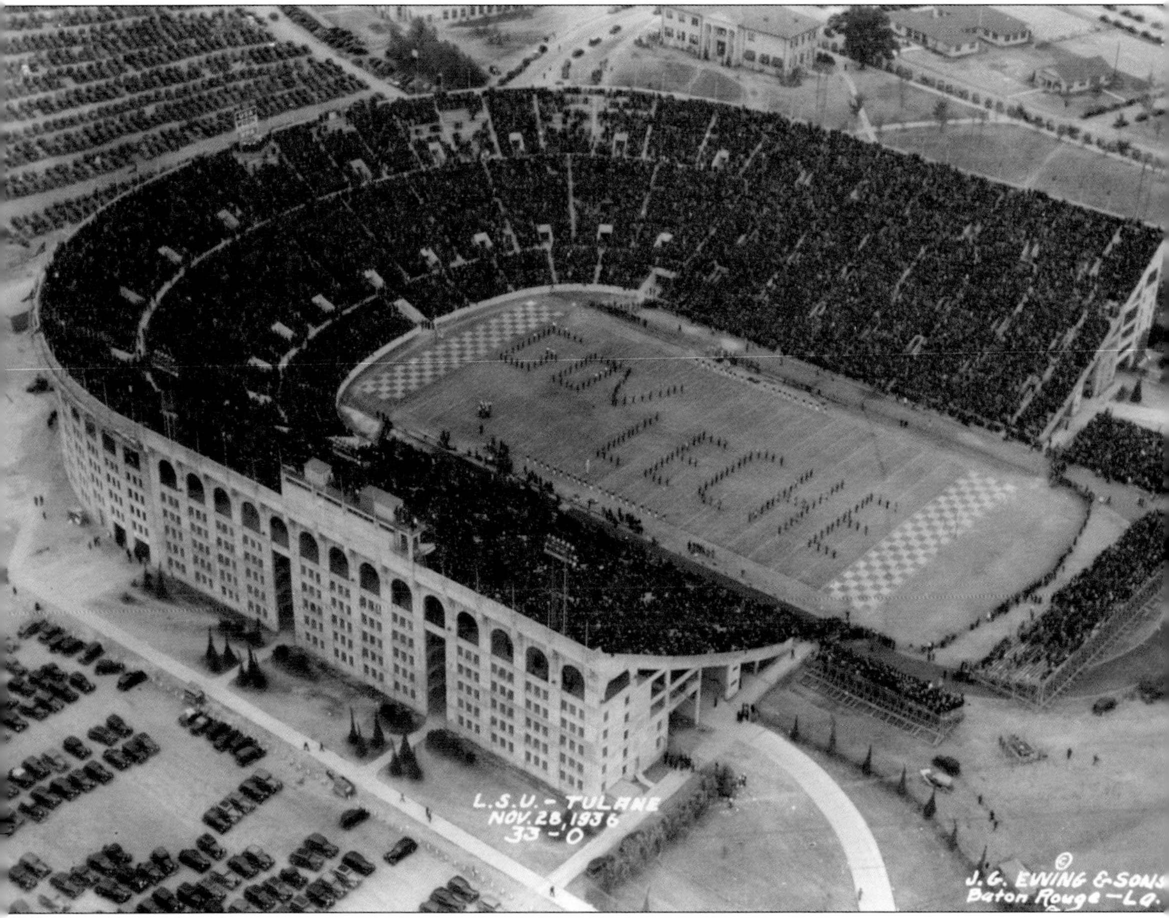

By the mid-1930s, the wraparound football stadium on Louisiana State University's new south campus was completed. This image depicts halftime ceremonies on November 28, 1936, during the LSU-Tulane game. The Louisiana State University marching band was in formation and created the words "Gov. Leche" in honor of newly elected Richard Webster Leche. The halftime moment was photographed by Jasper Ewing from high above Tiger Stadium. (LSUSC.)

Two

Historic Buildings

Old buildings often go unnoticed in today's world. Many old, iconic structures undergo transformations in the way of restorations, face-lifts, or renovations to the point where they no longer resemble historic structures. So, it seems that a few of the old could be easily forgotten.

In and around the downtown area, the number of historic buildings in Baton Rouge is remarkable. In this wonderfully preserved city, the streetscapes are filled with 19th-century landmarks, office buildings, museums, churches, and homes. Though there is a long list of buildings that have been razed over the decades, preservation efforts have been successful throughout the area. This chapter brings to mind both forgotten structures that have long disappeared as well as those architectural beauties that have survived the wrecking ball. Here, the reader will discover interesting facts about buildings of long ago that have been mostly forgotten—until now.

Through the lenses of amateur and professional photographers, visual treasures were created for the people of Baton Rouge. Without professional photographers Andrew D. Lytle, Jasper G. Ewing, and others, this city's graphic history would have been lost to future generations. Concurrently, during the period covered in this book, the introduction of the Kodak camera made photography possible for the casual amateur to chronicle life stories where professionals could not.

In this chapter, most images of historic buildings were artfully captured by photographers in a way that evokes solemnity. The portraitures are more than passing snapshots but rather visual stories about each place and time.

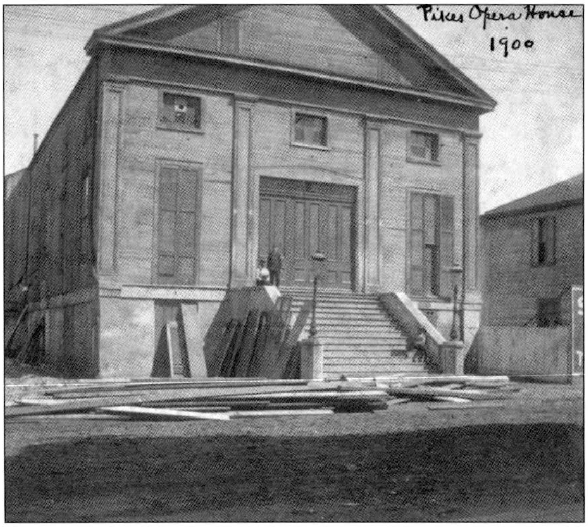

George F. Pike, an affluent businessman of book binding and printing in Baton Rouge, erected this barn-like structure in 1860. The building was called Pike's Opera House, or commonly known as Pike's Hall. During the Civil War, the building served as a hospital and later was converted for use as an auditorium for theatrical performances and social and political meetings. Pelican Hook and Ladder Company No. 1 held its annual ball in Pike's Hall. The Elk's Theatre was built in 1900 and replaced Pike's Opera House as the center for theatrical performances in Baton Rouge. (EBRPL.)

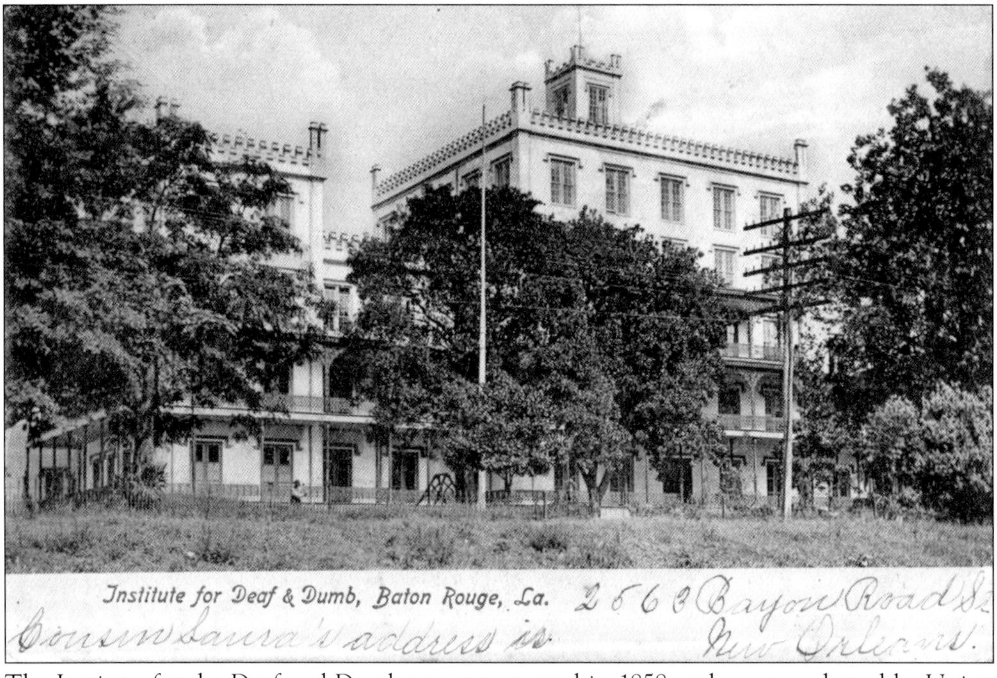

The Institute for the Deaf and Dumb was constructed in 1858 and commandeered by Union troops during the Civil War. Following a disastrous fire at the Seminary of Learning of the State of Louisiana (Louisiana State University) at Pineville, David F. Boyd, seminary superintendent, made arrangements for the school to move into a wing of the Institute for the Deaf and Dumb in Baton Rouge only a few days after the fire. The temporary relocation from Rapides Parish to East Baton Rouge Parish became permanent. In 1887, the university moved to the old US Army arsenal north of the city, and three years later, the State School for the Blind moved onto this location on Government Street. (EBRPL.)

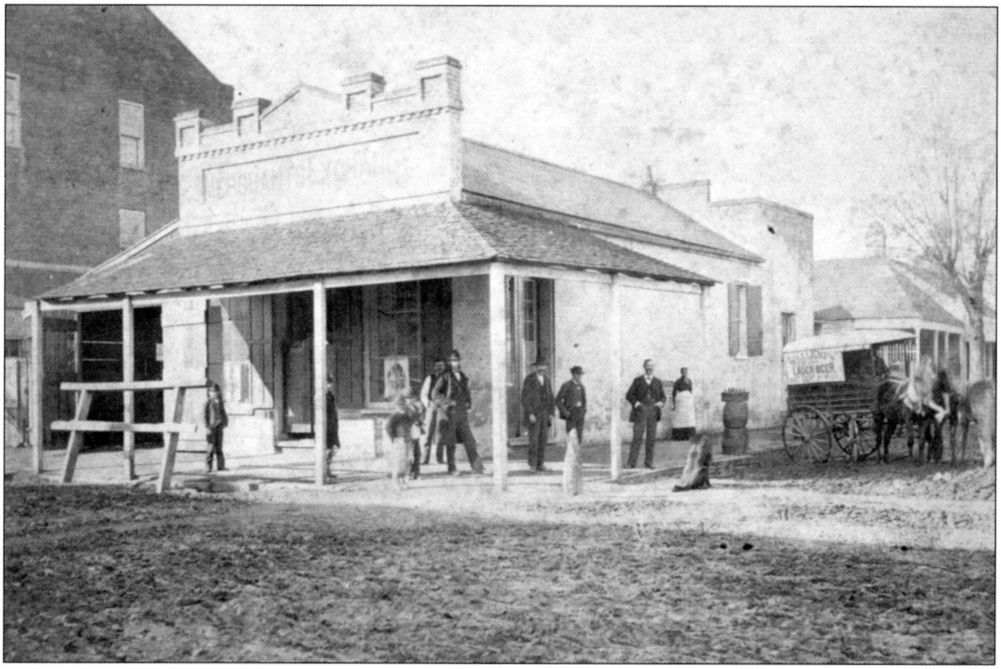

This rare photograph of the Merchants Exchange was taken around 1900. It depicts the rustic office building during a period when horse-drawn wagons were the norm and before the arrival of the automobile. The building was located at the corner of Third and Laurel Streets. (EBRPL.)

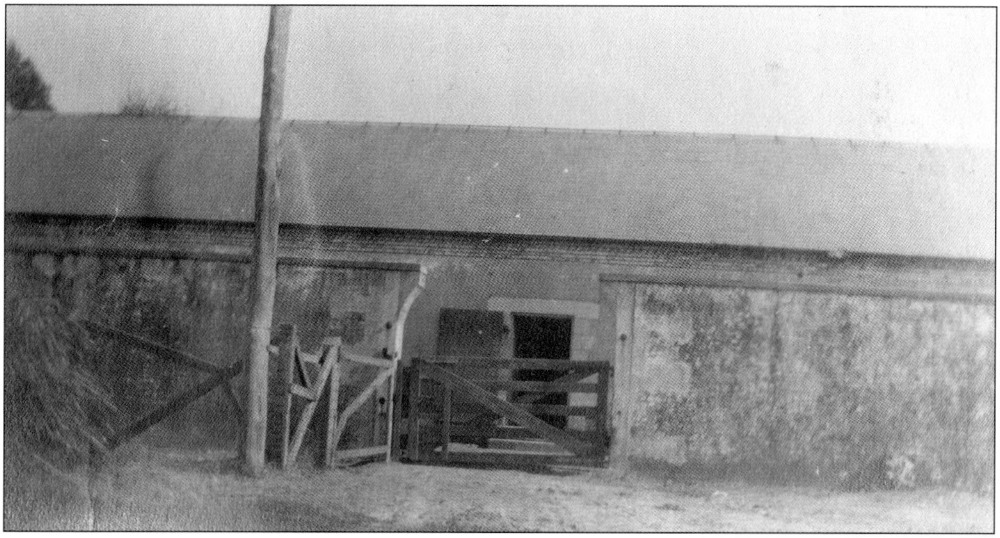

The old US Army arsenal powder magazine was constructed around 1836 to 1838. It once stored approximately 3,000 barrels of explosive powder during the Civil War. Between 1886 and 1926, the building was used as a veterinary hospital at Louisiana State University, when the campus occupied the arsenal grounds. Today, the building is Louisiana State Museum. This photograph was taken in 1914. (EBRPL.)

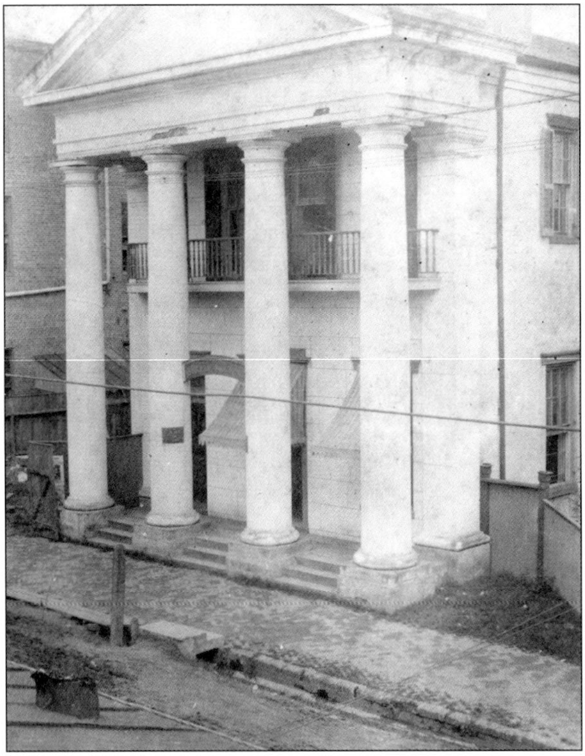

The Bank of Baton Rouge was organized in 1889 with William J. Knox as the bank's first president, Ollie B. Steele as vice-president, and Joseph Gebelin as cashier. The bank was located at 416 Third Street and reported as having the largest capital and surplus of any bank in Louisiana outside of New Orleans. Knox was previously an attorney with the firm Knox and Laycock. Steele was a state senator and public accountant, and Gebelin was previously assistant secretary of the state. This photograph was taken between 1900 and 1910. (EBRPL.)

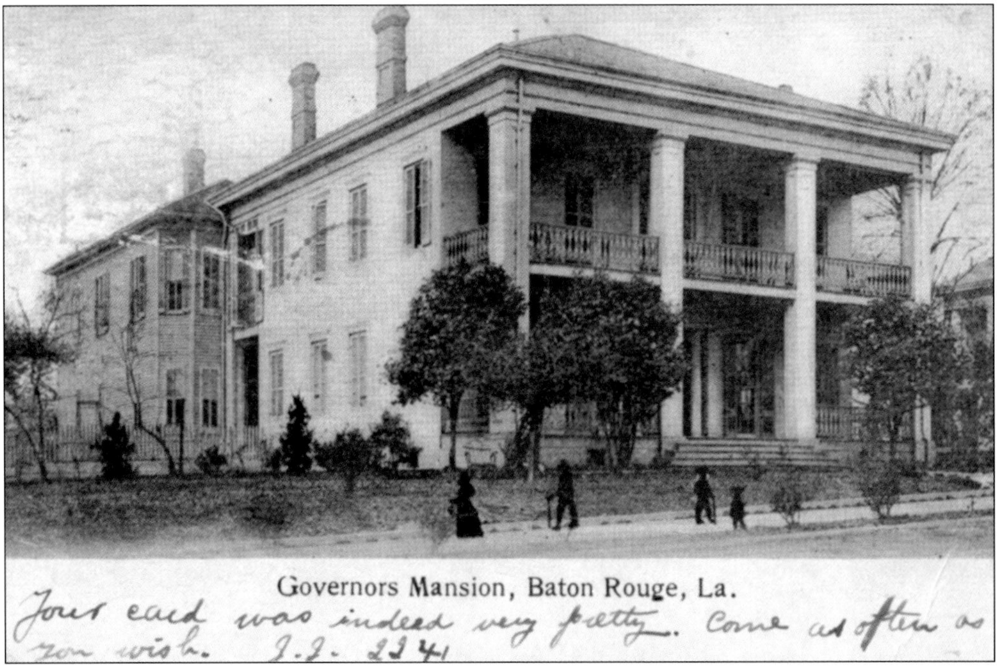

A prominent home built for Nathan King Knox around 1857 was later purchased by the state and served as residence for Louisiana governors until 1929. The governor's mansion, located on North Boulevard between St. Charles and Royal Streets, was replaced by a new governor's mansion at the same location in 1930. This photograph was taken around 1910. (EBRPL.)

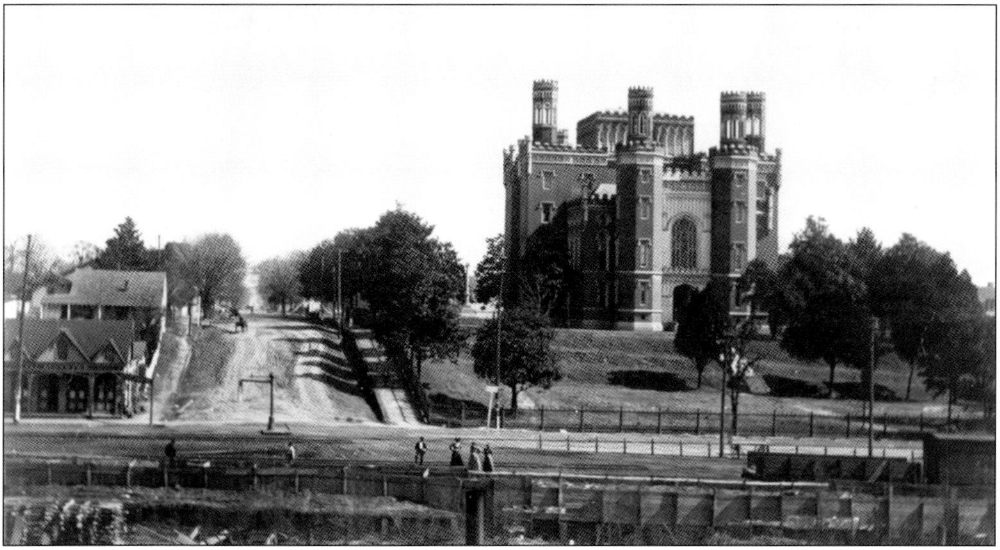

This majestic building was designed by renowned architect James H. Dakin, a New York native who moved to New Orleans and founded a reputable architectural firm. Construction began on Louisiana's state capitol in 1847. The walls were built of masonry and covered with stucco and scored to resemble stone. The building was first occupied for business by the Louisiana General Assembly in January 1849, but it was not officially completed until January 28, 1852. (SLL.)

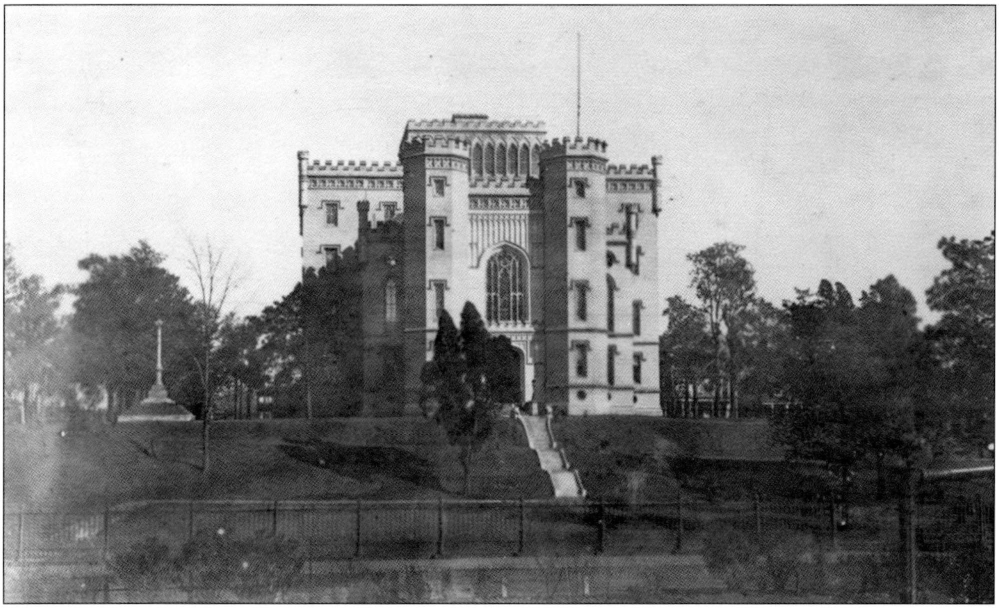

During the Civil War, the state capitol was occupied by Federal troops and used as a garrison until December 1862, when the troops set fire to the building and destroyed all but the exterior walls. Between 1880 and 1882, the structure was rebuilt under the direction of New Orleans architect William Alfred Freret. During this reconstruction, the magnificent stairway was added as well as more light to the interior provided by a large stained-glass canopy above the central spiral stairway. He also installed cast-iron turrets above the square tower corners. The cast-iron turrets were purposeless extensions and drew the attention and remarks of Mark Twain. The turrets were removed shortly before this photograph was taken by William B. Hart. (POVPC.)

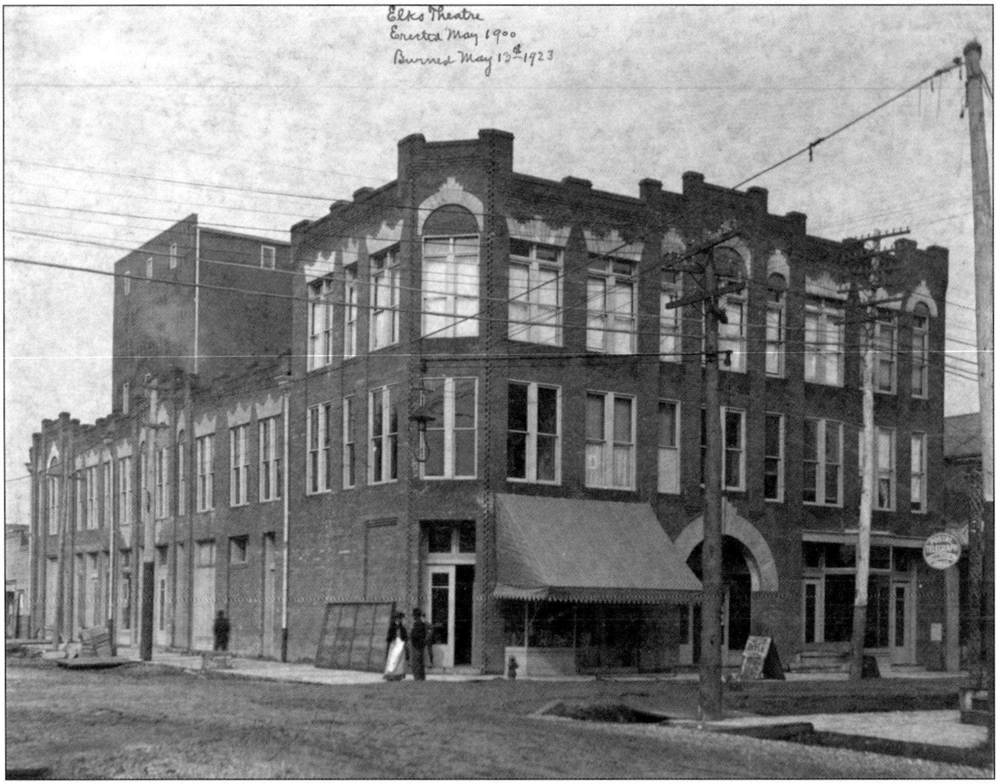

The Protective Order of the Elks was in need of a meeting hall and in 1900 committed to constructing a building, which would contain a theater, offices, stores, and lodge meeting rooms on the northwest corner of Florida and Third Streets. The meeting hall replaced Pike's Opera Hall as a center for theatrical performances. The theater was also a regular venue for the LSU Dramatic Club. Following the first stage performance of Hall Caine's *The Christian*, theatrical and musical performances in this playhouse became a mainstay for entertainment until the theater burned down in 1923. (Both EBRPL.)

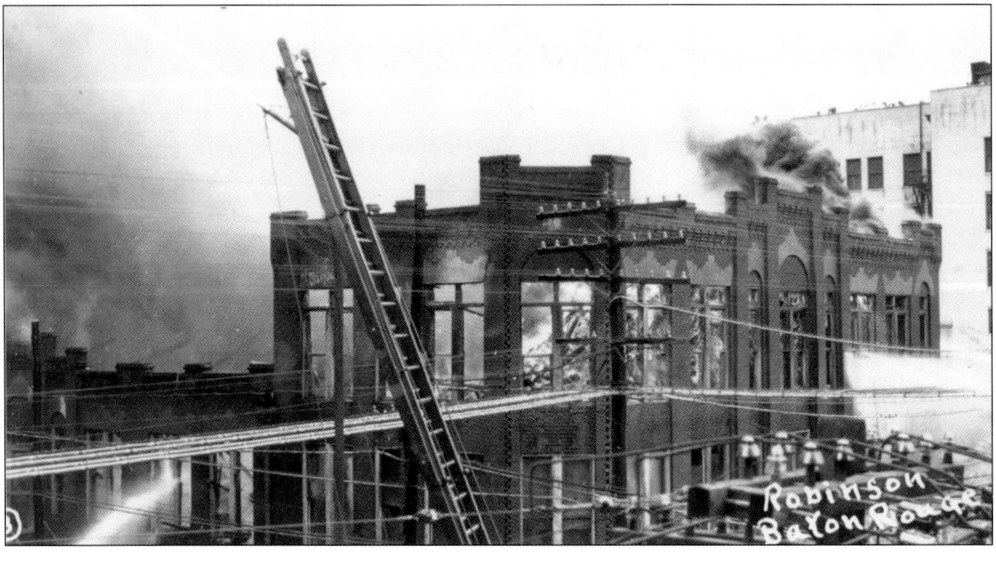

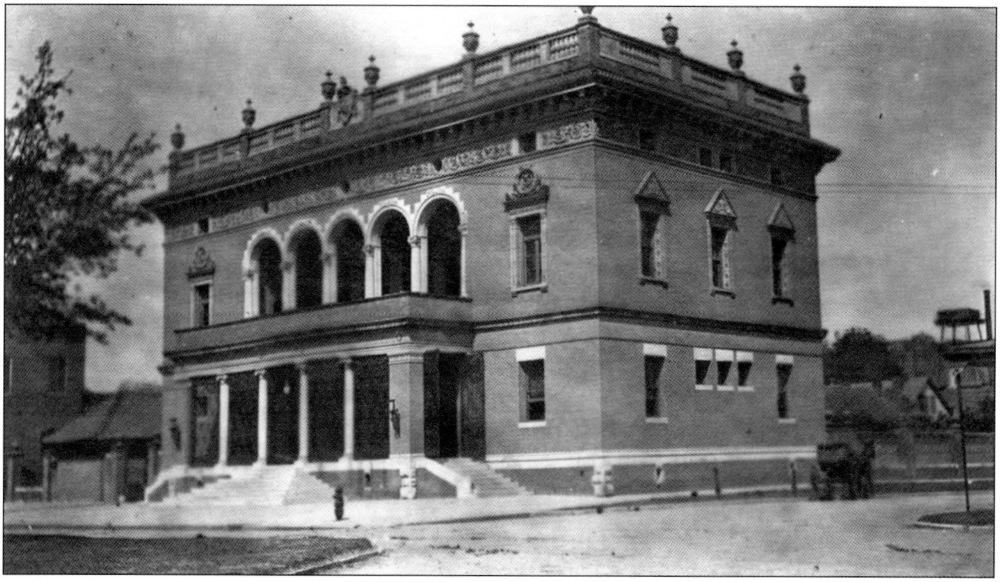

This yellow brick building served as the post office and federal courthouse from around 1895 to 1933. When completed, citizens of Baton Rouge believed it to be one of the most beautiful buildings in the city. In 1933, the federal building was transformed into the Baton Rouge City Hall and served as the seat of city government. A new post office building was constructed on Florida Street. The city made extensive renovations to the building in 1935, and it served as city hall until 1955. City National Bank purchased the building in 1956 and the next year leased it to the Baton Rouge City Club, Inc. (POVPC.)

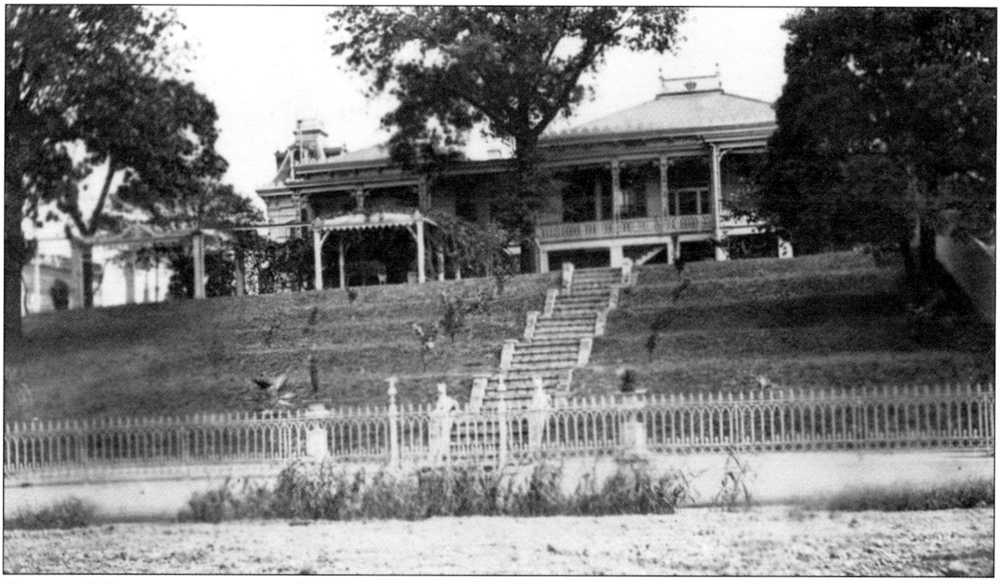

Some of the most exquisite homes in Baton Rouge were constructed along the natural bluffs overlooking the river. William Garig, one of the wealthiest men in the city, built a home that occupied half of the square bound by Front, Florida, and Lafayette Streets. The Garig House was a gray frame, cement-covered brick structure with bay windows and styled in the tradition of the 1880s. Its terraced lawn and formal garden could be seen from the opposite bank of the river. (POVPC.)

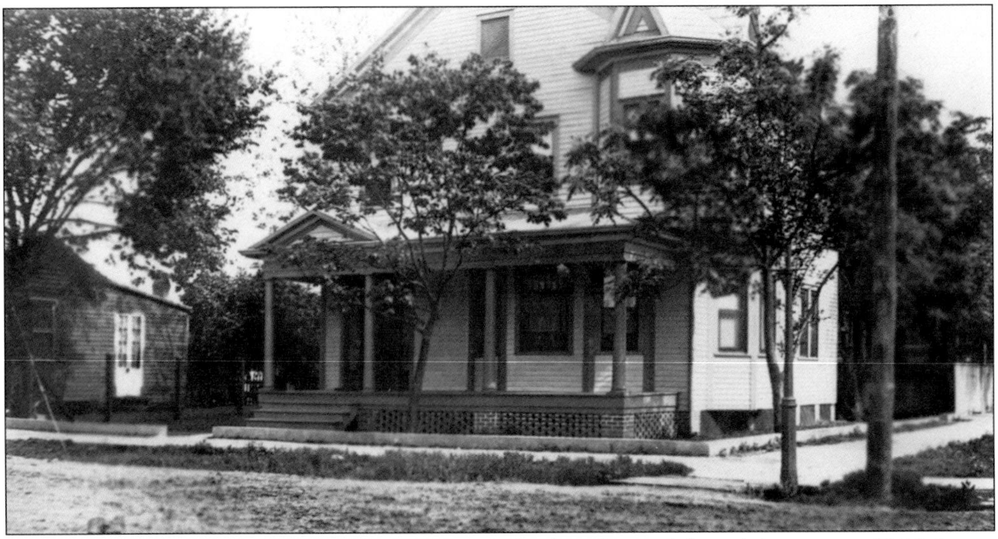

Beauregard Town was named for Elias Beauregard, who planned the subdivision in 1806. It was the second formal development in Baton Rouge. The houses in Beauregard Town consisted of a mixture of architectural styles such as Classical Revival and Colonial Revival, but perhaps the popular Late Victorian–style homes were most prevalent. The unidentified residence in this photograph is a typical style within the neighborhood of Beauregard Town. Most of the original homes were destroyed during the Civil War. Most of the remaining structures were built since 1900. (POVPC.)

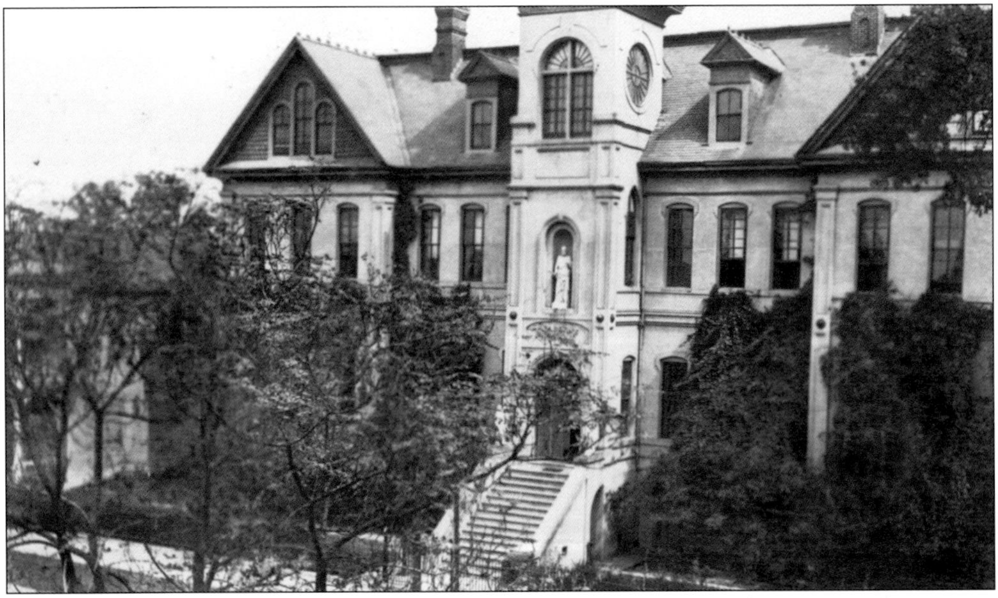

Four sisters of St. Joseph of Medaille arrived in Baton Rouge in 1868 for the purpose of managing a girls' orphanage. The orphanage was originally located on Seventh Street. In 1872, it became a boarding school and would be the first lasting Catholic school in Baton Rouge. At that time, it was known as St. Joseph's Academy Boarding and Day School. It was chartered by the state legislature in 1877 and graduated its first student, Josephine Bahlinger, the same year. The western facade of St. Joseph's Academy is shown here along Church Street, today North Fourth Street. The building was located on the northeast corner of Church Street and Florida Street. (POVPC.)

Washington Fire Company No. 1 fronted Church Street; the street name later changed to North Fourth Street. When it was built, the two-story firehouse was sandwiched between the large Ronaldson & Puckett Company general-merchandise store and the towering spire of the Methodist church. The Methodist church relocated to North Boulevard in 1925. For a period of time, the public library was housed on the second floor of the firehouse. (EBRPL.)

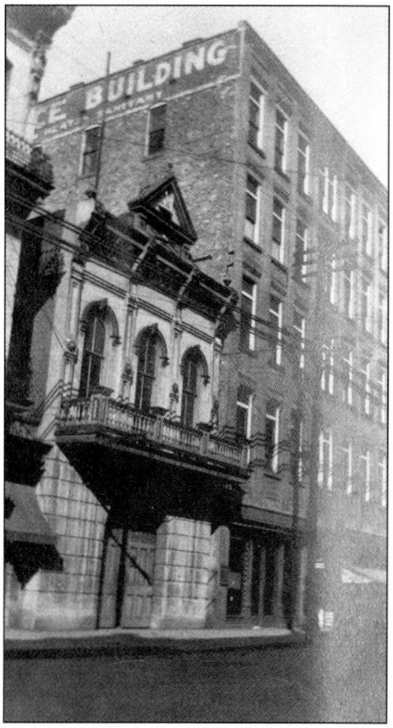

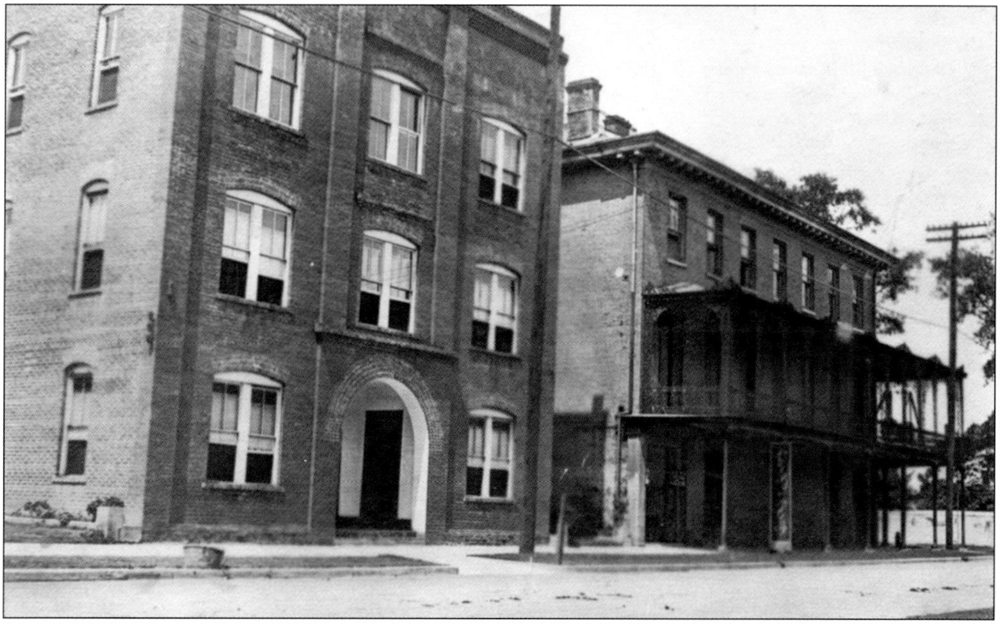

Visible on the left, Baton Rouge Sanitarium was founded by Dr. Thomas Puller Singletary, who also served as the coroner of Baton Rouge in 1911. The building on the right housed the board of trade, which was located on the northwest corner of Florida and Church Streets. Officers were board president Solon Farnbacher (also director of Louisiana State Bank), first vice president A. Dougherty Jr., second vice president Eugene Cazedessus (also first vice president of the Bank of Baton Rouge), third vice president Dr. Charles McVea, treasurer Alex Grouchy Jr., and secretary Fred B. McQueety. The second and third floors above the board of trade consisted of boarding rooms. Photographer William B. Hart temporarily resided on the third floor. The board of trade building was converted to a business college by 1916. (POVPC.)

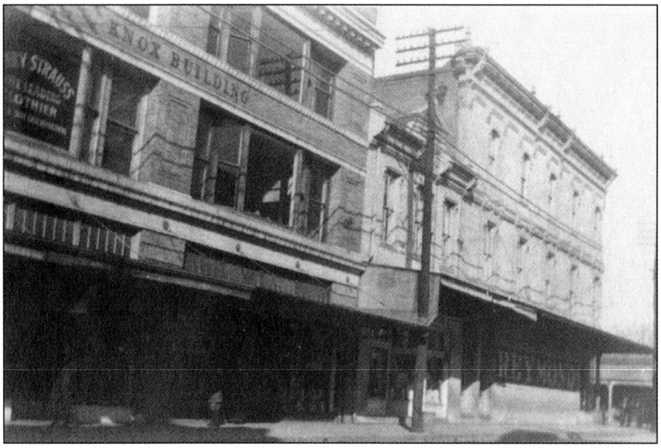

Reymond Dry Goods Company (right) was established in 1902 by Samuel I. Reymond. The dry goods business was first located on the corner of Third and Main Streets. It was later moved to a new high-rise building at the corner of Third and Florida Streets. The Knox Building (left) was constructed by Nathan Knox, a prominent business promoter and developer in Baton Rouge. (EBRPL.)

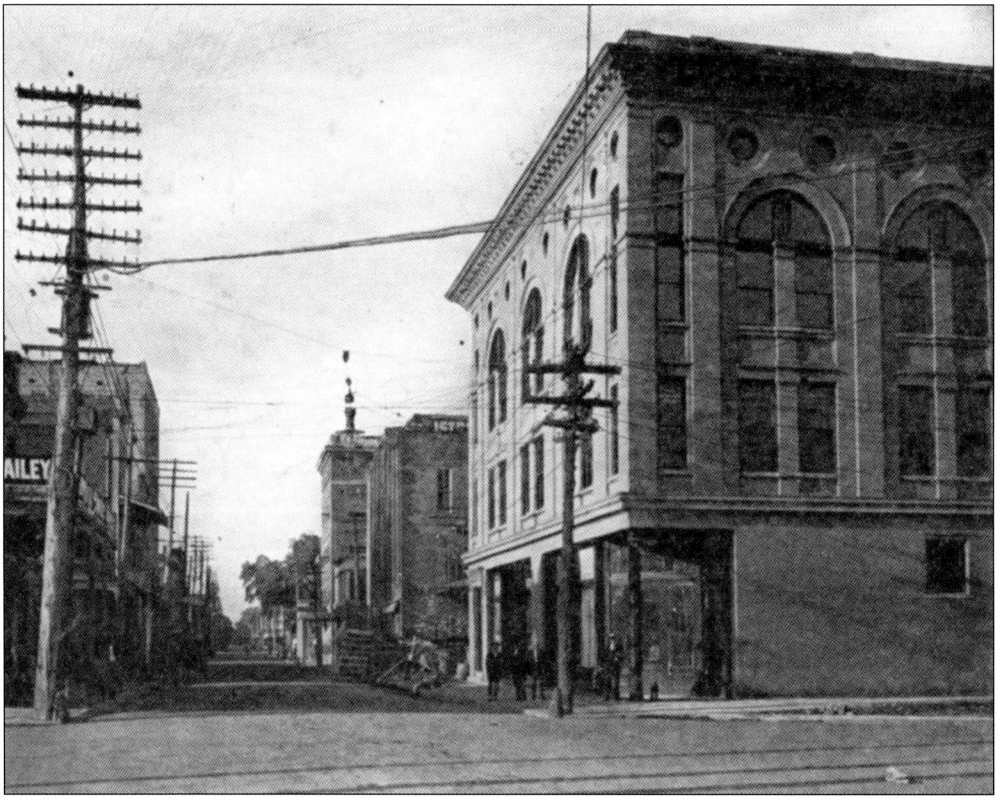

This view of North Third Street at Convention Street captures the architectural beauty of the Masonic temple in 1910. The lodge moved to this building in 1907 after utilizing space in the Ronaldson and Puckett Building for many years. The first commercial tenant here was Paulsen & Son Drug Store. Later tenants were Walgreens, Tic-Toc Shoes, and Capital Area Legal Society. Shown on the same block beyond the lodge are the Mayer Hotel, Louisiana National Bank, and the Istrouma Hotel. (EBRPL.)

In 1914, the Louisiana Theater was a popular entertainment venue on Third Street. The theater opened in July 1913 and was among the earliest silent moving-picture theaters in Baton Rouge. It predated the Greek Revival–style Columbia Theater, built in 1920, which was also on Third Street. (EBRPL.)

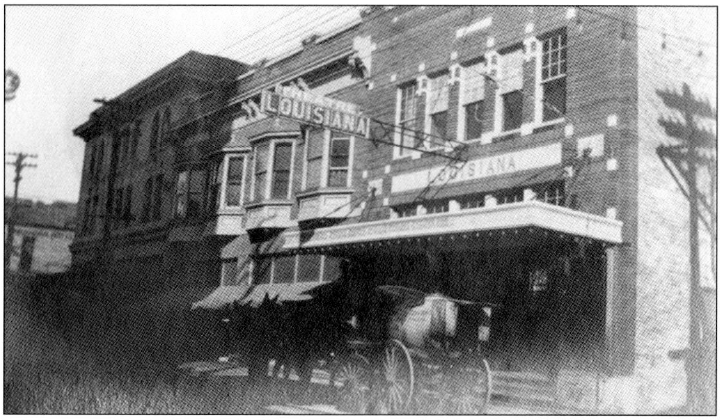

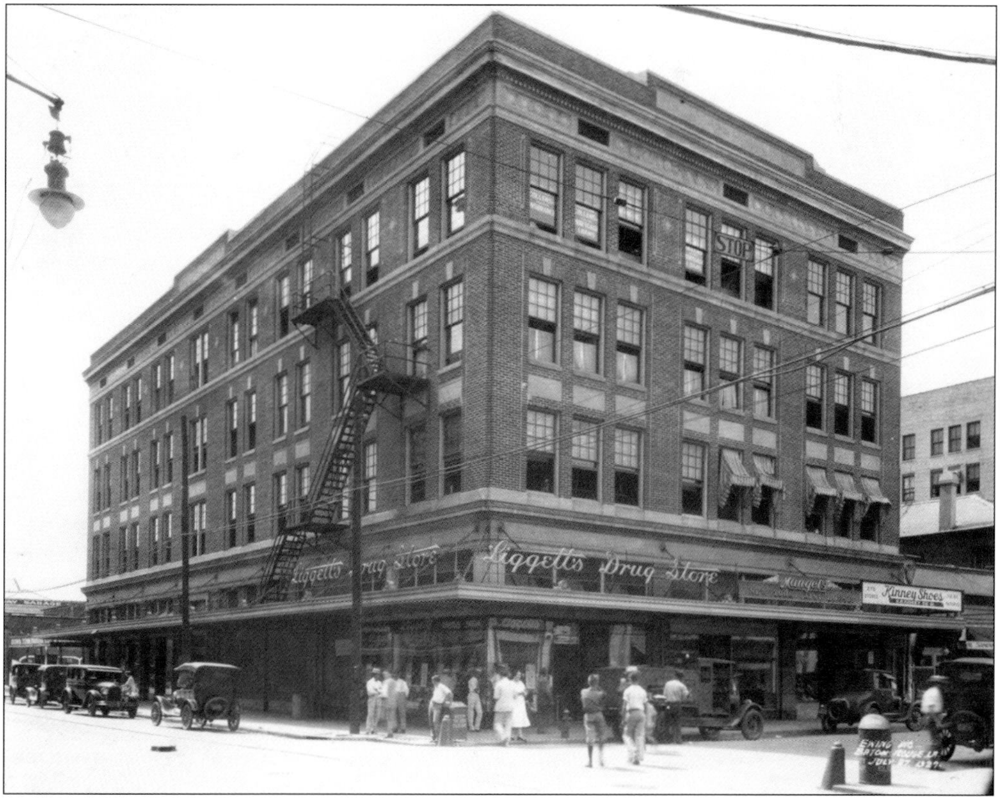

This photograph by Jasper Ewing captures the architectural details of the Triad Building at 301 Third Street, which still stands on the northwest corner of Third and Florida Streets. The office building was constructed in the 1920s by three local businessmen. Retail tenants at street level featured the large modern pharmacy of Liggett's Drug Store, Mangel's New York Waist House, and Kinney Shoes. The building was mostly noted for Liggett's, a drugstore that was one of 672 stores across the nation owned by Louis Kroh Liggett. The chain store was advertised as the South's largest self-service drugstore and featured an expanded sideline of products. Today, the building is known as the Taylor Building. (EBRPL.)

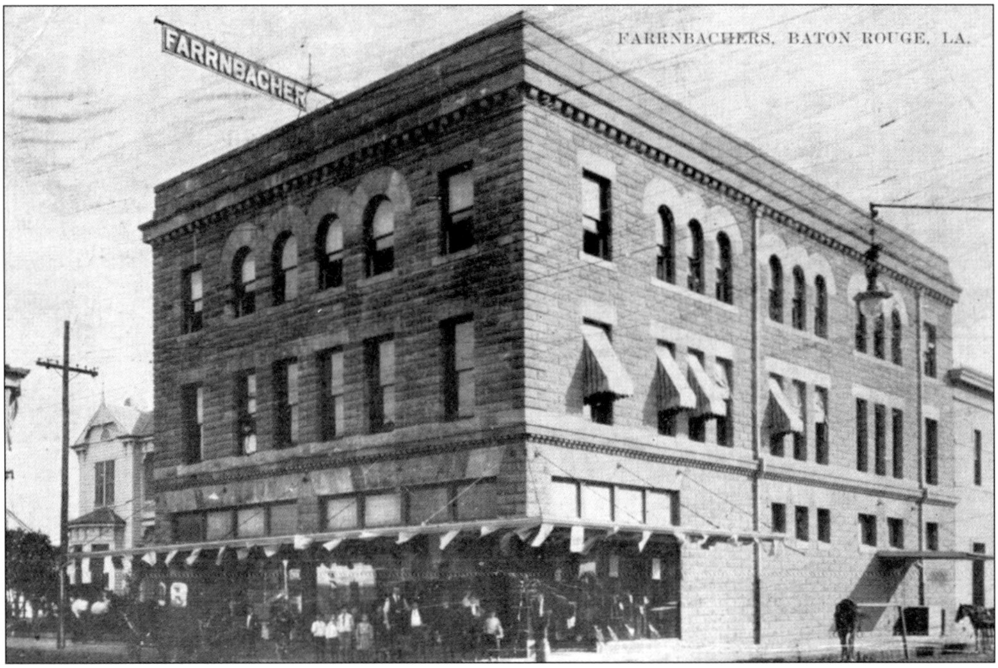

Farrnbacher Dry Goods and Clothiers was located on the southeast corner of Main, in the 700 block, and St. Anthony Streets. The store was one of Baton Rouge's retail icons and a competitor of Rosenfield's Dry Goods, S.I. Reymond (later Dalton's), and Henry Strauss Clothiers. The store was established by Bavarian-born Jacob Farrnbacher, who later diversified his investments into insurance and banking. (EBRPL.)

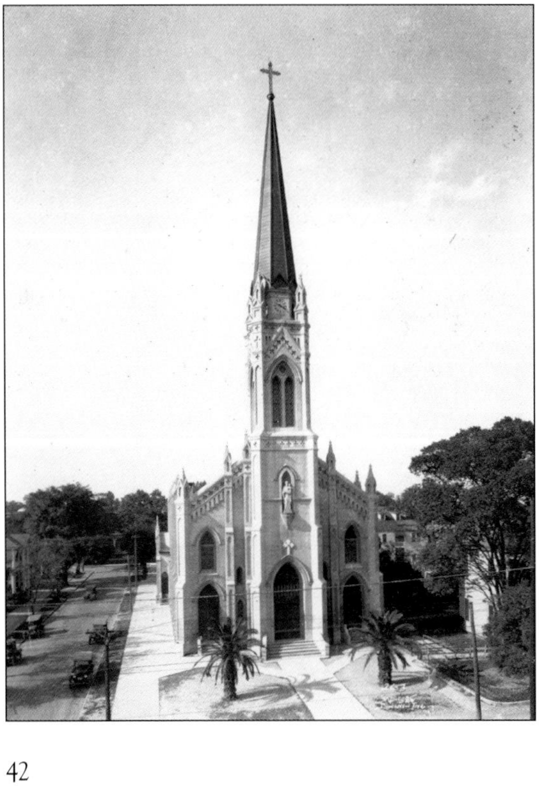

St. Joseph's Catholic Church is one of the oldest and largest churches in Baton Rouge. St. Joseph's was originally named Nuestra Señora de los Dolores, or Our Lady of Sorrows. The first Mass at St. Joseph's was conducted in 1792. The site was located north of the present-day Louisiana State Capitol and on the site of the original Our Lady of the Lake Hospital, overlooking University Lake, today Capitol Lake. St. Joseph's present church building was completed in 1856 in the Gothic Revival style on the corner of Main and Church Streets. The building was designated to be the cathedral of the Diocese of Baton Rouge in 1961 and later listed in the National Register of Historic Places. (EBRPL.)

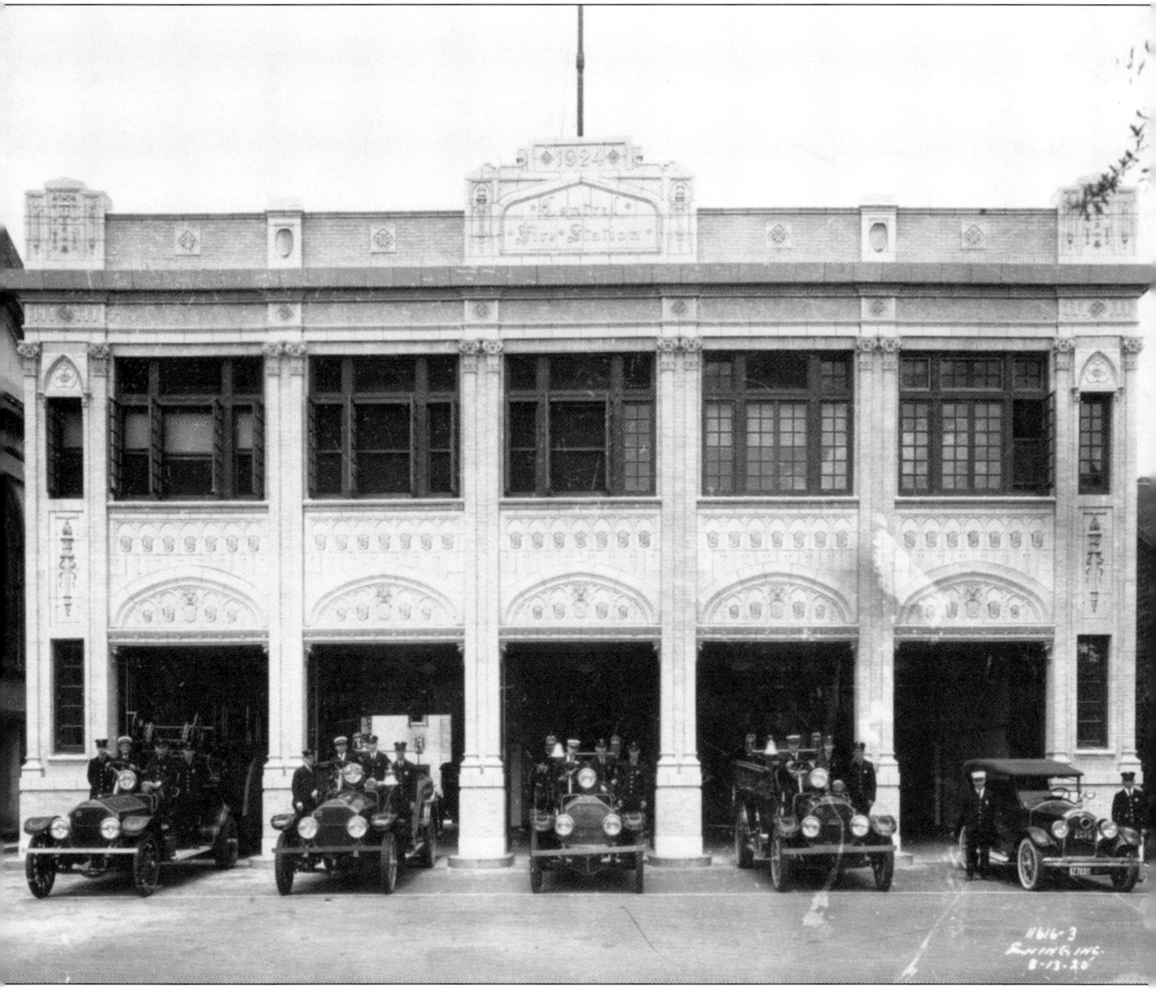

Central Fire Station was one of four modern stations built in Baton Rouge in 1922. The firehouse is located at 425 Laurel Street. The building was renamed Bogan Fire Station in honor of Robert A. Bogan, who was the first paid fire chief. He served from 1918 to 1959. Firemen display new apparatuses and vehicles for Jasper Ewing in this 1923 photograph. (EBRPL.)

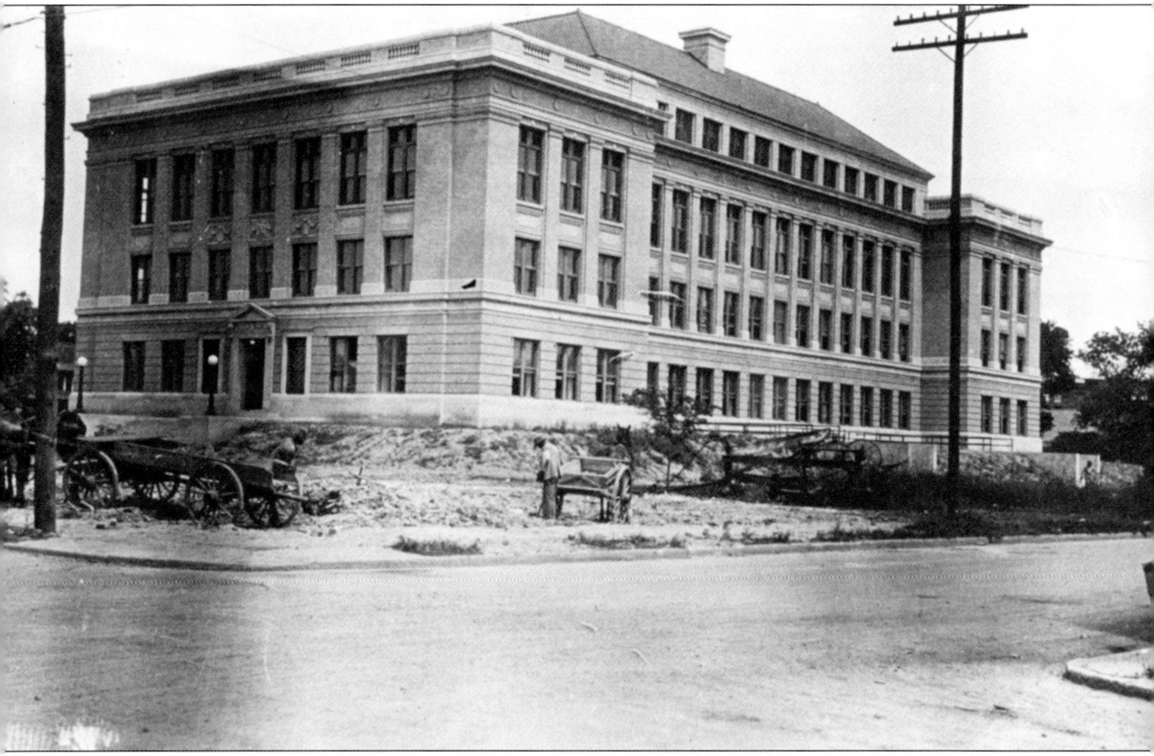

The East Baton Rouge Parish Court House was built in 1923. It occupied an entire city block bordered by St. Louis, St. Ferdinand, Africa (later renamed Louisiana), and Court Streets. Court Street ran east-west between the courthouse and the city market. The modern building was fitted with two electric, manually controlled elevators running from the basement to the third floor and a third elevator designated for the parish jail located on the fourth floor. (EBRPL.)

Unlike many weaker banks that quickly failed after the 1929 stock market crash, Citizens Bank and Trust Company opened its doors in January 1930 after building assets through bank mergers. The modern brick structure was located at 1604 Main Street. (EBRPL.)

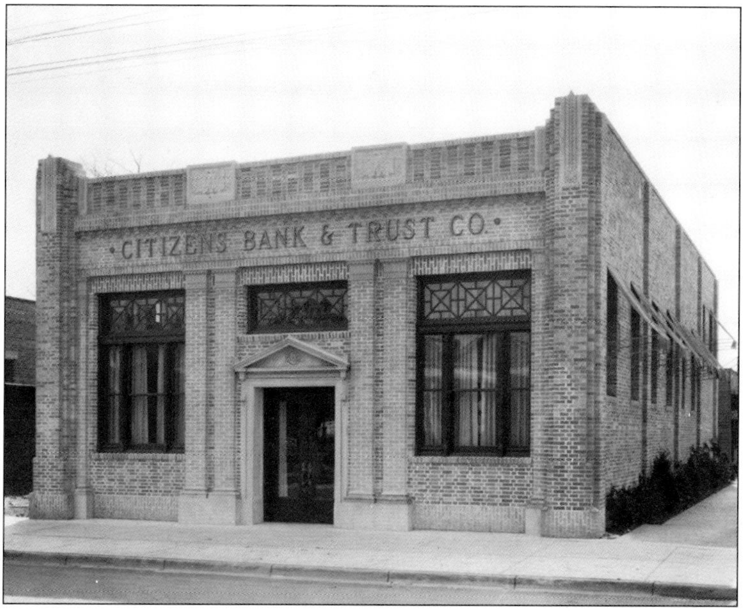

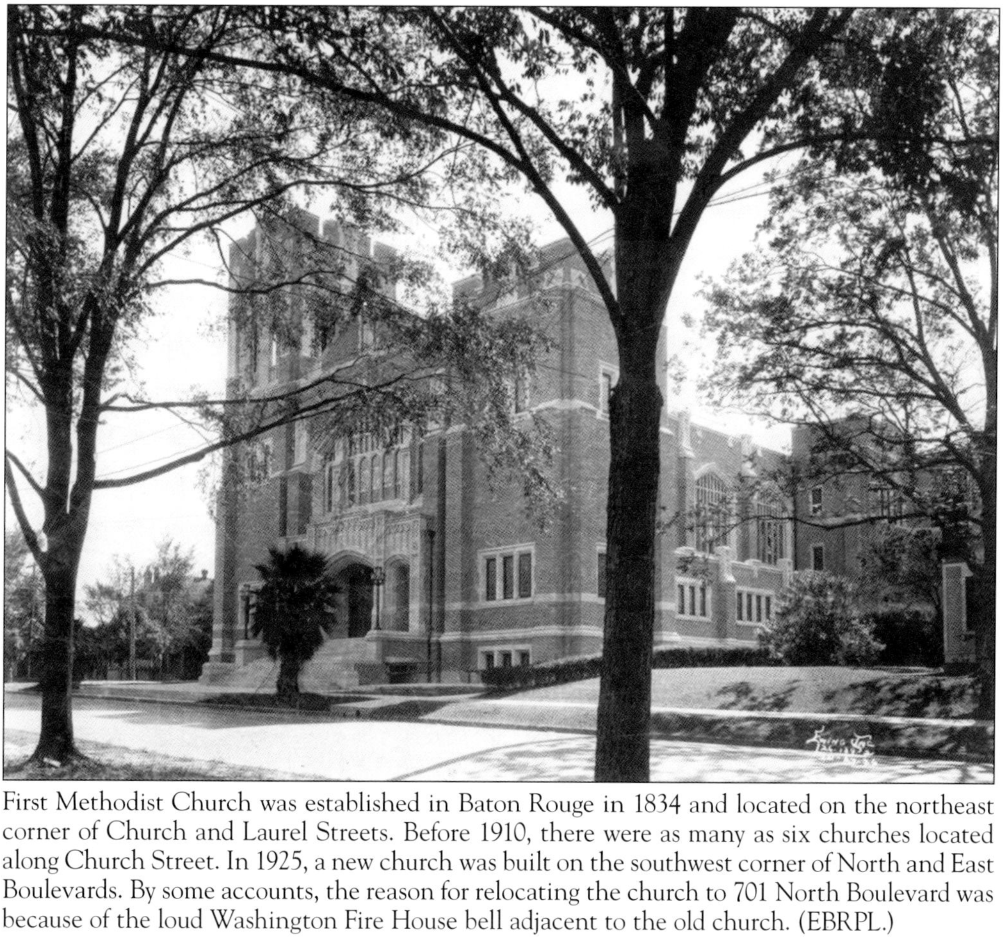

First Methodist Church was established in Baton Rouge in 1834 and located on the northeast corner of Church and Laurel Streets. Before 1910, there were as many as six churches located along Church Street. In 1925, a new church was built on the southwest corner of North and East Boulevards. By some accounts, the reason for relocating the church to 701 North Boulevard was because of the loud Washington Fire House bell adjacent to the old church. (EBRPL.)

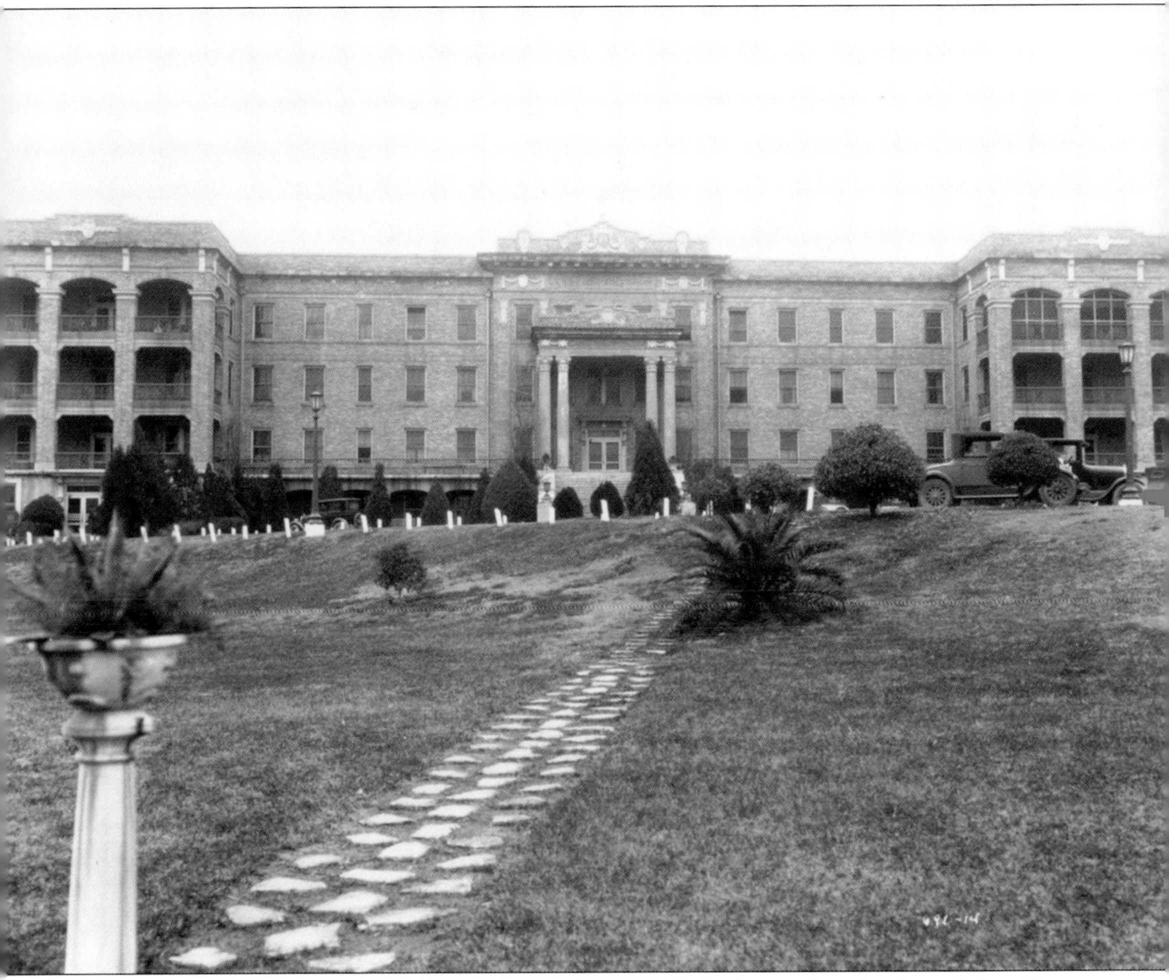

Five Franciscan Missionaries of Our Lady and Mother de Bethanie Crowley from Calais, France, came here for the purpose of serving the sick and needy. Together, the Franciscan sisters and a group of physicians opened Our Lady of the Lake Sanitarium on the banks of University Lake (later Capitol Lake), located north of the downtown campus of Louisiana State University. The 17-acre site and 100-bed hospital was replaced in 1977 by the current facility located on Essen Lane. The older sanitarium was razed in 1980 to make way for Louisiana state offices. (EBRPL.)

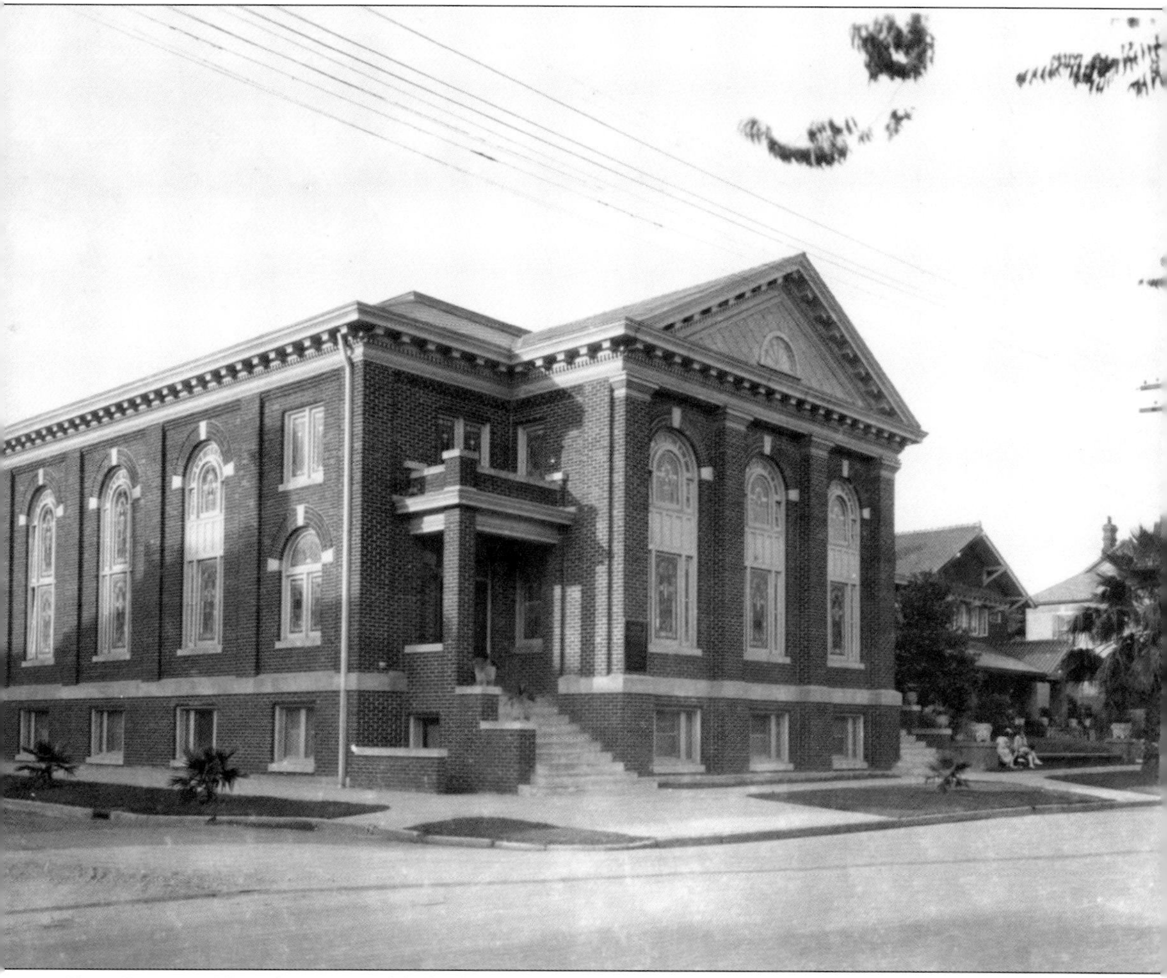

First Baptist Church was established in Baton Rouge around 1874 in a building that faced Florida Street. The building pictured here, constructed around 1920, was replaced by a larger one at the same location on Convention Street. The newer church, annex, and parking area encompassed the entire block bound by Fifth, Sixth and Florida Streets. This image was taken around 1927. (EBRPL.)

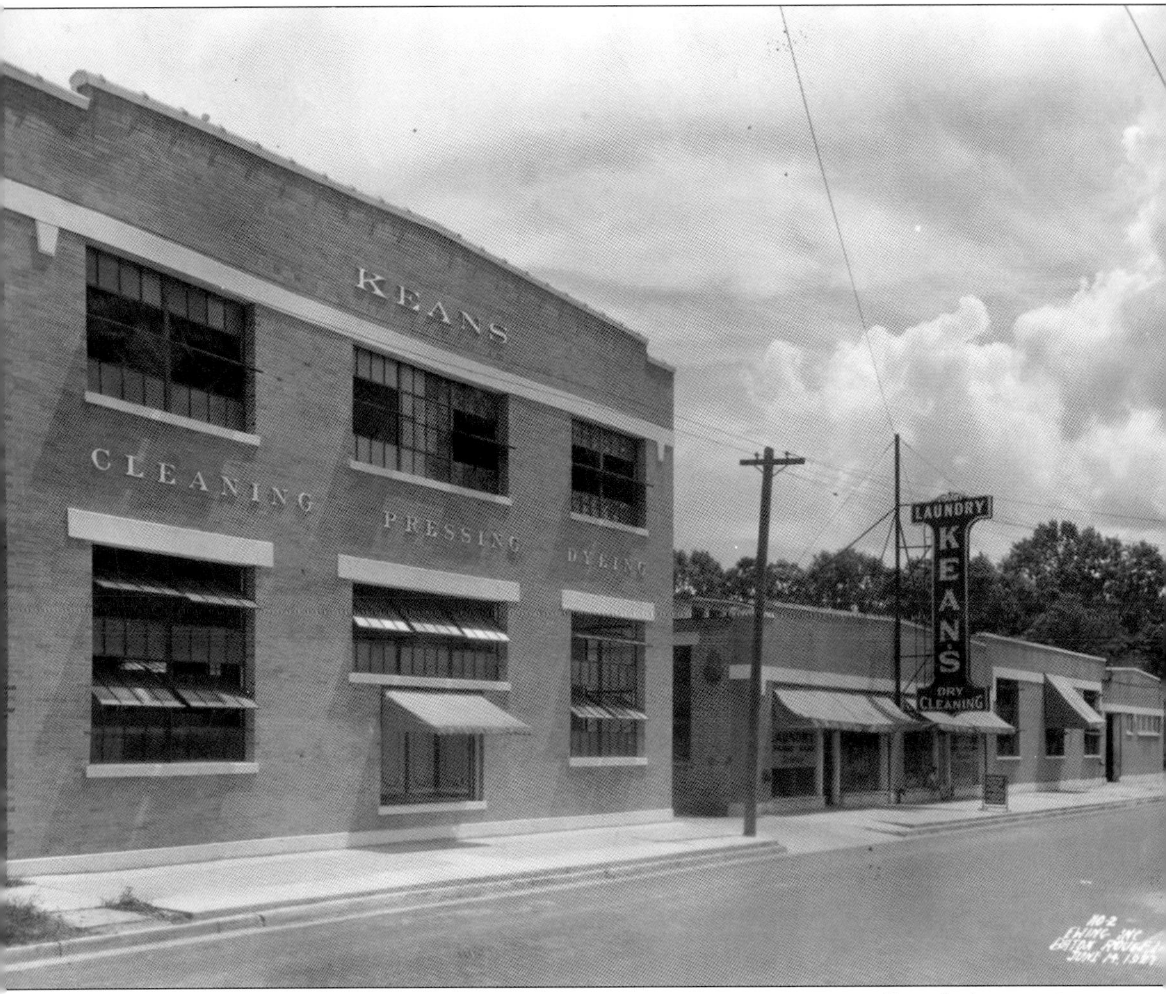

Kean's Laundry was located on the 1800 block of Convention Street. Initially called Kean's Fine Dry Cleaning, it was founded by John Selby and Frank H. Kean in 1900. In the beginning, the cleaning business focused on laundering collars for LSU students in a wood-frame building on Government Street. The name was changed to Kean Brothers in 1906 and moved to Third Street. In 1924, Kean's moved to Convention Street after a fire destroyed the Third Street business. (EBRPL.)

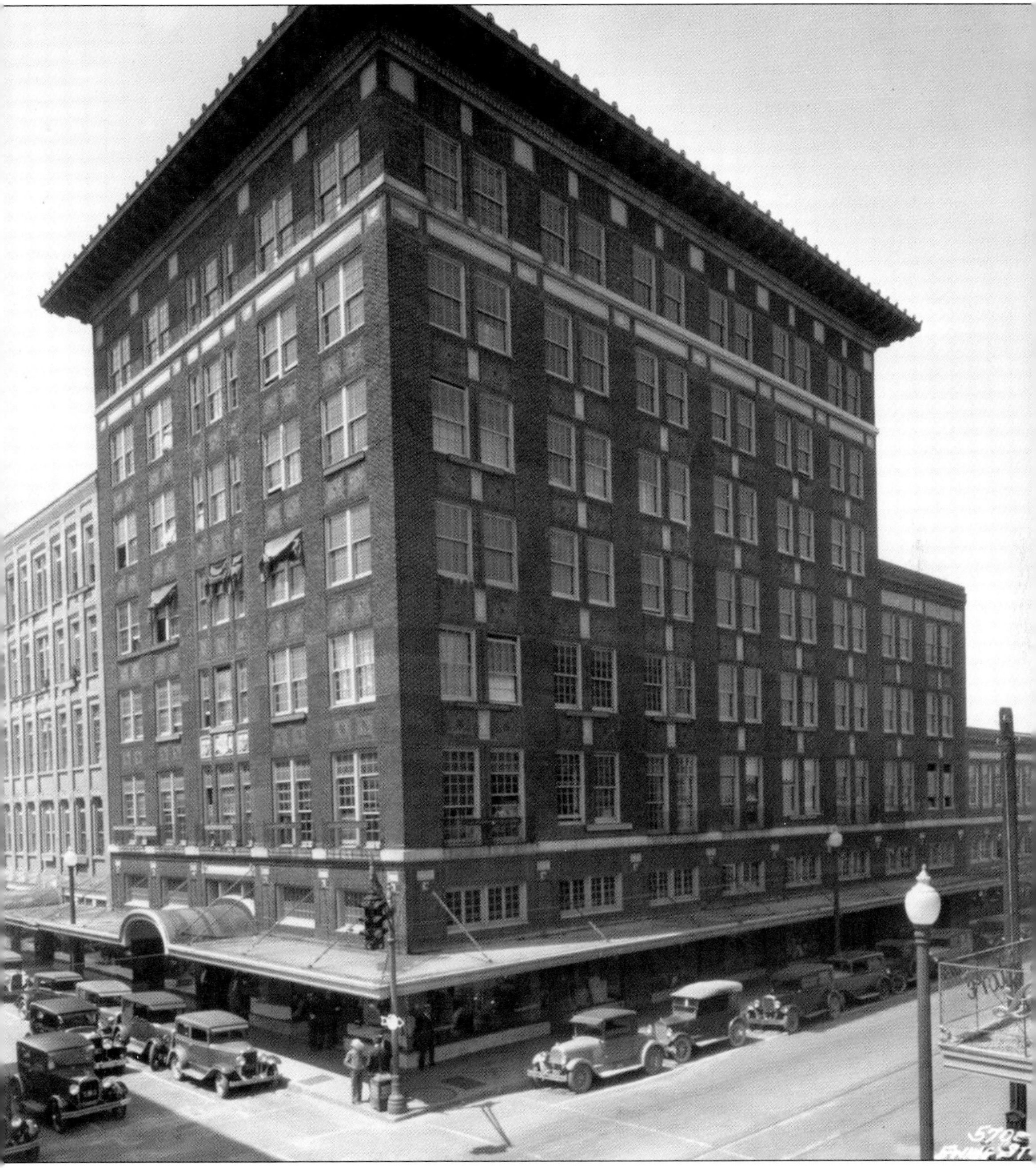

Samuel Isett Reymond, at the age of 21, established S.I. Reymond Co., Ltd. (later Dalton's) in 1902 after apprenticing for 11 years as a salesman in the dry goods business. Reymond Dry Goods Company was formerly located at Third and Main Streets. The new Reymond Building, a high-rise, fireproof structure, was constructed on the corner of Third and Florida Streets. Welsh & Levy Clothing Company moved into the old Reymond Dry Goods Company store in February 1907. (EBRPL.)

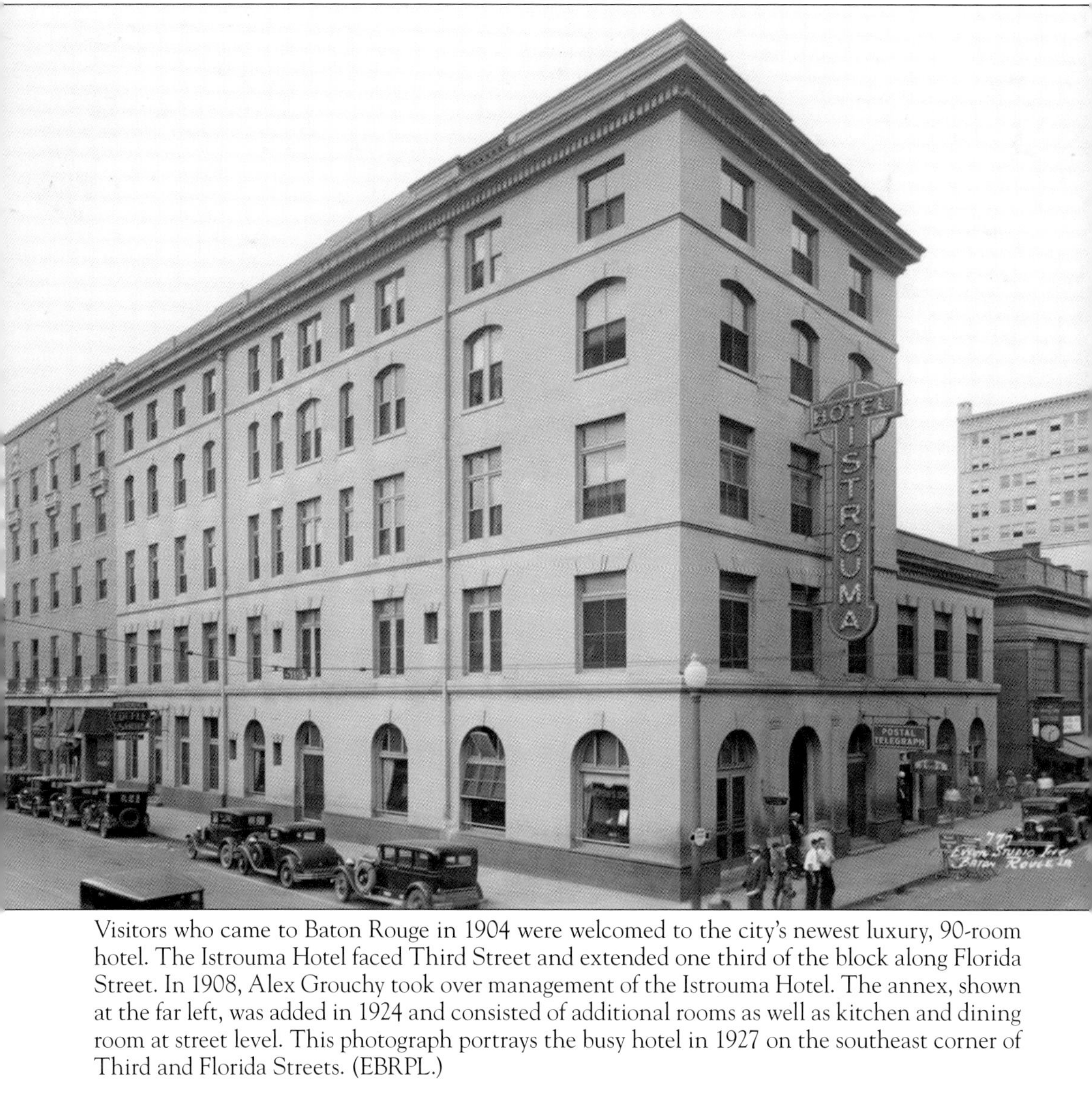

Visitors who came to Baton Rouge in 1904 were welcomed to the city's newest luxury, 90-room hotel. The Istrouma Hotel faced Third Street and extended one third of the block along Florida Street. In 1908, Alex Grouchy took over management of the Istrouma Hotel. The annex, shown at the far left, was added in 1924 and consisted of additional rooms as well as kitchen and dining room at street level. This photograph portrays the busy hotel in 1927 on the southeast corner of Third and Florida Streets. (EBRPL.)

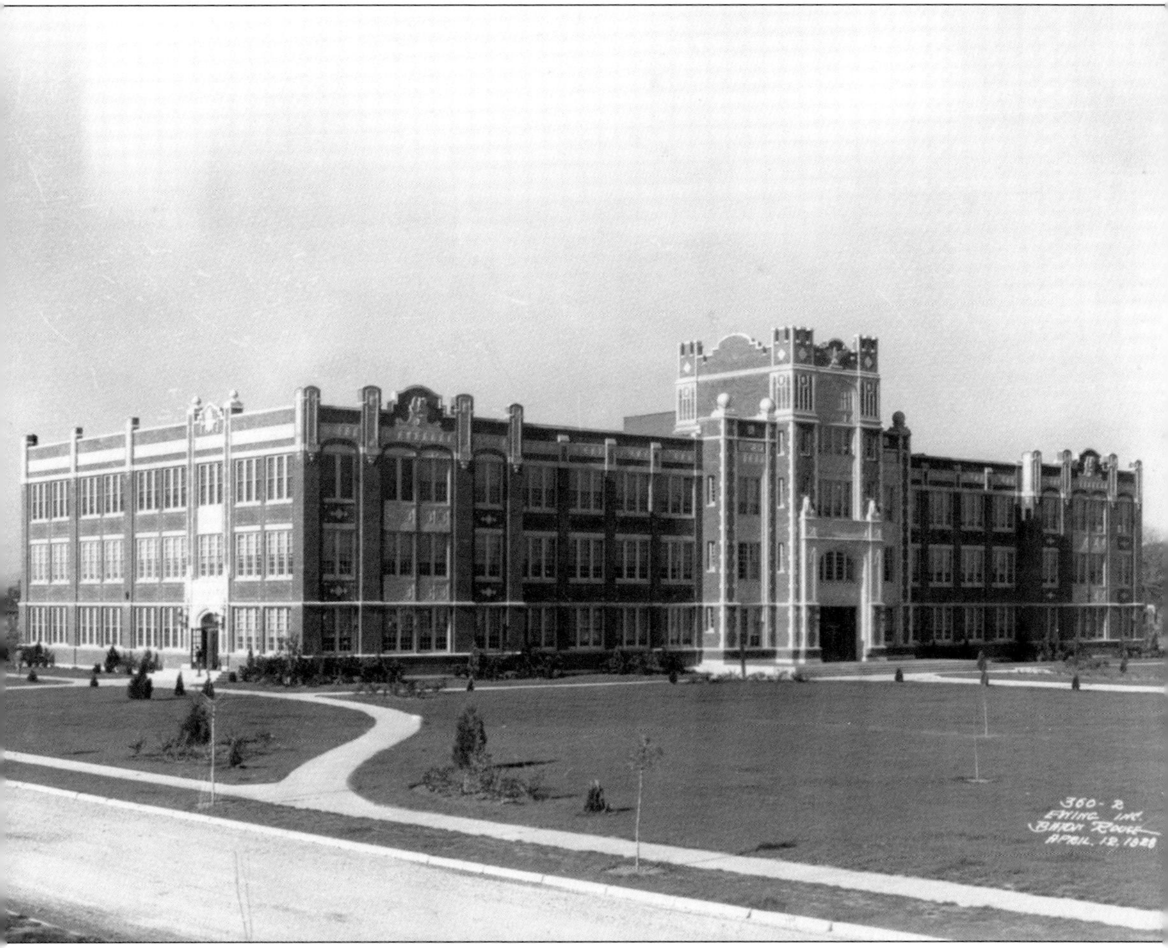

Baton Rouge High School was established in 1903 on Tenth Street between North Boulevard and Convention Street. In 1913, a new brick structure was built on the northeast corner of Tenth and Florida Streets. The school was moved again in 1925 to a new location and occupied the entire 2600 block on the north side of Government Street between Ogden and Eugene Streets. This building, on Government Street, has remained the home of Baton Rouge High School since 1925. (EBRPL.)

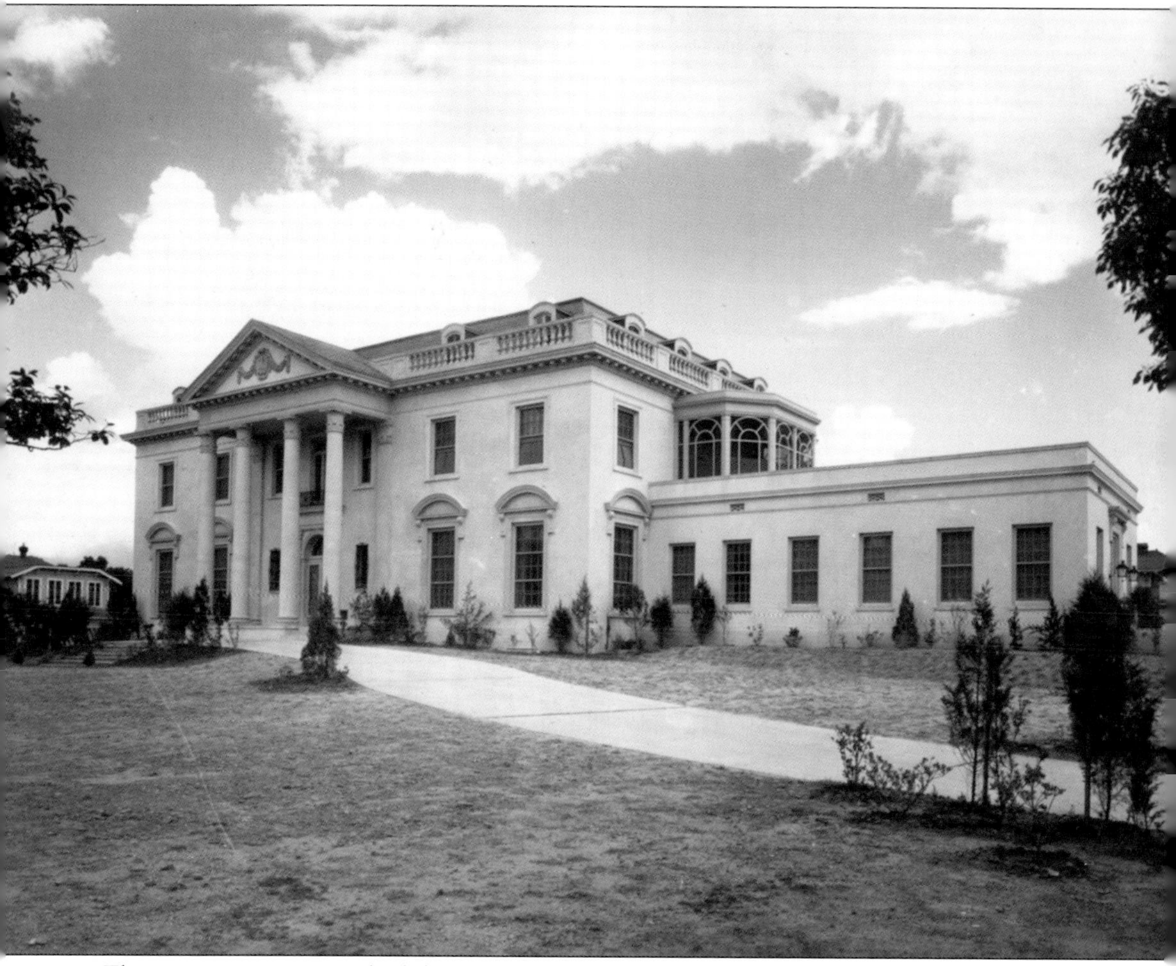

This governor's mansion, built by Huey P. Long in 1930, was located on the southeast corner of North Boulevard and St. Charles Street. This was the site of the previous governor's mansion built in 1857. Gov. Huey P. Long required the design of this building to resemble a stucco Georgian mansion constructed to the likeness of the White House in Washington, DC. (EBRPL.)

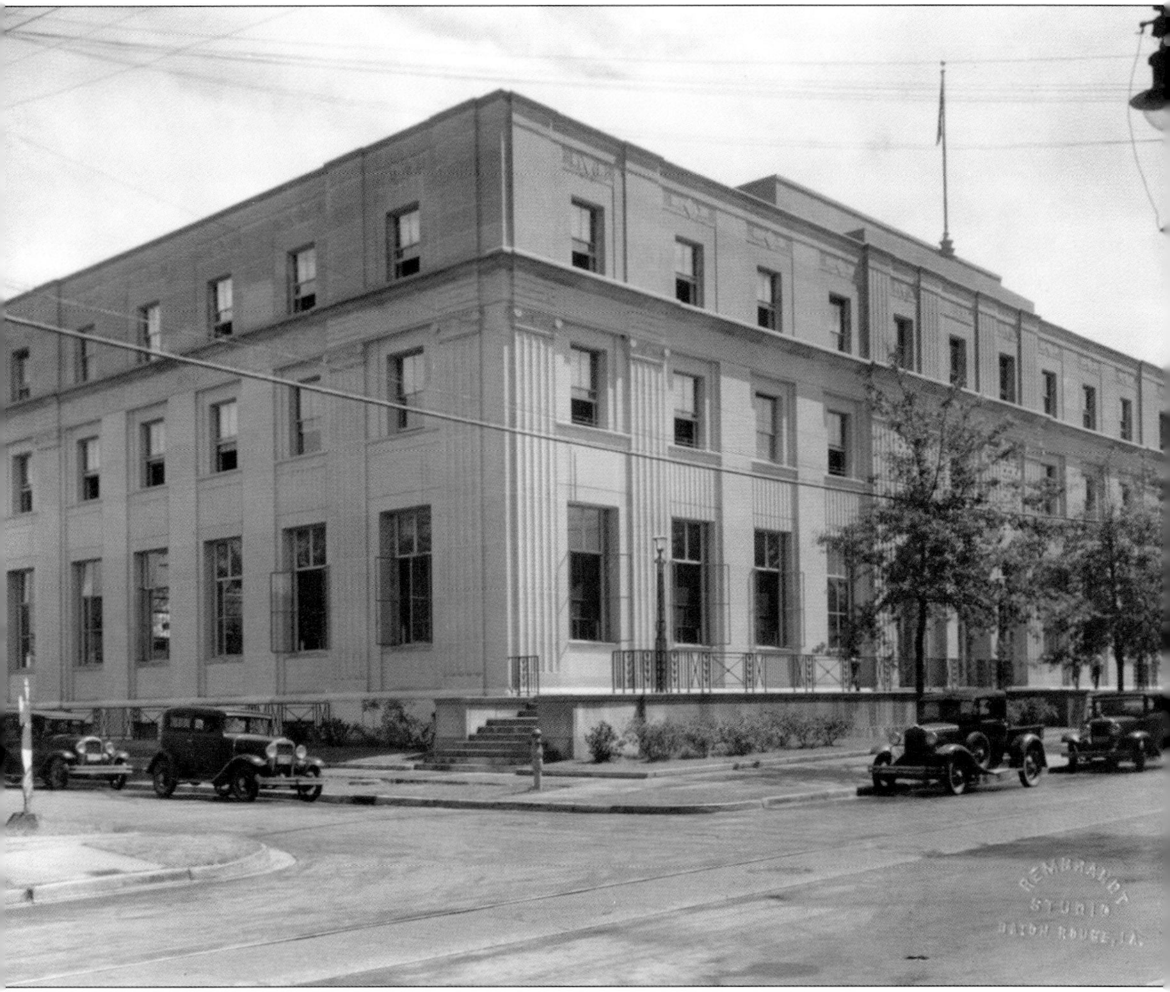

The combination courthouse and post office on the northwest corner of North Boulevard and North Fourth Street had outlived its usefulness by 1933. This modern building, on the 700 block of Florida Street, became the new federal court and post office facility in 1934. The Art Deco–style building is representative of the modern styles of architecture used in the design of many public buildings during the 1930s. (EBRPL.)

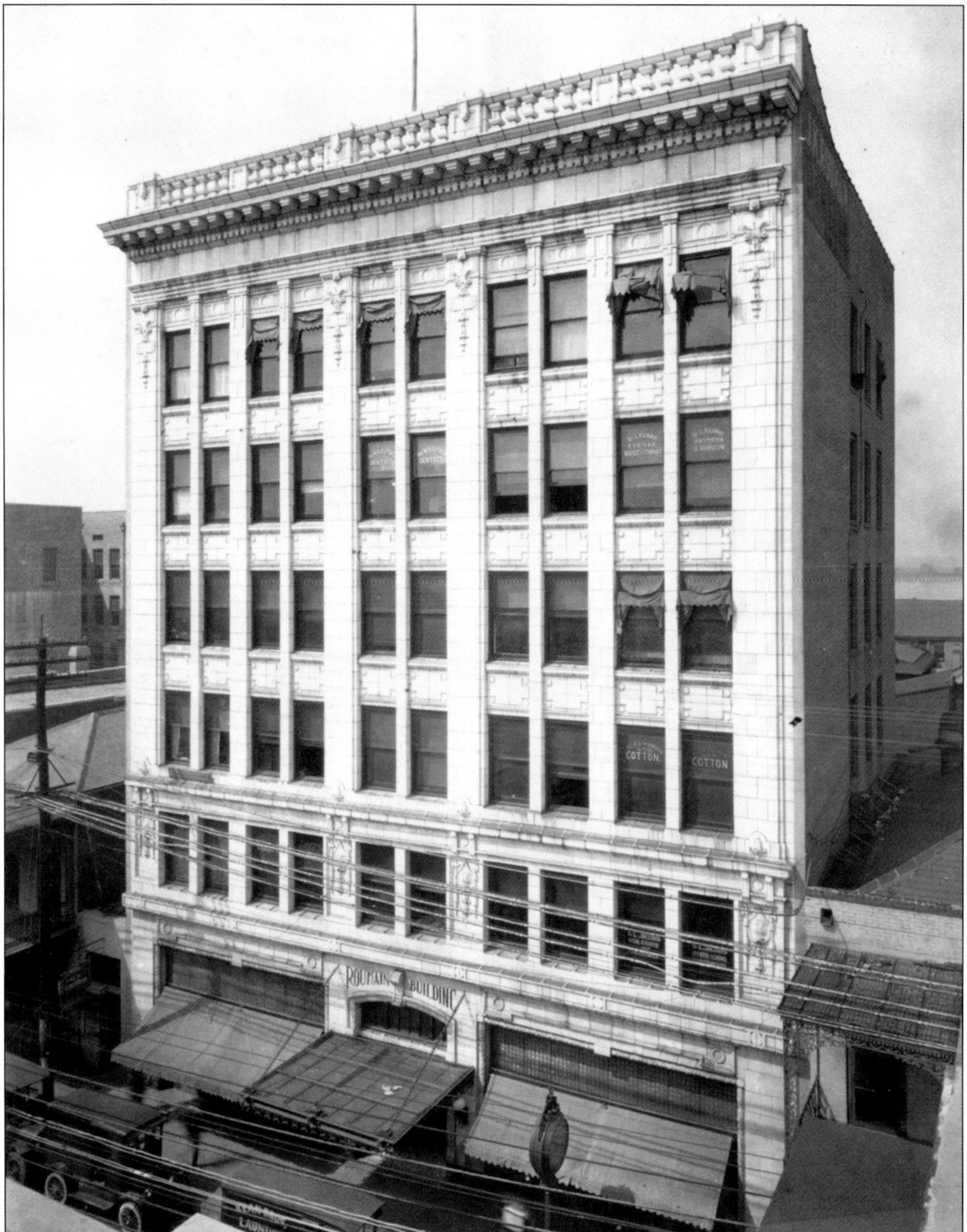

The Roumain Building was popularized as Baton Rouge's first skyscraper in 1913. It was named for owner Joseph K. Roumain, a wealthy watchmaker and jeweler. The building was designed by New Orleans architects Favrot and Livaudais and embellished in the style of Beaux-Arts architecture. It was added to the National Register of Historic Places in 1985. (EBRPL.)

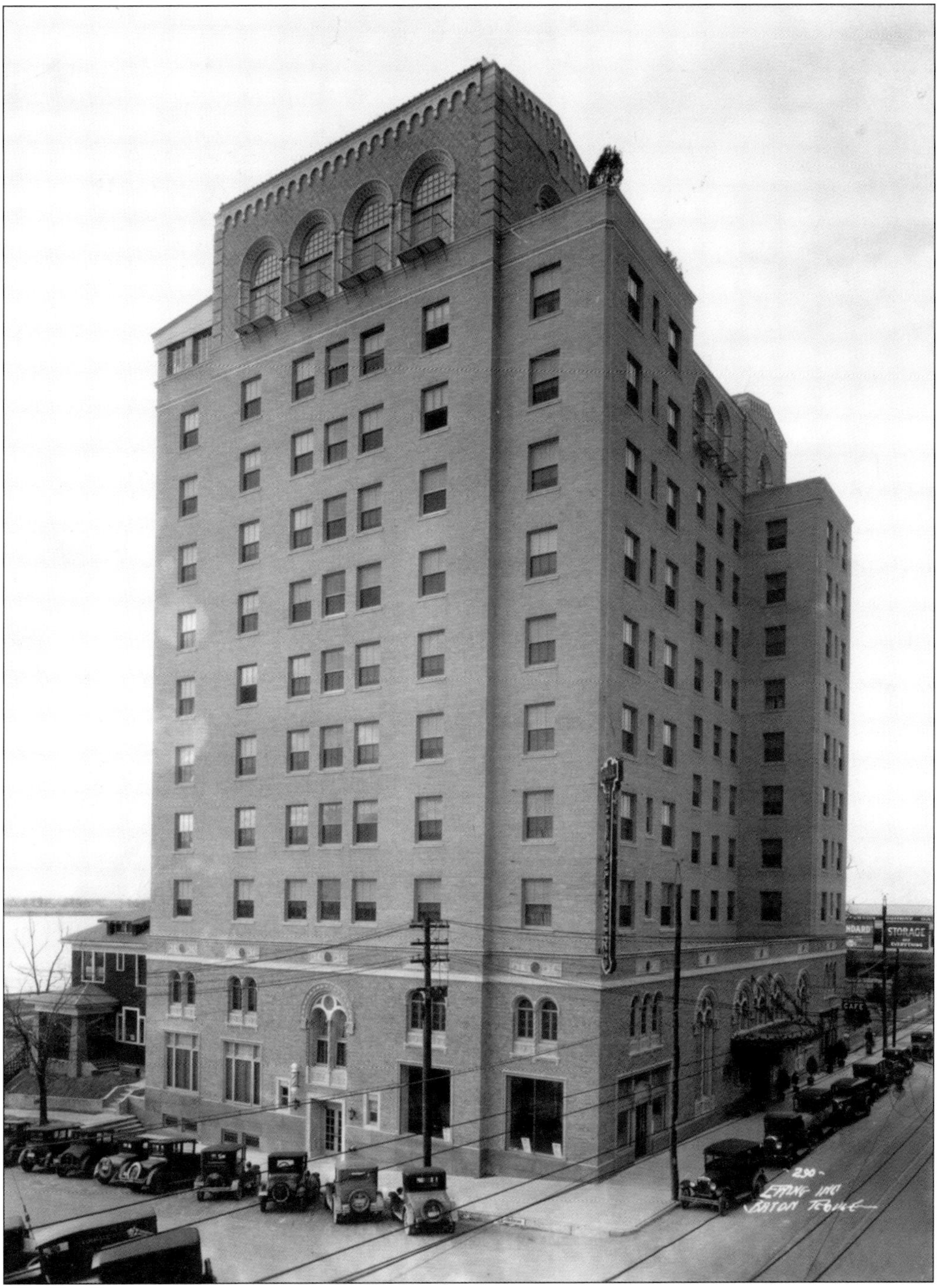

The Heidelberg Hotel was designed by architect Edward Nield and built in 1927 at the corner of Lafayette and Convention Streets. The hotel served as a frequent dwelling of Louisiana governor Huey P. Long, who accessed a secret tunnel beneath the street for his many rumored rendezvous. The building later served as the Capitol House Hotel and today as the Hilton Baton Rouge Capitol Center Hotel. It was listed in the National Register of Historic Places in 1982. Jasper Ewing took this photograph shortly after its opening. (EBRPL.)

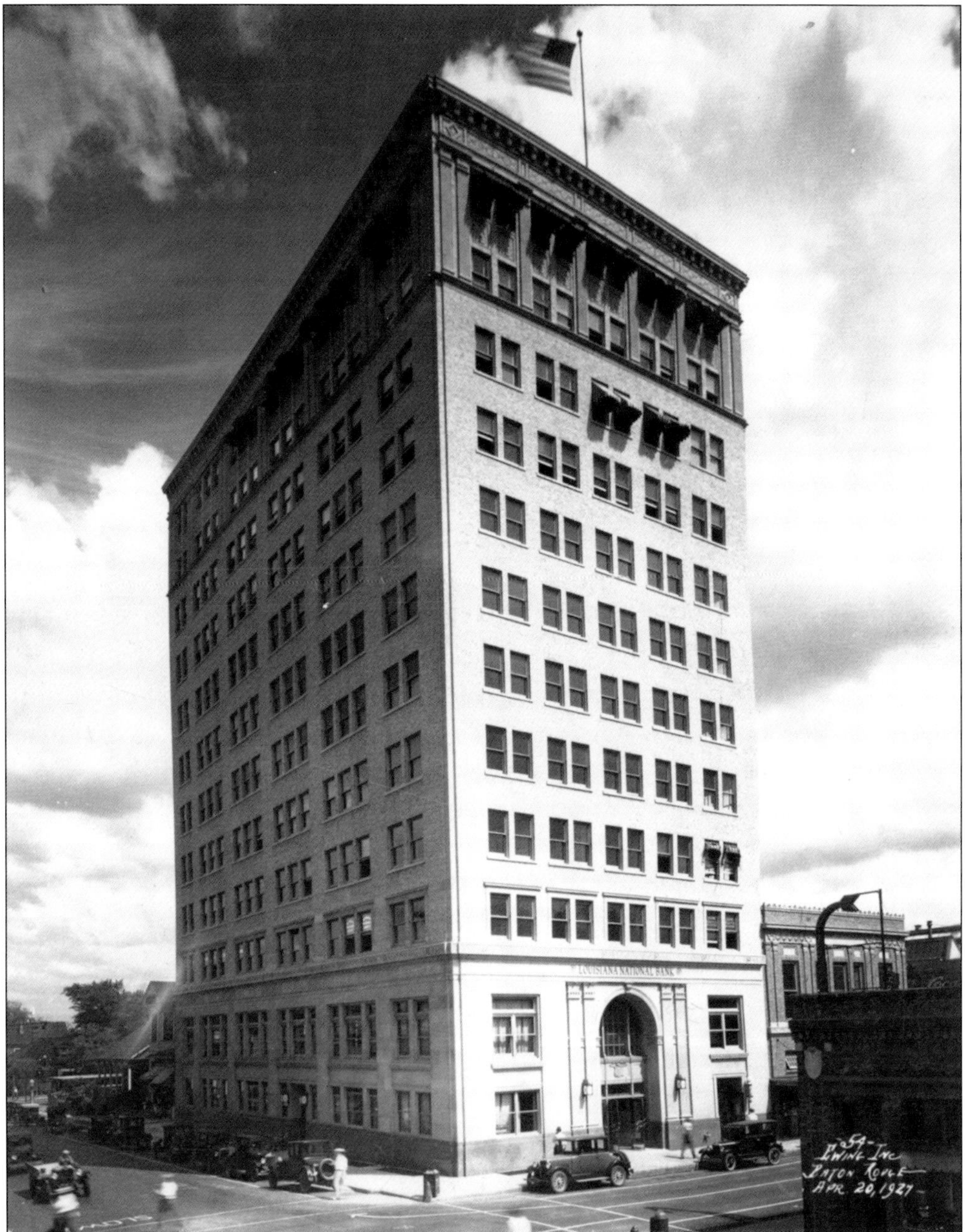

For Baton Rougeans, Louisiana National Bank, established in 1910, was one of this city's leading financial institutions. In 1926, a modern building was constructed at 150 Third Street. It was the first skyscraper in the city of Baton Rouge. An enormous building in its day, the 12-story structure consisted of more than 92,000 square feet of office space. (EBRPL.)

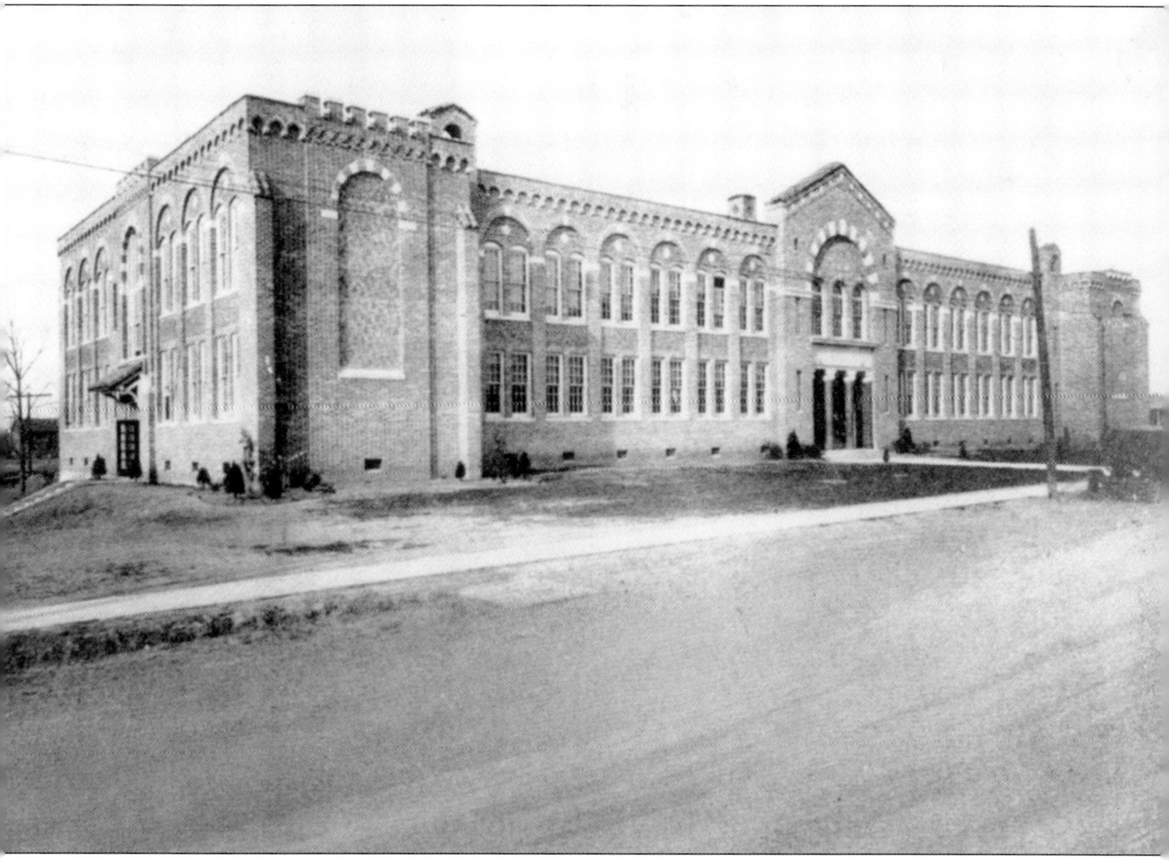

The first African American school in Baton Rouge was originally named Hickory Street School in 1907. By 1913, it opened as Perkins Road School at a new location near Sixteenth and Bynum Streets. In 1927, the school was relocated to East Boulevard (later named Thomas H. Delpit Drive), between Howard and Louise Streets, and was named after President McKinley. McKinley was the oldest high school in the state of Louisiana, established for African Americans, and the building was added to the National Register of Historic Places in 1981. (LSL.)

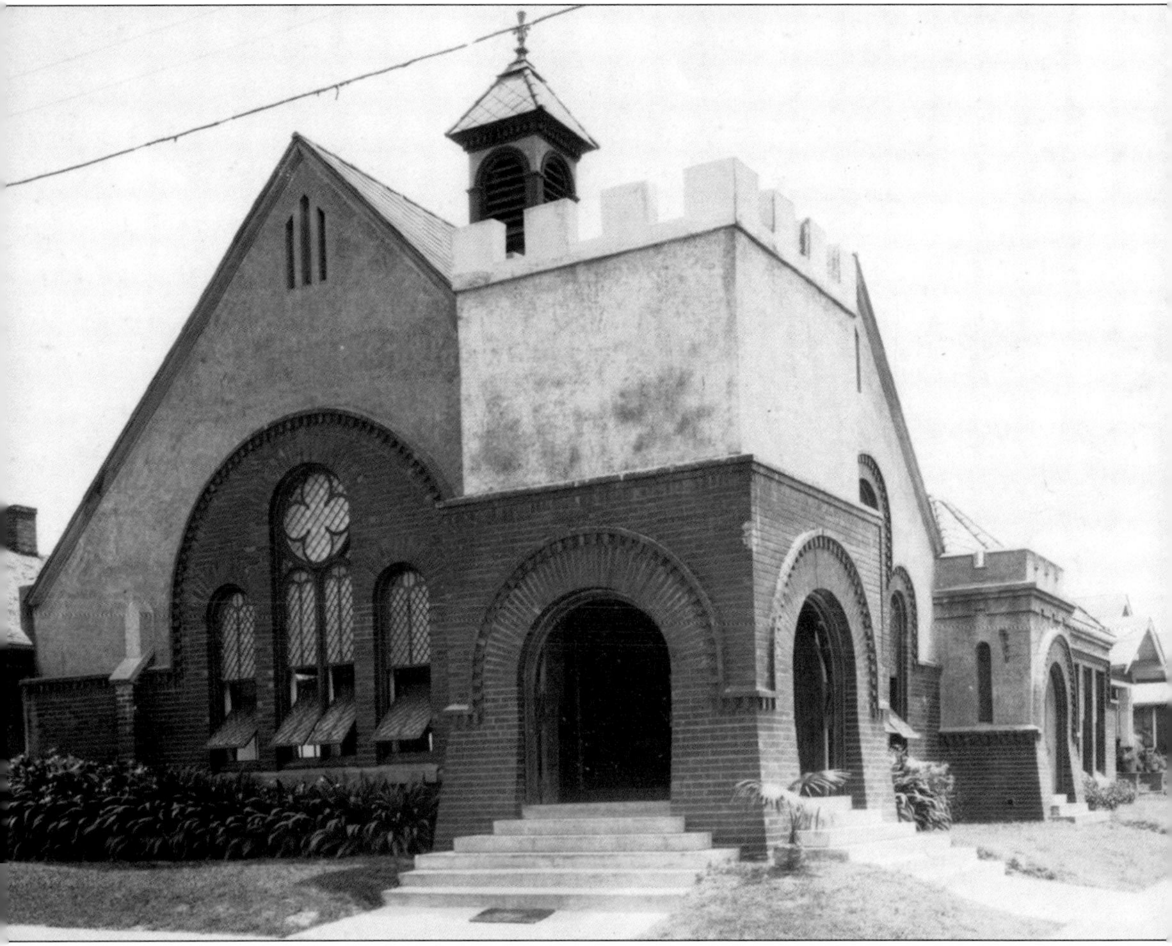

The Christian church was located at the corner of East and North Boulevards on the edge of Beauregard Town. During the 1920s, it was transformed into the Women's Clubhouse, which was a consortium for 15 ladies' organizations. The Woman's Clubhouse was a popular gathering place for social events and meetings. (EBRPL.)

Three

Trains, Planes, and Automobiles

In this chapter, artists have captured images of the forgotten and unremembered ways in which people and freight arrived at destinations from the late 1800s to the early 1900s. During that time, most images outside of a photographer's studio portrayed some form of transportation. Planes, trains, and automobiles were relatively new to Baton Rouge compared to wagons, ships, and boats of the 1800s. Because of the importance of these newer modes of transportation, Baton Rouge was able to come into its own.

Railroads played a key role in growth and expansion of Baton Rouge. Prior to the Civil War, rail connections to Baton Rouge were segmented and without any direct lines to other cities. By 1883, the first direct line was completed from Baton Rouge to New Orleans. By 1893, the Yazoo and Mississippi Valley Railroad ran from New Orleans to Memphis, and during the period covered in this book, trains were able to cross the river by ferryboat. Around the turn of the 20th century, railroads were nearing their peak on several levels, but it was soon thereafter that the automobile stole the limelight for travel.

By 1910, aviation began to play a role in cities across the nation. The new technological marvel of flying machines brought aviation races and air shows from the larger cities to Baton Rouge. The earliest aviation mishaps in Louisiana claimed two experienced aeronauts: John B. Moisant of New Orleans and William G. Purves of Chicago. Purves was the first aeronaut known to visit Baton Rouge. The first airmail flight between cities in the United States was in 1912 when French aviator George Mestach, the "Birdman," arrived at his destination on the campus of Louisiana State University on April 10, 1912.

The debut of automobiles affected everyday life in Baton Rouge. The proliferation of autos and buses eventually brought about the demise of railroad and trolley car travel in the capital city. The social impact caused by the automobile encouraged city dwellers to visit distant rural landscapes and country folks to visit and shop within the city. And its effect was to the extent that teenagers gained liberation with driving freedom.

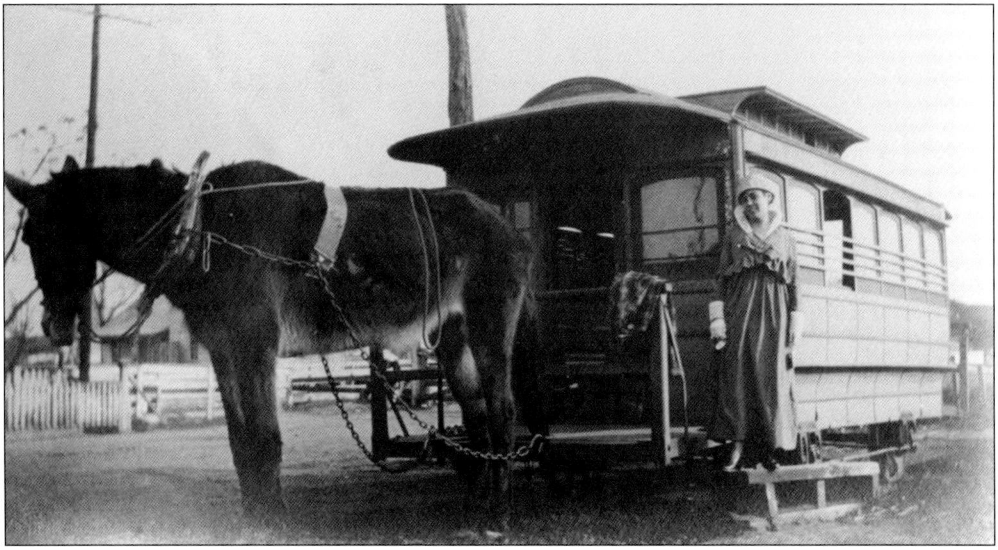

Mule-drawn trolleys began operating in 1890 with the initial charter by Baton Rouge Street and Railway Company. By 1893, the trolleys were already considered obsolete because of the more efficient electric motor–driven trolleys. Approximately four miles of Belt Line railway ran down the middle of Main Street, Third Street, North Boulevard, and St. Louis, Government, Dufrocq, and Convention Streets. One of the most popular routes was to the Baton Rouge Fairgrounds. (EBRPL.)

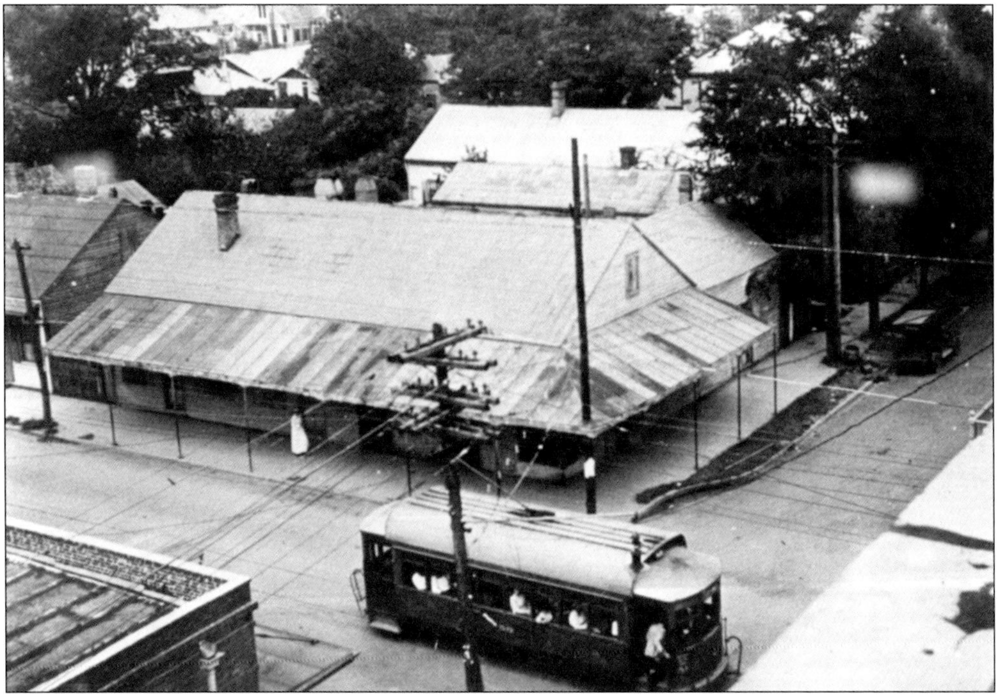

In this c. 1915 photograph, one of Baton Rouge's electric trolleys traverses the intersection of Main and Hypolite Streets (later North Sixth Street). By the mid-1920s, revenue was decreasing for the electric trolley industry, and the motor bus gradually took over to replace the rail line routes. By April 23, 1936, a farewell ceremony was held at the corner of Third Street and North Boulevard to bid the streetcars goodbye. (EBRPL.)

During the early 1920s, despite the proliferation of automobiles, streetcars were still the most efficient mode of transportation to get around the city. Shown here is one of Baton Rouge Electric Company's streetcar barns used for storage and maintenance of the trolleys. This barn was located on Goat Street. (SLL.)

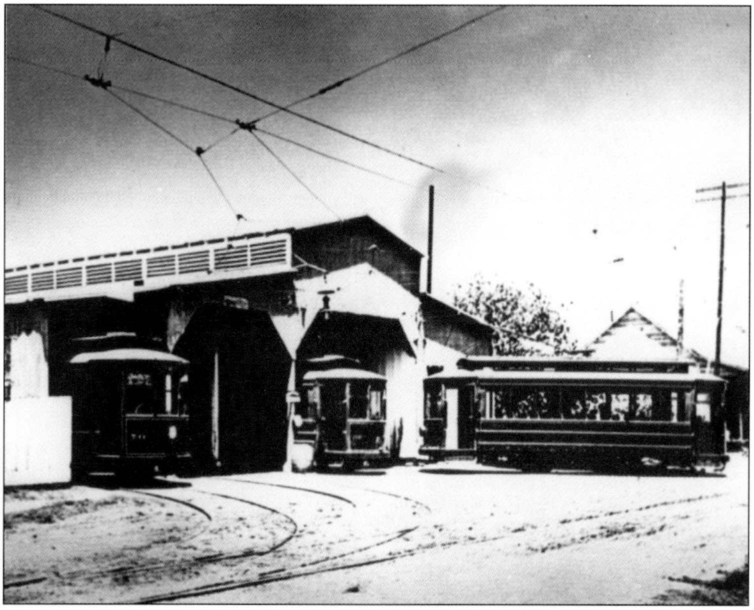

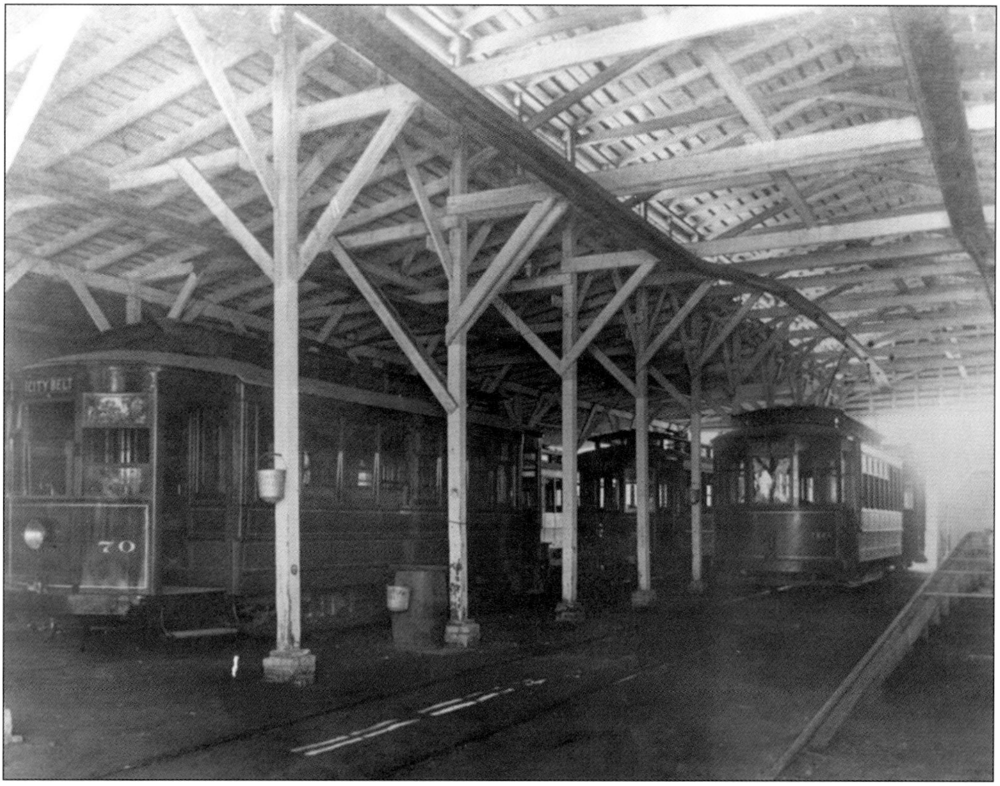

Here, Belt Line No. 30 and No. 70 have joined other trolleys at the end of a busy day. Some of the car barns were located on Government Street between Twelfth and Thirteenth Streets and housed as many as 18 trolleys. In 1925, Baton Rouge Electric Company bought three gasoline-powered buses that serviced between downtown and Louisiana State University's new south campus. All of the electric trolleys were eventually replaced by 1936. (SLL.)

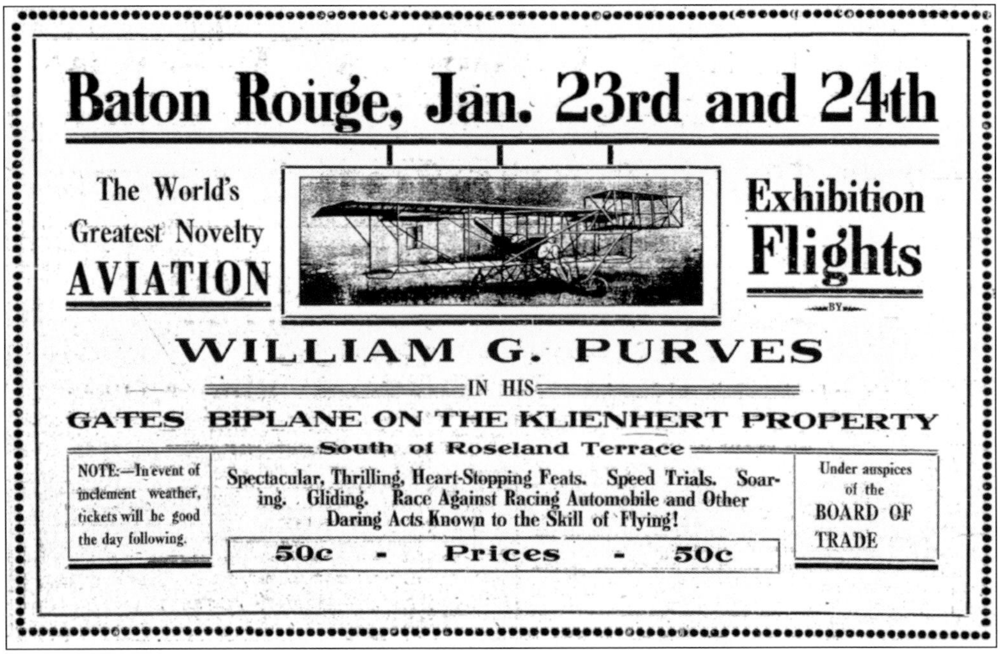

Promoters placed this advertisement in the *Daily State-Times–New Advocate* announcing an event by the first aviator to come to Baton Rouge. William G. Purves planned to do aerobatic performances over the Kleinert property near the site of the former Baton Rouge Fairgrounds. Zodak Realty, developers of Roseland Terrace subdivision, was joined by the board of trade in sponsoring Purves's aerial exhibition. A photograph of the Gates biplane was included in this advertisement on Friday, January 20, 1911. (TABR.)

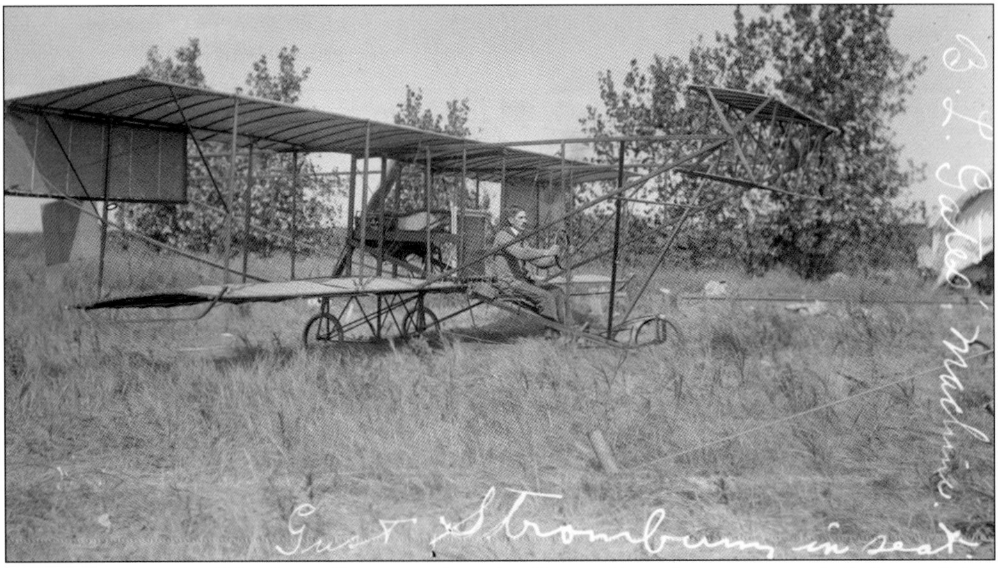

Preparations on the B.L. Gates flying machine by Gustav Strombum were made before a flying exhibition in Baton Rouge. William G. Purves was scheduled to perform aerial maneuvers and races against automobiles in this biplane at Kleinert's pasture on February 22 and 23, 1911. The field was located southeast of Baton Rouge on what is now known as Kleinert Terrace subdivision. (CHM.)

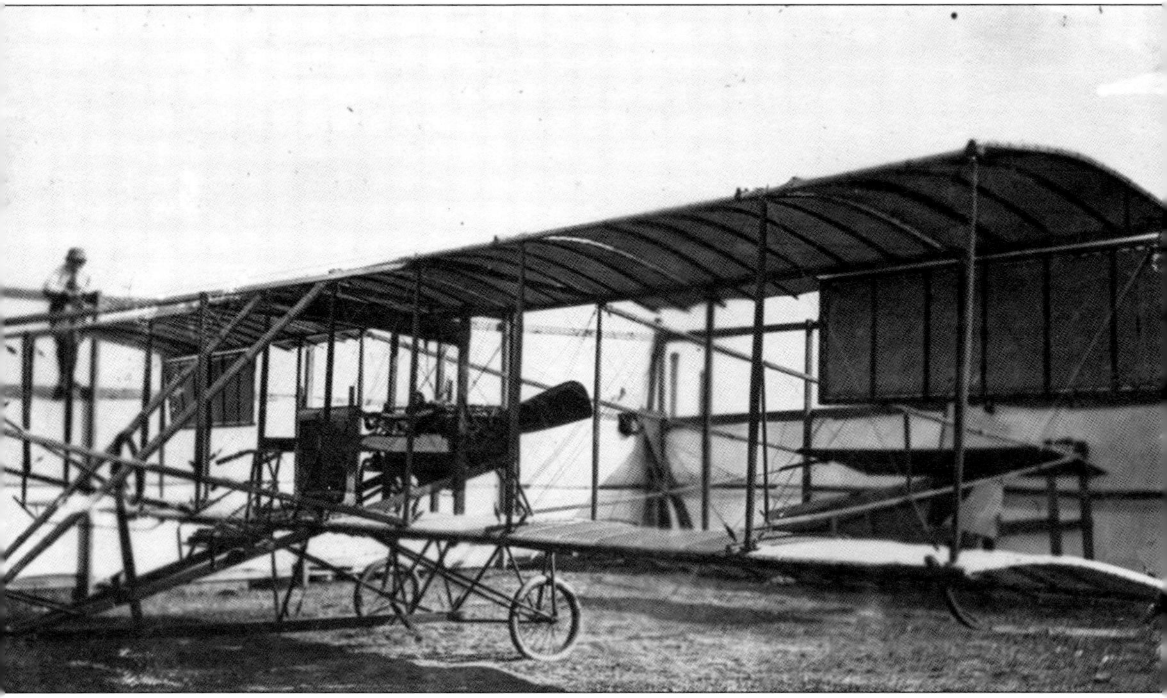

William G. Purves's Gates biplane, secluded in a temporary compound and out of public view on the morning of January 22, 1911, awaited its debut for an aerial performance above Kleinert's field. Photographer William B. Hart snapped this image, the only known photograph taken in Baton Rouge of the famous biplane, before its fatal demise. The event did not take place as scheduled and was postponed until March. A vivid account of the first aeronaut to visit Baton Rouge was told by St. Clair Favrot in a letter to the *State Times* newspaper in 1926. (POVPC.)

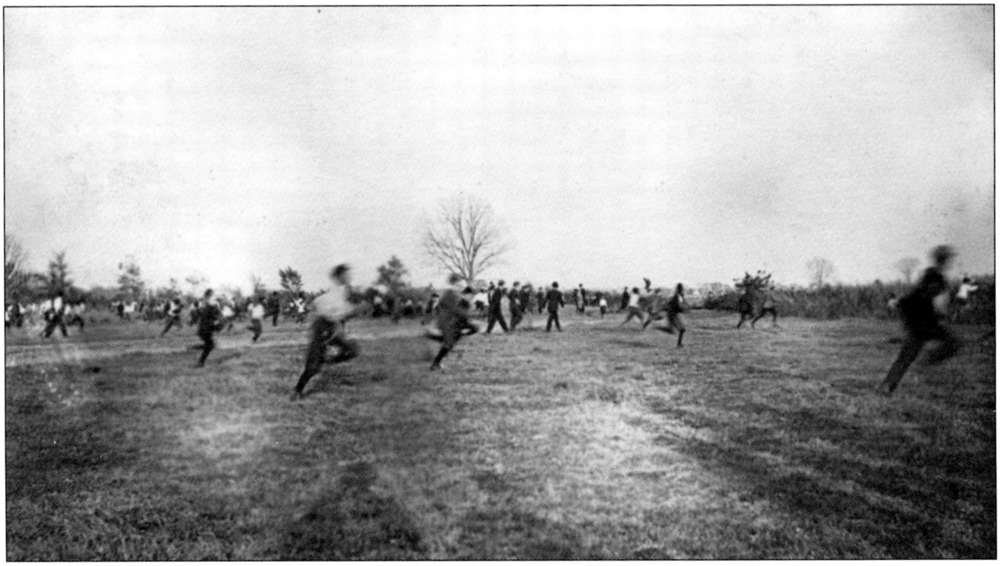

Exhibition flying was an aviation event in other parts of the country never before performed in Baton Rouge. William G. Purves was to perform aerobatic stunts, speed trials, and racing against automobiles for the purpose of promoting a new subdivision called Roseland Terrace. The highly touted fête never came to pass. On March 5, 1911, William B. Hart captured images of spectators running to the fallen biplane on Kleinert's field. The pilot, a nationally renowned aviator, died from injuries sustained after crashing his Gates biplane on his initial flight. (POVPC.)

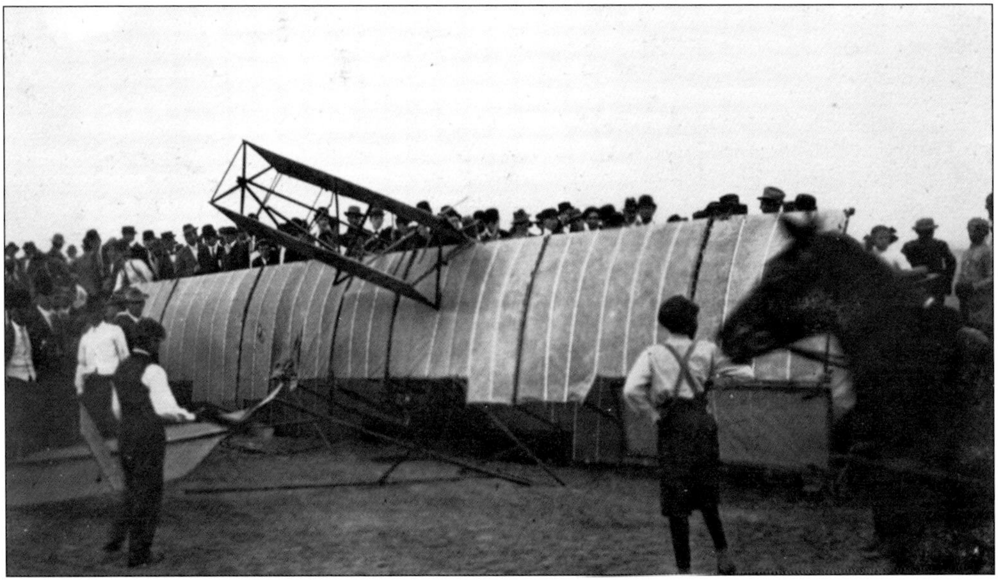

All hopes were eliminated on March 5, 1911, when the aeronaut and his plane fell to the ground after struggling for altitude. A wagon arrived at the scene of the accident to take the aviator to Dr. Singletary's sanitarium. The heavily damaged Gates biplane was surrounded by spectators who rarely, if ever, saw a flying machine. A little over a year later, on April 10, 1912, George Mestach transported 32 pounds of mail from New Orleans to Baton Rouge, landing on LSU's campus after 91 minutes in the air, marking the second airmail delivery in the United States. (POVPC.)

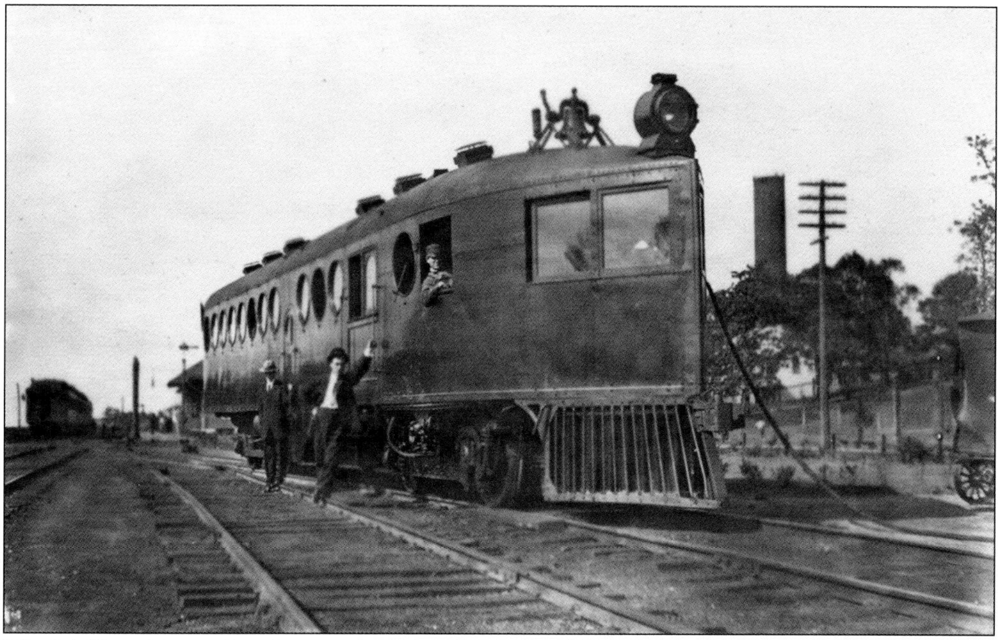

The McKeen Motor Car Company of Omaha, Nebraska, was a builder of internal combustion–engine railroad motor cars. McKeen produced a design that was ahead of its time. Unfortunately, internal combustion technology was not, and the McKeen cars never found a truly reliable power plant. The company produced at least one style of gasoline-engine locomotive. This gasoline mechanical car was in use in 1912 between Baton Rouge and New Orleans. McKeen cars had the distinctive "wind-splitter" pointed aerodynamic front end and rounded tail. In this photograph, the engineer and crew await refueling. Visible in the background are the Baton Rouge Waterworks standpipe and the Old State Capitol fence along Natchez Street (later River Road). (POVPC.)

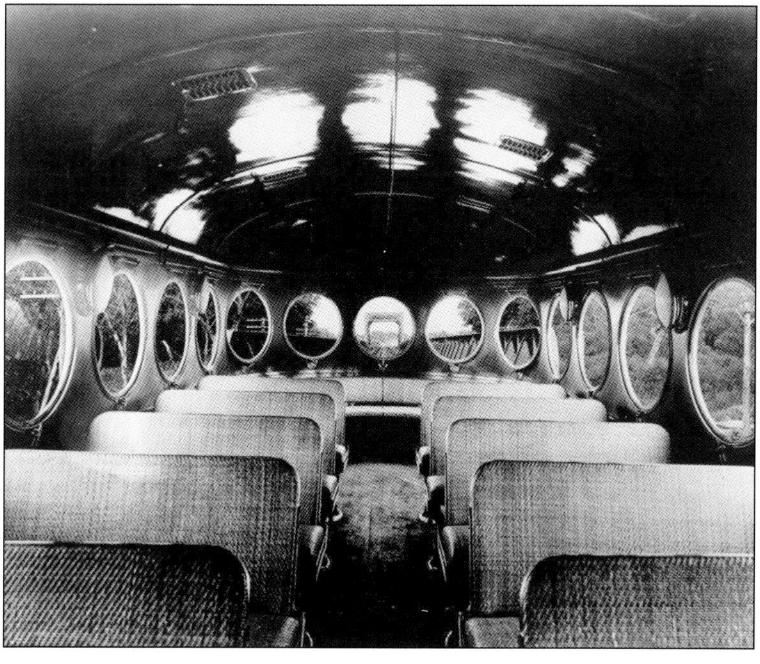

The interior of McKeen Motor Cars presented a distinctive panoramic view for passengers and was widely preferred by passengers traveling through Louisiana and Mississippi. The porthole windows were also a McKeen trademark, adopted for strength. This car seated approximately 75 persons, depending on the locomotive's other uses like mail and parcel transport. (NSRM.)

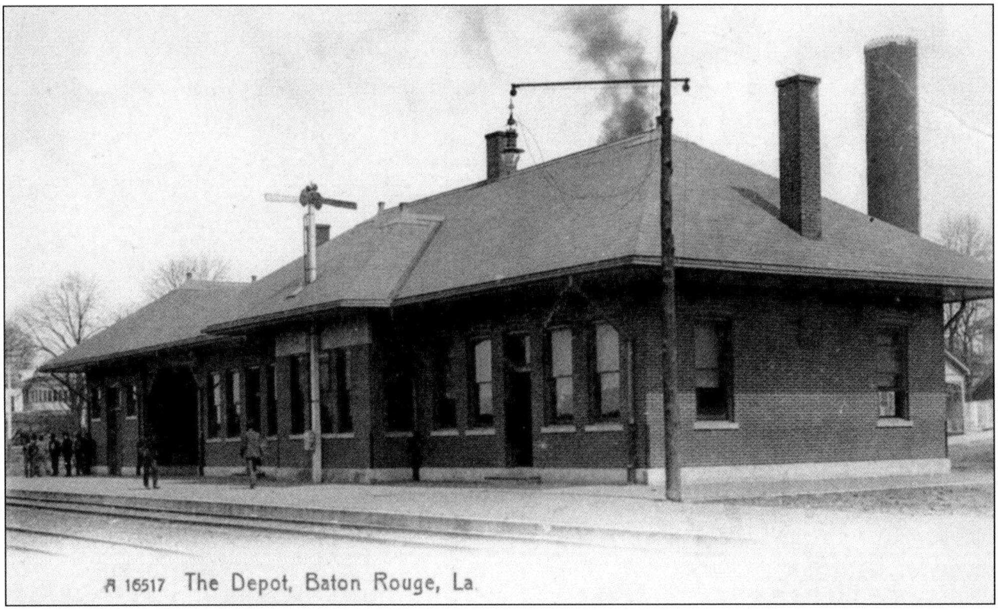

This view of the original Yazoo and Mississippi Valley Railroad Depot was photographed from the river side of the tracks. The building was razed in 1925 to make way for a new Illinois Central Railroad Depot, which was completed in 1926. The site was that of military bombardment in 1862, when Admiral Farragut ordered his ship to fire upon Baton Rouge. The old depot today is occupied by the Louisiana Arts and Science Center Riverside Museum. The old Baton Rouge Water Company standpipe is visible on the far right on the Lafayette Street bluff behind the depot. (EBRPL.)

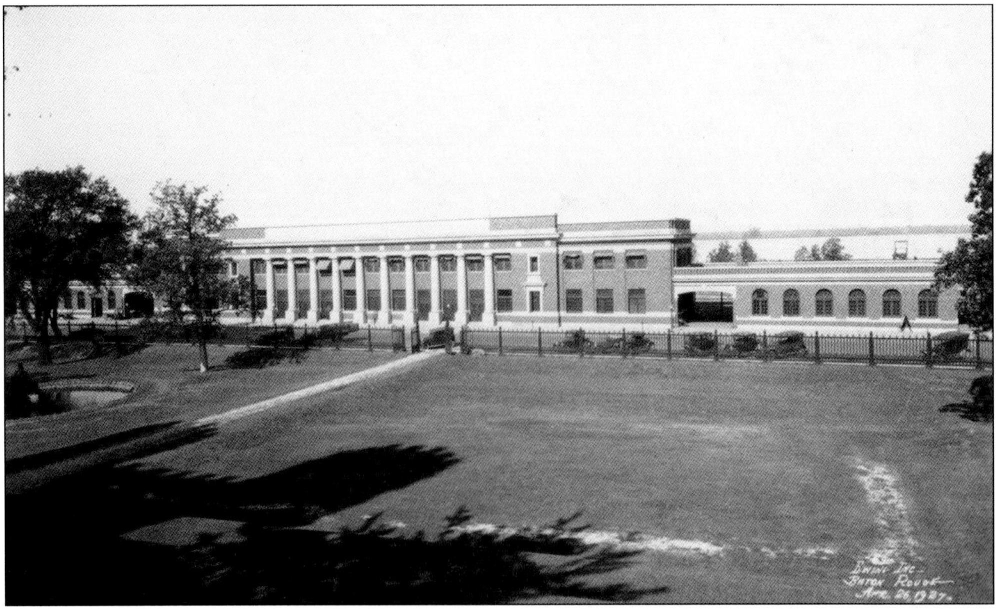

The original Yazoo and Mississippi River Valley Railroad Depot was razed in 1925 to make way for the new Illinois Central Railroad Depot, shown here, which was completed in 1926. This view of the depot fronts Natchez Street and the Old State Capitol. The depot and railroad tracks were wedged between Natchez Street and the Mississippi River. (EBRPL.)

Baton Rouge Fire Department officials pause for the photographer on a downtown street around 1910. The image illustrates a transitional time when horse-drawn carriages and the emerging motor car were sharing the roadways. Gasoline-powered vehicles had yet to be purchased by the city's fire department. (EBRPL.)

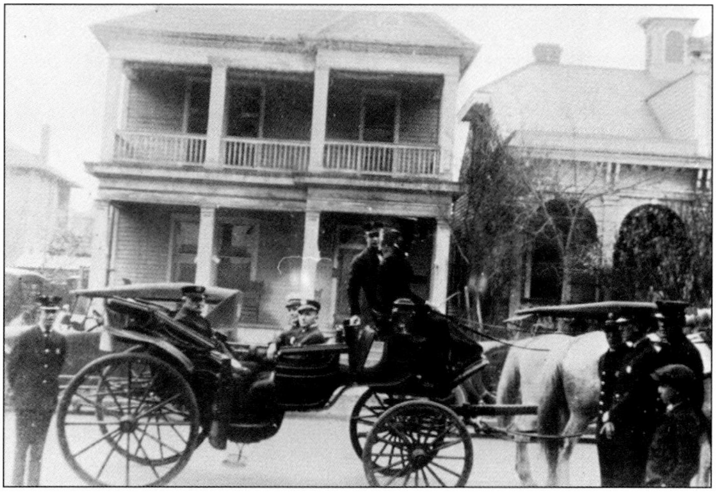

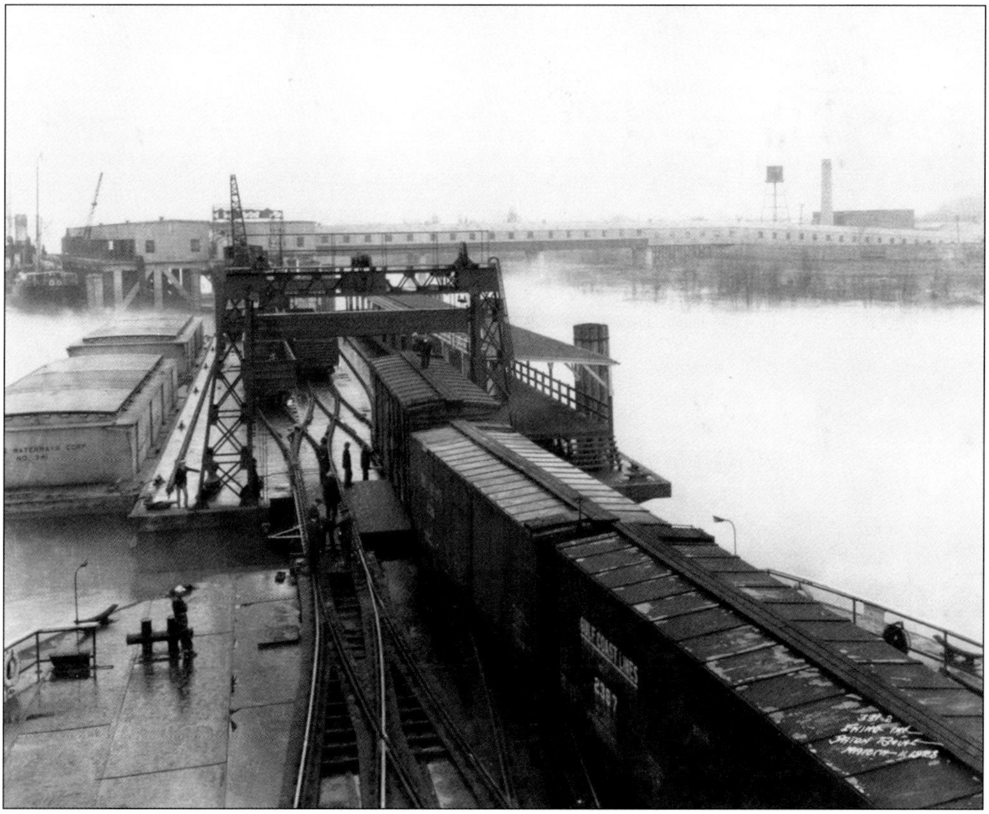

Until 1940, trains crossed the river at Baton Rouge by way of a train ferry. On the west side of the river, the eastern terminus of the Grosse Tete–Opelousas Railroad was at Anchorage, Louisiana, a small community north of Port Allen. The train ferry took on as many as a dozen Pullman passenger cars or twice as many tank cars and boxcars. The passengers disembarked at a small west-side depot and crossed the river to Baton Rouge by way of the passenger ferry. This image provides a rare glimpse of how railcars were off-loaded from barges in the river. The Baton Rouge Municipal Dock, shown in the background, was completed in 1926. The concrete and steel structure provided access for loading services with bulk cargo. (EBRPL.)

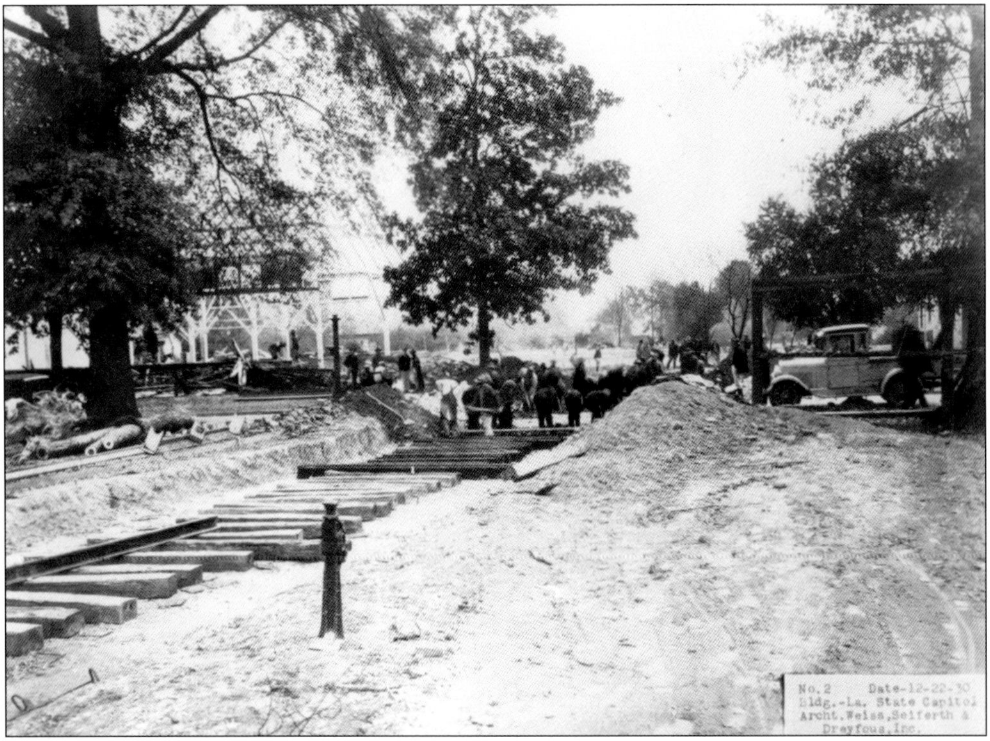

By December 1930, the new Louisiana State Capitol was under construction on the grounds of Louisiana State University's vacated downtown campus. An exclusive railroad spur was built for the purpose of transporting the heavy building materials directly to the site. This image shows workmen laying railroad ties leading up to the capitol's foundation. (SLL.)

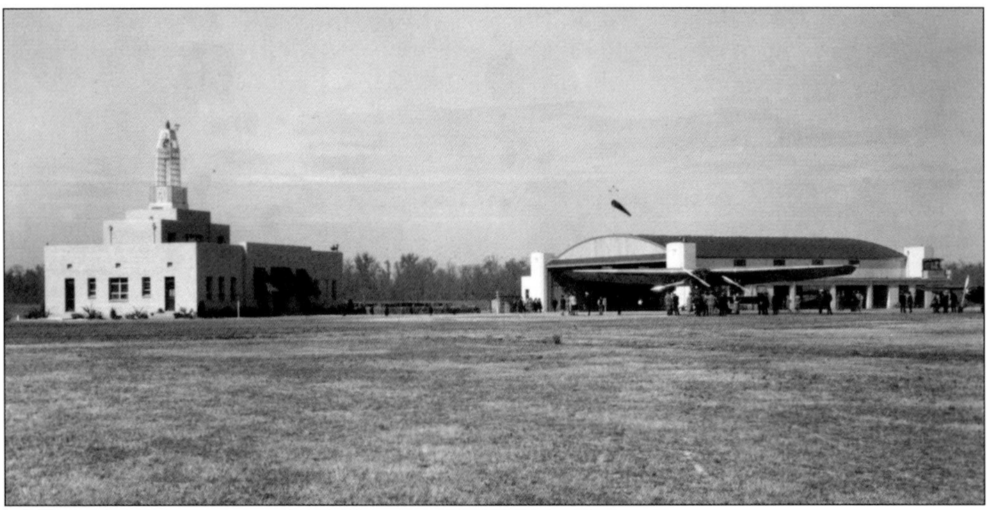

Baton Rouge Municipal Airport was dedicated on June 17, 1931. Pre-dedication advertisement boasted that the facility was among the best in the South, with the most elaborate lighting systems of any airport in the country. The 200-acre site initially consisted of a large hangar and a terminal with a rotating beacon. Eastern Airlines briefly flew commercial flights to the airport but found the runways too short and discontinued use of it in 1939. Known as the Downtown Airport, the facility was closed in 1975. (EBRPL.)

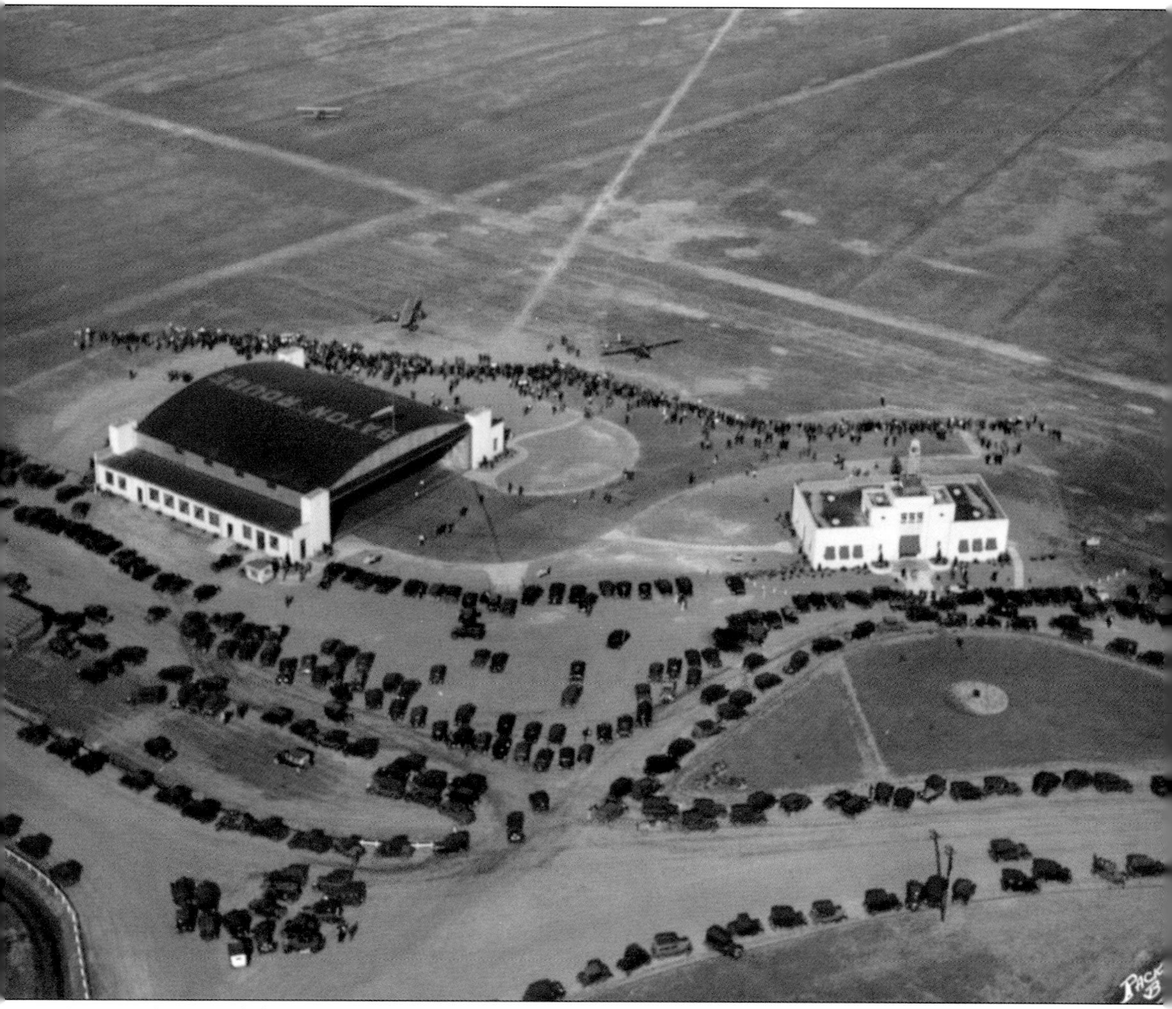

An aerial view of the Baton Rouge Municipal Airport provides a unique look at the expansive landing field and modern buildings. Located on the west side of a 200-acre turf field, the two-story terminal and hangar buildings were considered the most advanced facilities of the era. In 1933, the airport manager was E.W. Kleinpeter. The airport had two commercial aviation operators: American Airways Incorporated and E.W. Kleinpeter flying service. (EBRPL.)

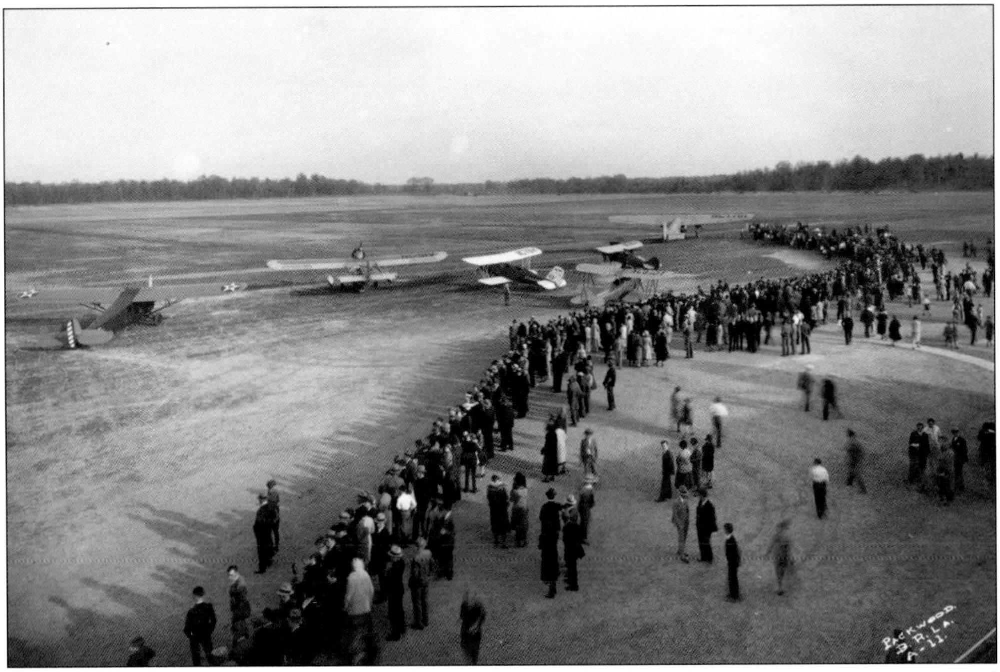

In this 1931 photograph, a variety of aircraft are seen on display at the Baton Rouge Municipal Airport for a special occasion. The large gathering of spectators may have been for the dedication ceremony of the airport. Shown in the upper right is a Ford Tri-Motor, nicknamed the "Tin Goose." The 12-seat plane was the first commercial passenger plane. (EBRPL.)

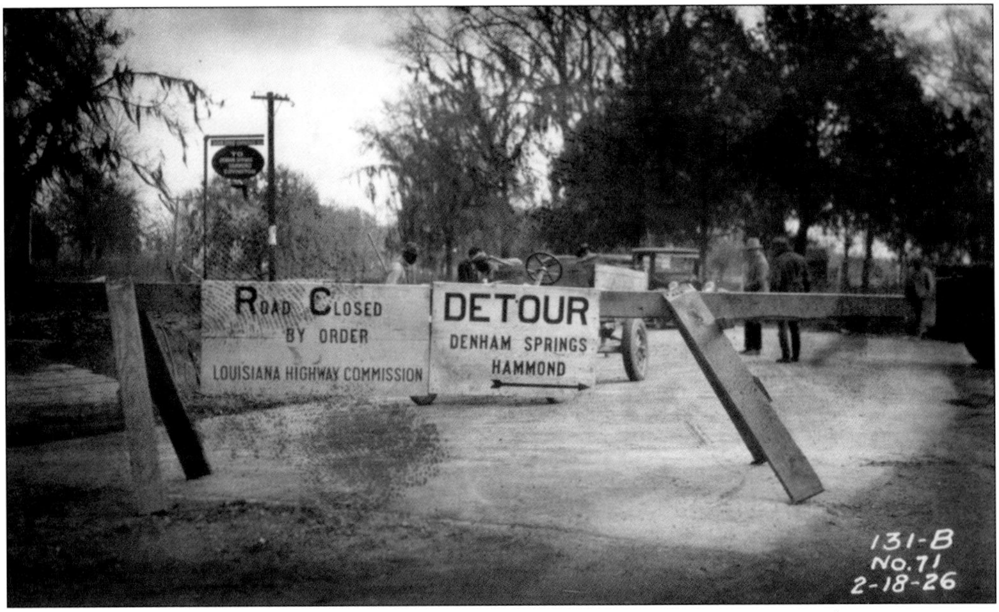

While the main route from Baton Rouge to Hammond, US Highway 190, was under construction in 1926, traffic was diverted to alternate parish roads. A progressive road-construction plan called the Good Roads Movement was strongly supported and spearheaded by Gov. J.Y. Sanders as early as 1909. The program continued to be a priority with successive governors to the middle of the 1920s. (SLL.)

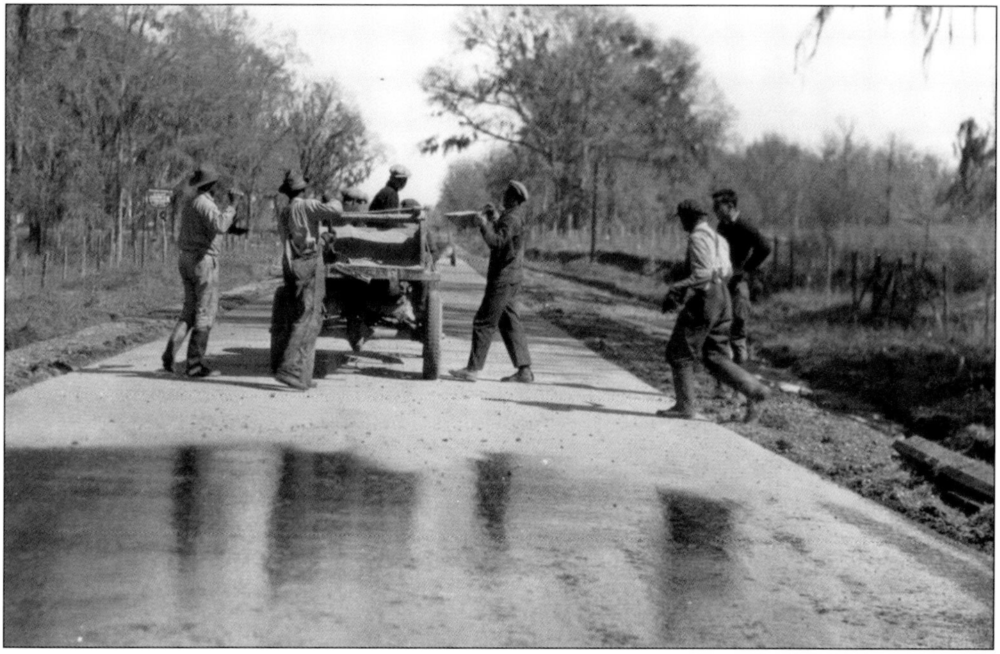

Residents in the 1920s witnessed the continuation of an aggressive road-construction program throughout the state that was started during Governor Sanders's administration. In this 1926 photograph, the road to Hammond is almost complete. The Hammond Highway was part of a two-lane intrastate route called US 190. In Denham Springs, the road was called the Baton Rouge Highway. (SLL.)

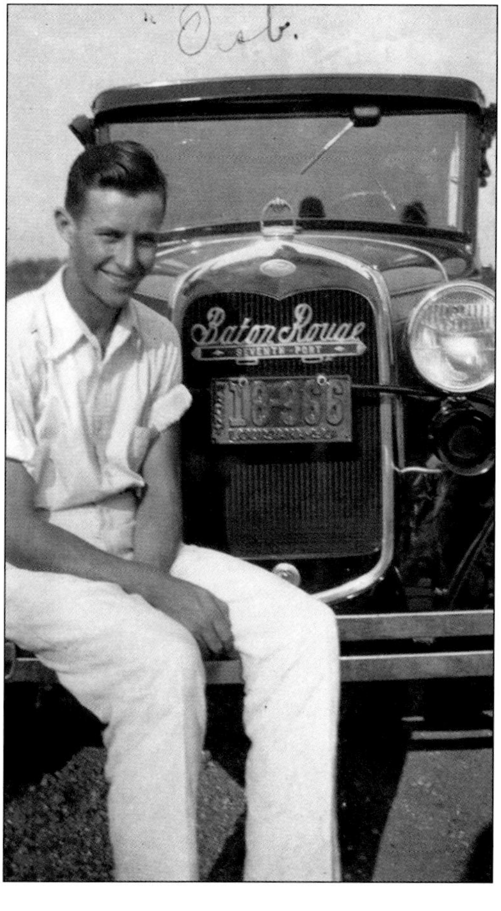

In this c. 1930 photograph, a young man sits proudly in front of what may have been his first automobile. The vehicle displays a grill placard engraved, "Baton Rouge–Seventh Port." The promotional ornament had a deeper meaning for the period and implied that Baton Rouge was a wide-awake, progressive city, and in 1922 it was the seventh-largest shipping port of the United States. This photograph is from the scrapbook of Velma Poché. (EBRPL.)

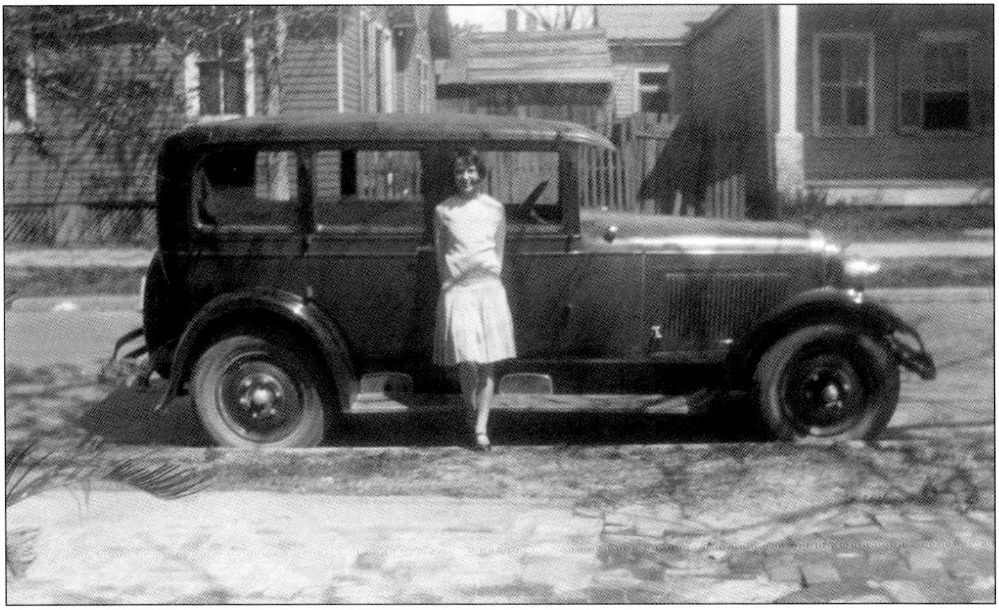

This photograph of an unidentified young lady was taken around 1928 in front of a four-door Dodge sedan on Seventh Street in Baton Rouge. The lady's clothing style features the popular look of the dropped-waist skirt as representative of times. The automobile was considered a toy for the rich but increasingly gave the general public and travelers the freedom to travel when and where they wanted. (EBRPL.)

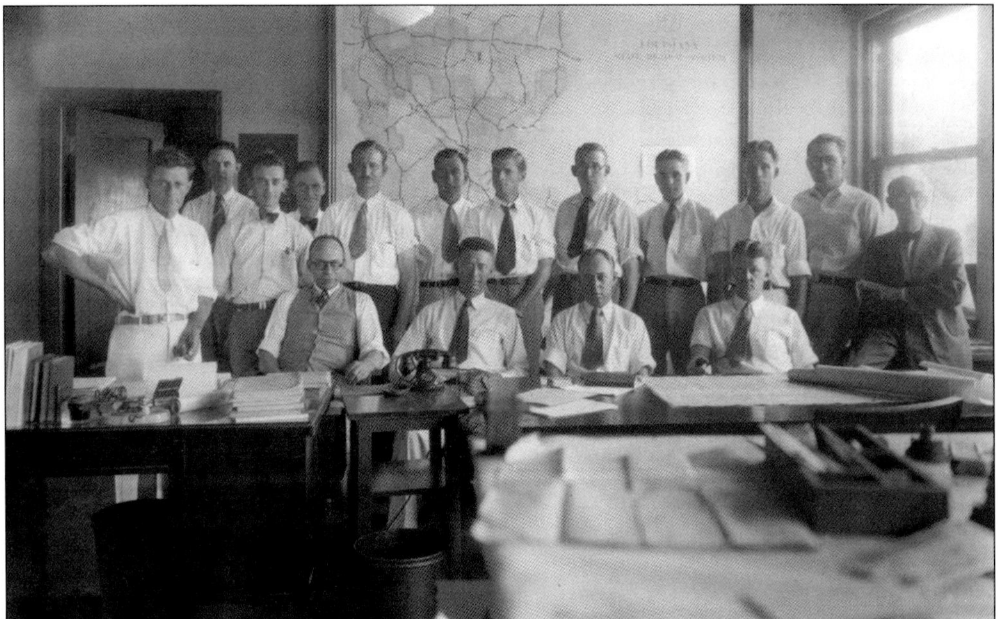

Louisiana Highway Department engineers of the early 1930s were faced with some of the greatest civil-engineering challenges in Louisiana's history. Their tasks included a long list of highway and bridge designs throughout the state under great political pressure. Among their greatest tasks were bridge crossings of the Mississippi River and numerous other significant rivers around the state. (SLL.)

Four

SIGHTS AND SCENES

This collection of scenes captured by photographers between the 1890s and 1930s describes what the casual person would have observed around Baton Rouge. Here, photographs depict scenes from the heart of the business district to the oldest residential subdivisions.

After the Civil War, residential and commercial growth was very slow; however, after 1900, a wave of progress changed the landscape. Photographers took advantage of taller structures for better vantage points to show how much the city had changed. Rooftops gave great bird's-eye views of the skyline and a sense of the city's remarkable growth.

A favored residential part of the city for the photographer was Beauregard Town. Even in the early 1900s, Beauregard Town was praised as a historic subdivision and part of Baton Rouge's splendor. The subdivision was filled with charming raised wooden structures, most having deeply set verandas along shaded streets that crisscrossed in grid-like patterns. The home styles varied from bungalow to Colonial Revival and Late Victorian architecture. The subdivision's boundaries were trimmed with wide boulevards featuring promenades and trolley lines. These are some of the forgotten views of downtown Baton Rouge. The views were pleasing to the eye of any visitor.

A short distance away and on the eastern edge of the city were scenes of modern homes built during the 1910s in one of the most advanced subdivisions of the era. Captured on film by A.F. Cazedessus, a prominent real estate developer and business owner of Zodak Realty, were barren tracts of land and sparsely scattered, newly constructed homes in the Roseland Terrace subdivision. His intrepid plan for the subdivision marked a new beginning in Baton Rouge's residential growth.

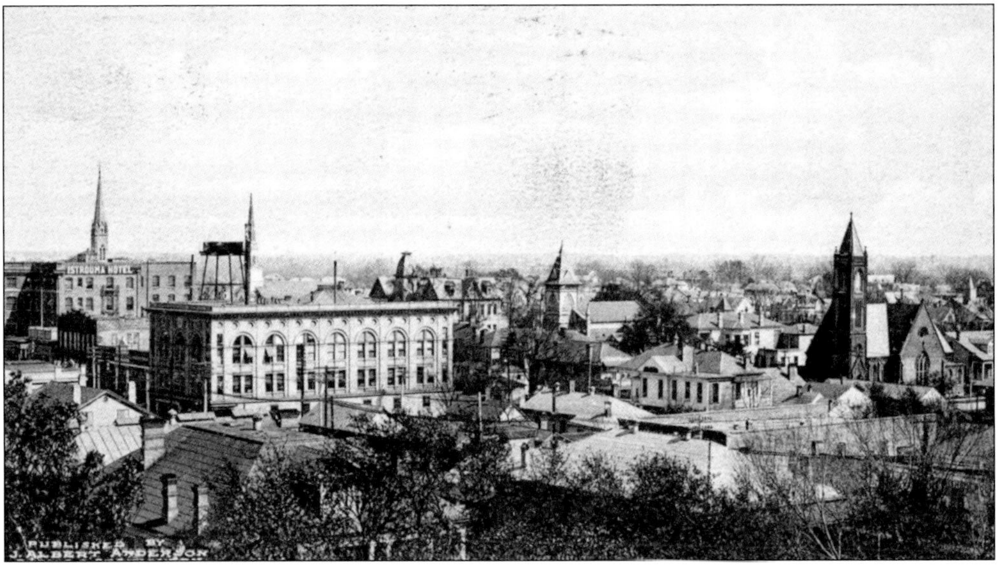

A 1911 rooftop view of downtown Baton Rouge from the old Louisiana State Capitol looking toward the northeast area of town provides a compelling explanation for the naming of Church Street (later renamed Fourth Street). Steeples and bell towers adorn the Church Street skyline from Main Street southward to Convention Street. Beginning at the far left are St. Joseph's Church, Washington Fire Hall No. 1, a Methodist church, St. Joseph's Academy Boarding and Day School, a Presbyterian church, and an Episcopal church. Also visible from this vantage point are two popular hotels on Third Street: the Istrouma Hotel and Mayer Hotel. (EBRPL.)

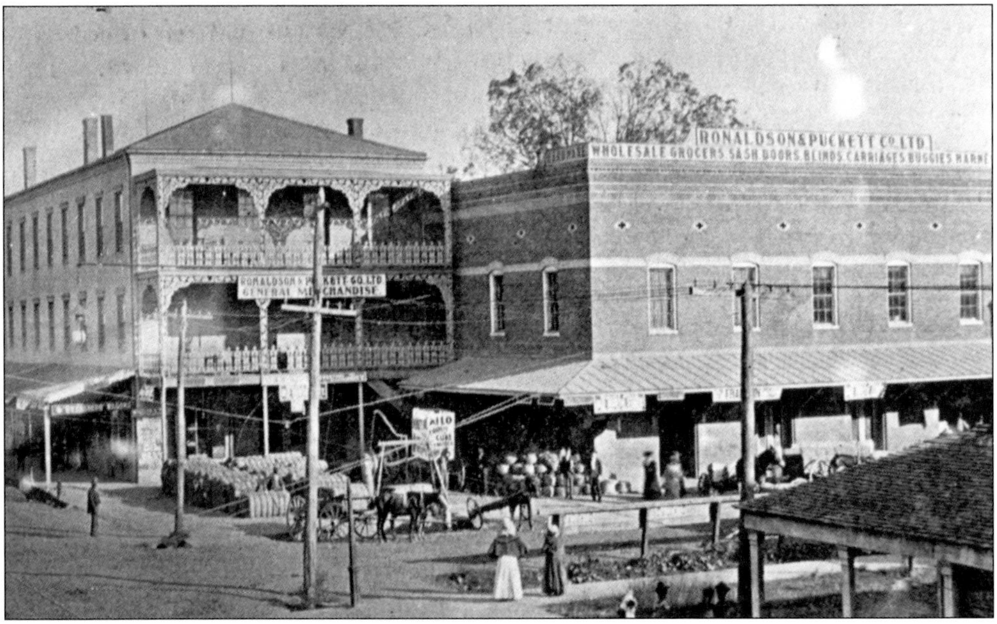

In 1901, Ronaldson and Puckett was one of the largest wholesale and general-merchandise concerns in Baton Rouge. Its inventory consisted of everything from home furnishings to business supplies. Ronaldson and Puckett also leased meeting space to St. James Lodge No. 47 until 1906, when its new lodge hall was completed. Ronaldson and Puckett was located at the corner of Main and Church Streets. (SLL.)

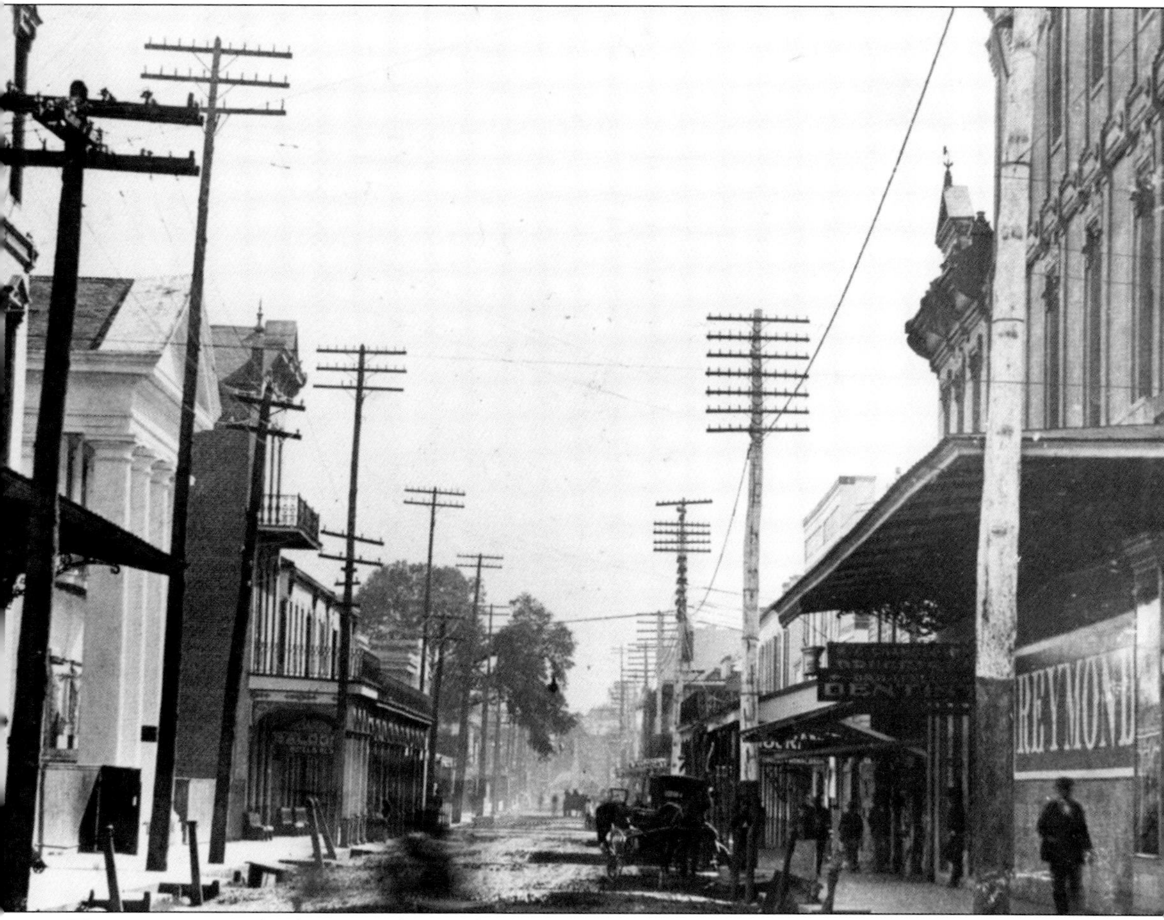

This perspective, looking south on Third Street toward North Boulevard, depicts the busy commercial corridor as it looked in the early 1900s before Mayor Robert A. Hart's aggressive program to pave downtown streets. Faintly visible at the far end of the street is Baton Rouge's Confederate monument, erected by the Confederate Monument Association in 1886. (EBRPL.)

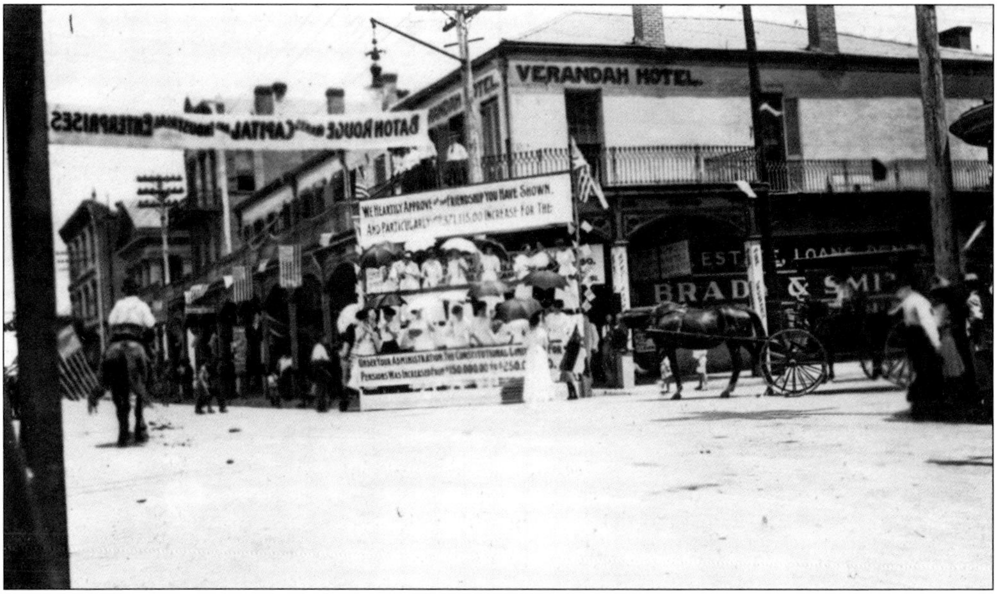

The Verandah Hotel was located on the corner of Third and Laurel Streets and was once operated by the Lorente family. Here, at the annual firemen's parade, supporters of Gov. Luther E. Hall constructed a viewing stand with signs expressing approval of a constitutional increase in pension appropriations and workmen's compensation. Visible on the far left are the large round columns of the Bank of Baton Rouge. (POVPC.)

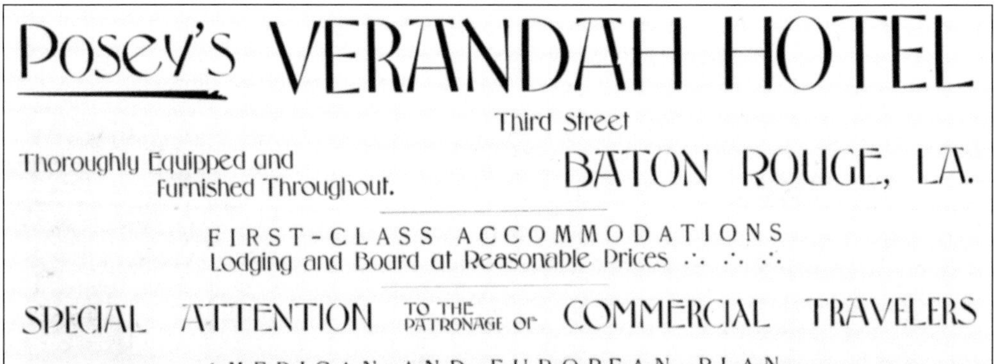

The Elks' Souvenir of Baton Rouge displayed this advertisement for the Verandah Hotel, managed by Frank Posey. The hotel provided some of the finest accommodations and meals in all of Baton Rouge. The adjacent Verandah Saloon, managed by John "Noon" Roux and Joseph Gangloff, was known as one of the finest saloon establishments in the region. (ESBR.)

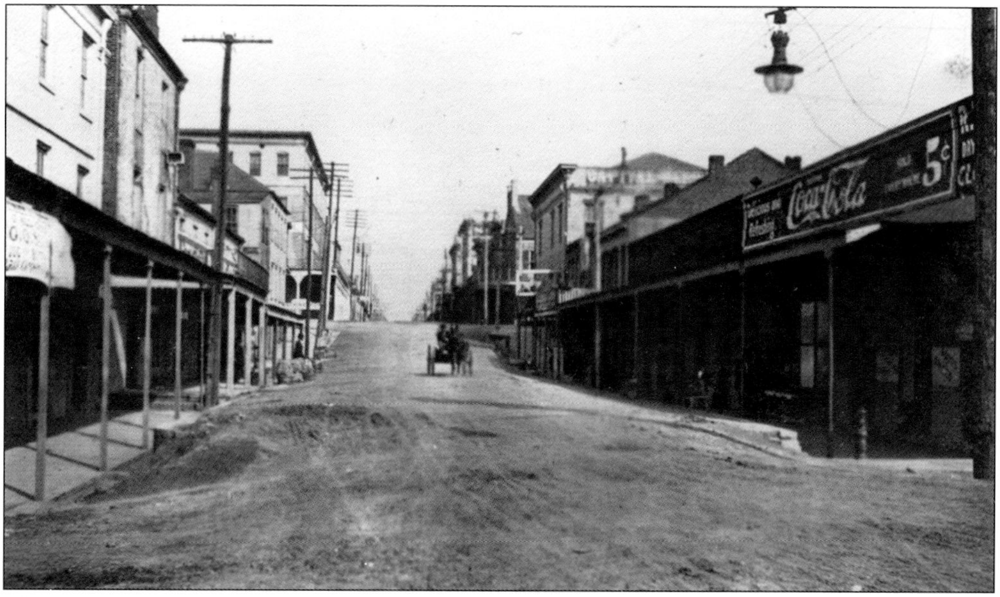

This view of Main Street looks east from near the Baton Rouge ferry landing. Just beyond the crest of the bluff, Main Street intersects with Lafayette Street. The trolley tracks were located in the middle of Main Street and then turned and ran south down the middle of Lafayette Street. Visible on the crest of the ridge, on the left, is Hotel Grouchy, which was the previous site of the famous Harney House Hotel. Across the street from Hotel Grouchy was the studio of A.D. Lytle, a famous Civil War photographer. On the right side is the Florence Coffee House, at 130 Main Street, which was built in 1850 and owned by John and Lucas Florence. (POVPC.)

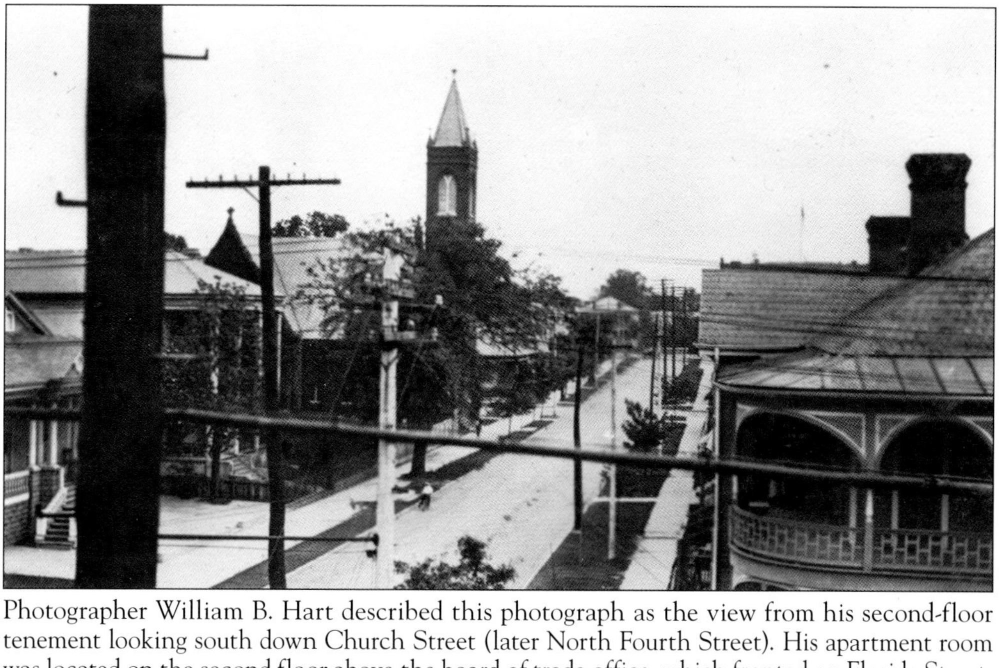

Photographer William B. Hart described this photograph as the view from his second-floor tenement looking south down Church Street (later North Fourth Street). His apartment room was located on the second floor above the board of trade office, which fronted on Florida Street, adjacent to Dr. Singletary's sanitarium. The steeple of the Episcopal church is shown in the center at Convention Street. (POVPC.)

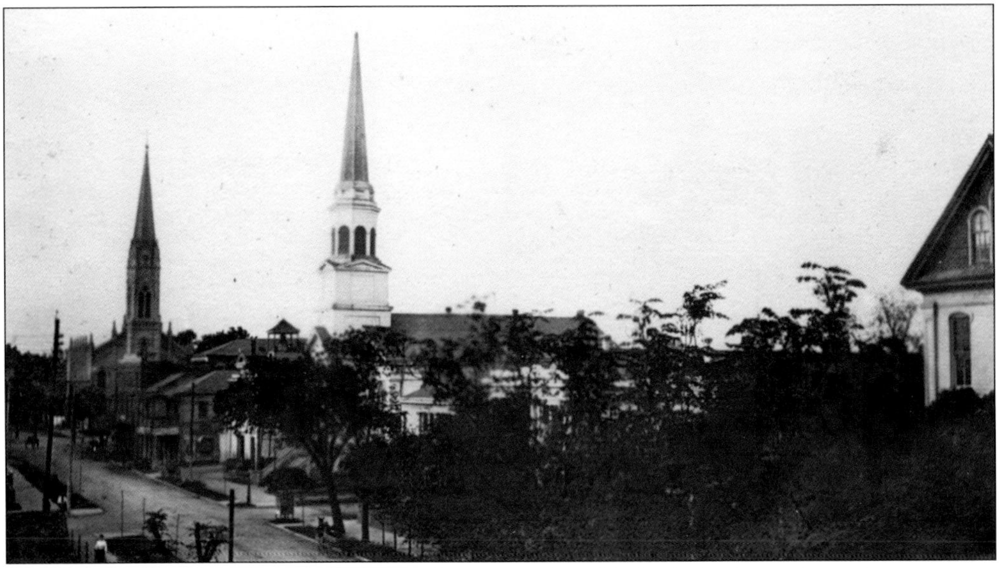

A view looking north of Church Street depicts St. Joseph's Catholic Church on the northeast corner of Church and Main Streets, and prominently displayed one block south is the Methodist church, located on the corner at Laurel Street. A glimpse of St. Joseph's Academy is seen on the far right. Visible between St. Joseph's and the Methodist church is Washington Fire Company No. 1, with its bell tower showing above the tree line. (POVPC.)

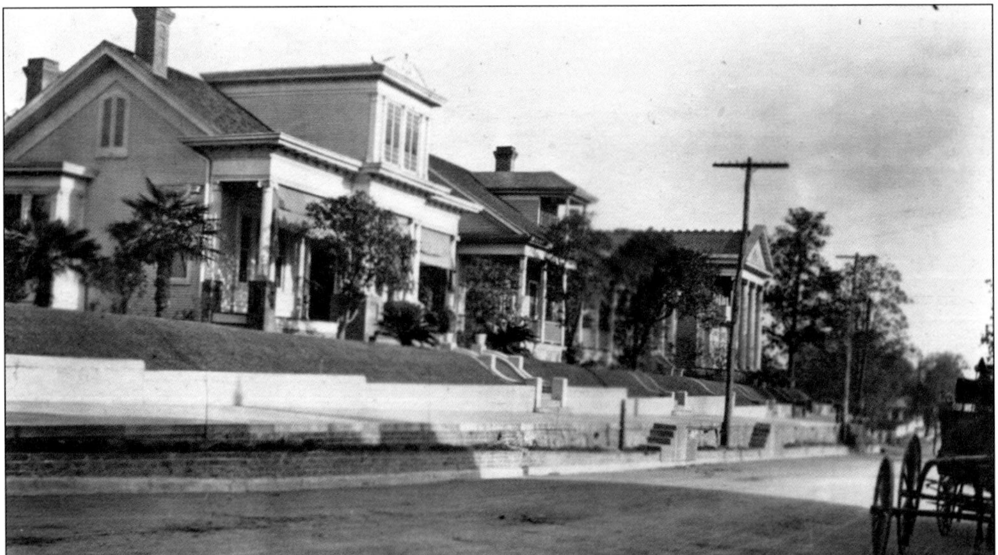

This scene in Beauregard Town depicts homes that were on the high side, on the 200 block, of Phillippe Street (also spelled St. Philip Street). Here, one block southeast of the Old State Capitol, is a sample of the collection of architectural styles that existed in 1912. The home on the far left was that of Joseph Gebelin, a prominent Baton Rouge figure who served as assistant secretary of state of Louisiana, police jury president, city councilman, board member of the Bank of Baton Rouge, and founding member of the Baton Rouge Country Club. In recent times, this scene became part of the plaza area of the Baton Rouge Centroplex. (POVPC.)

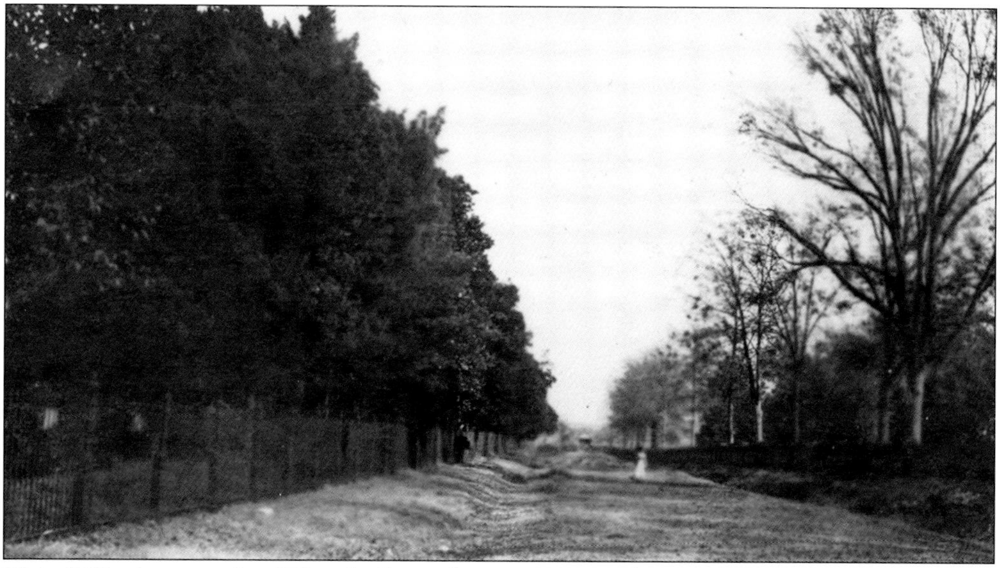

This 1912 photograph of Florida Street between Magnolia Cemetery (left) and National Cemetery (right) was taken before paving was extended east of Church Street. Historically, this area was the site for the Battle of Baton Rouge. In the battle, Confederate forces hid amongst the tombs and trees in Magnolia Cemetery and subsequently launched an attack against the Union forces. (POVPC.)

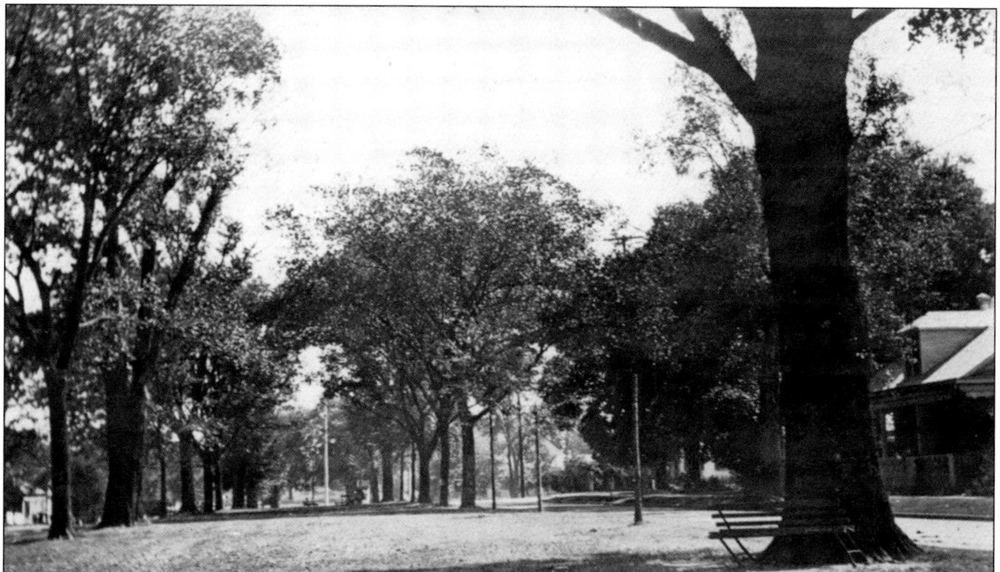

A familiar view for many Baton Rouge residents was this scene of North Boulevard looking east from the intersection of Church Street. Though Beauregard Town, located on the right side of this photograph, was laid out in 1806, most of the structures from that period were destroyed by fire or bombardment during the Civil War. Many of the buildings in Beauregard Town were constructed between 1900 and 1930. (POVPC.)

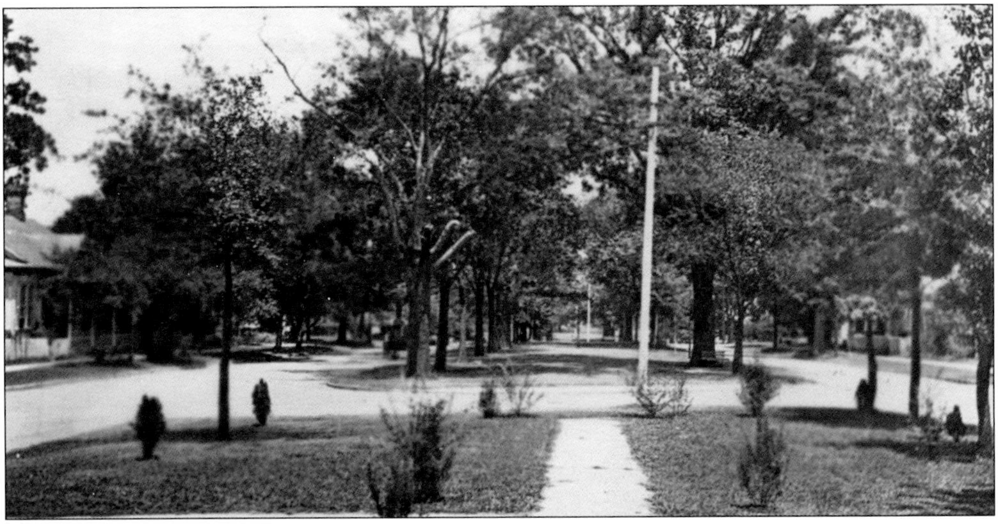

The east-west corridor of North Boulevard was equally attractive 100 years ago. It was an impressive promenade that formed the northern boundary of Beauregard Town, the second-oldest subdivision in Baton Rouge. The street was called the Boulevard by residents and was a favorite gathering place for family outings or civic events. (POVPC.)

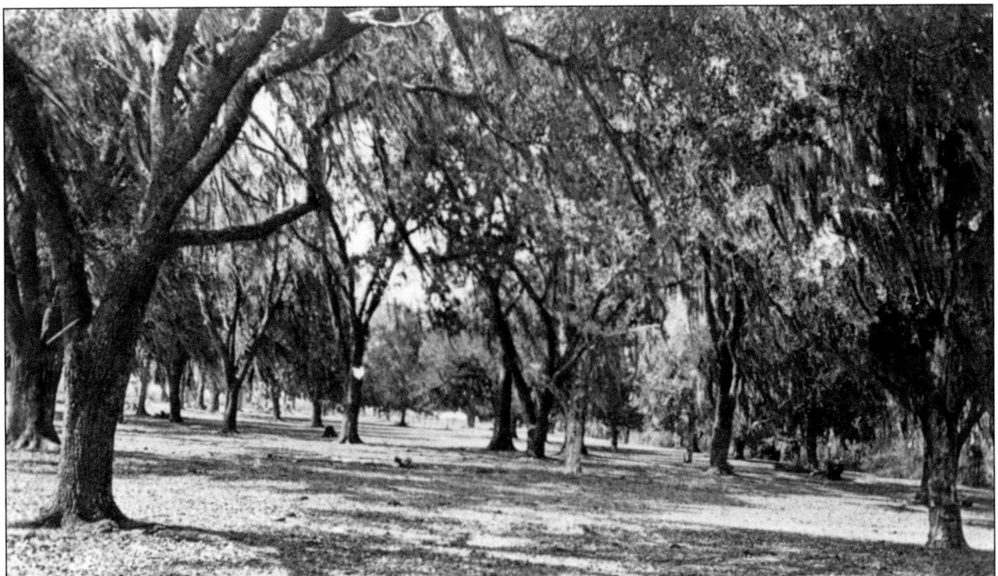

Hundred Oaks Farms was a tranquil and desirable place for a picnic or outing in 1912. The entrance to the plantation meandered through a large oak orchard that appeared to be endless. Appropriately named Hundred Oaks, the plantation was previously known as Richland Plantation from the antebellum period. The area later became known as Perkins Grove, Bonnie Grove, and Hundred Oaks Plantation. Platted by Mundinger and Payne in 1919, Hundred Oaks Farms subdivision was carved from the original plantation, flanking both sides of Perkins Road, formerly known as Middle Highland Road. Hundred Oaks was situated north of the Louisiana Railway & Navigation Company Railroad. The remainder of the plantation was further divided between 1920 and 1949 into subdivisions named Suburb Hundred Oaks, Hundred Oaks, Zeeland Place, and Hundred Oaks Park. (POVPC.)

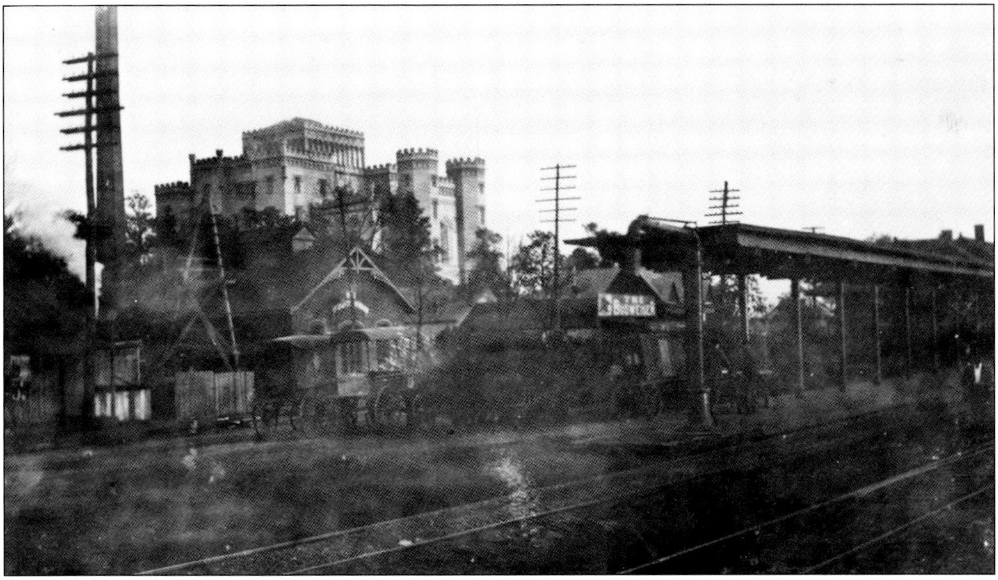

This scene depicts a busy area near the river along Natchez Street. Standing tall on the far left is the 77-foot-high brick chimney of the water company, and in the background is the Old Louisiana State Capitol. The Yazoo and Mississippi Valley Railroad Depot, loading area, and two cafés on the northeast corner of Natchez Street and North Boulevard are visible in the foreground. (POVPC.)

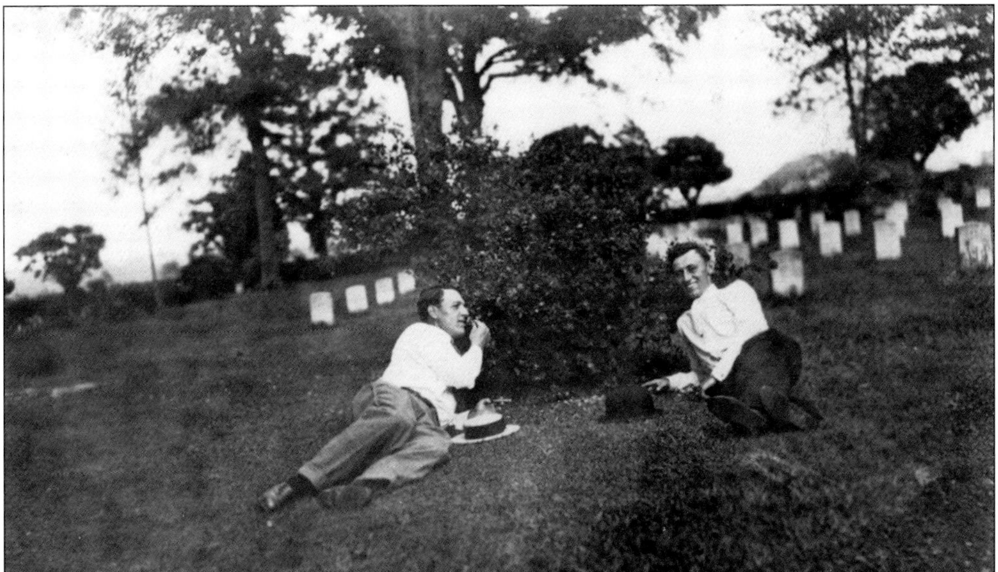

Brothers William B. "Sweet" Hart (left) and Jesse Hart visit the National Cemetery at Baton Rouge in 1912. The entrance to the US National Military Cemetery was on Dufrocq Street (later North Nineteenth Street) between Convention and Florida Streets. Designated as a national cemetery in 1867, soldiers from area battlefields were buried on this site. Within two years of its construction, 2,925 soldiers were interred here. (POVPC.)

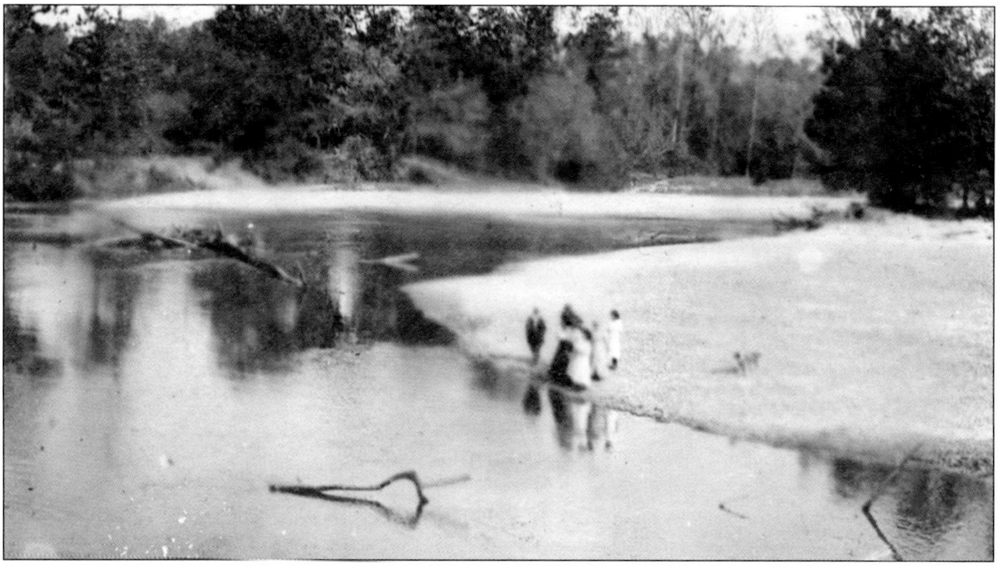

Some 11 miles east of Baton Rouge, the natural meandering Amite River formed a beautiful and lush boundary between East Baton Rouge Parish and Livingston Parish. The Amite River was a favorite place and attraction for a day trip of fishing, picnicking, swimming, or simply basking on the many sandy beaches along its banks. Pictured here are family and friends of photographer William B. Hart experiencing the natural scenic beauty of the Amite River during a time when the waters were clean and clear. A great number of people who lived along the Amite River found that water from the stream was dependable for consumption and domestic use. (POVPC.)

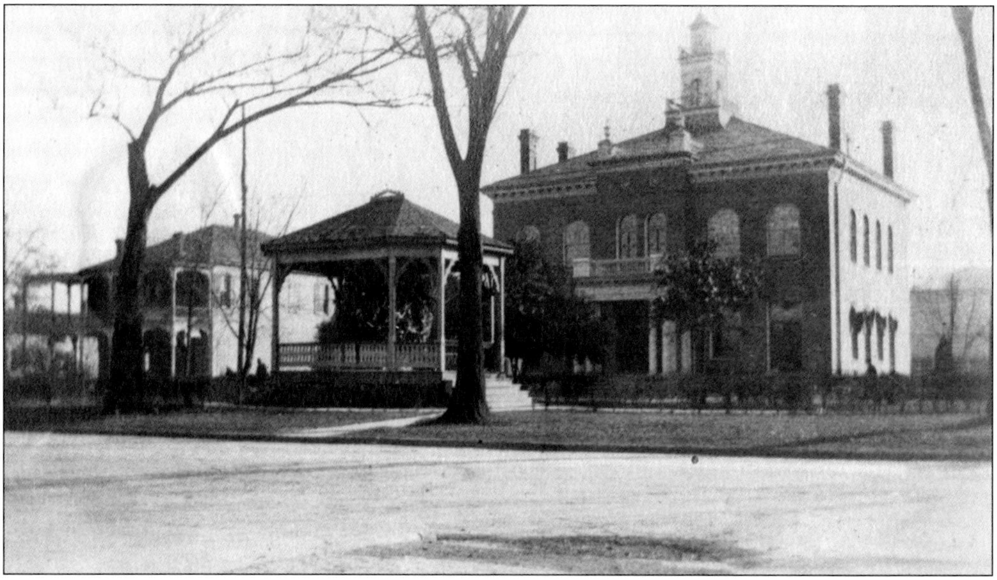

A large bandstand in the median of the Boulevard (formally North Boulevard) served as a gathering and meeting place for many Baton Rouge civic events. One of Baton Rouge's earliest parks was that of the median area of North Boulevard. It was a wide promenade that provided for picnics and gatherings as well as a place for peddlers to sell their wares. This scene also features city hall, which was part of an improvement boom 10 years earlier under the leadership of Mayor Robert A. Hart. (EBRPL.)

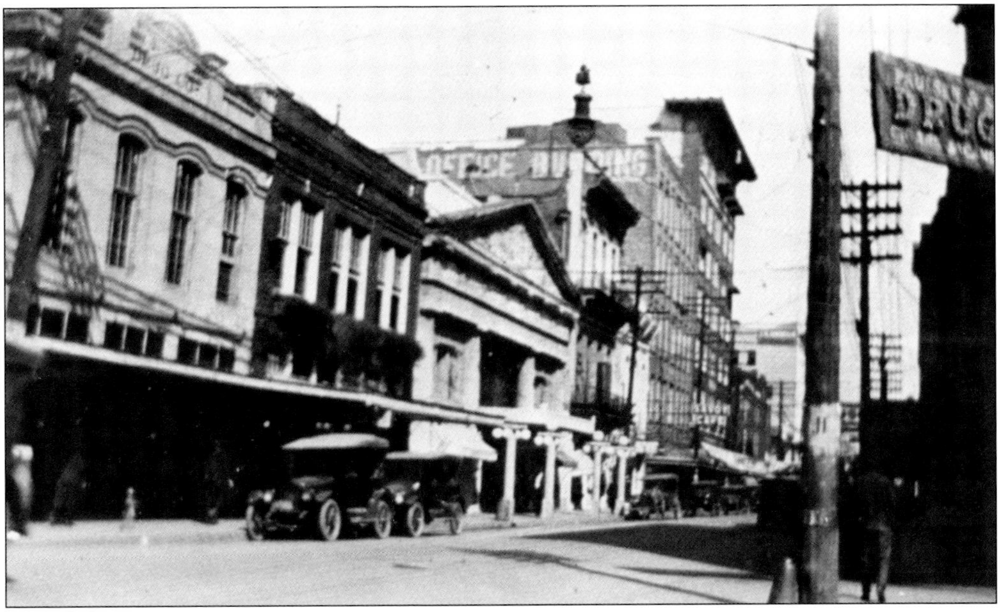

In 1925, Baton Rouge's growth and progress was evident, as seen in this Third Street view looking northwest. In the upper right is the street corner sign of Paulson and Son Drugstore. Prominently in the center of the city block is the uniquely designed Columbia Theater, built in 1920 by the architectural firm of Prather & Stephens. The theater was considered the South's most thoroughly equipped and scientifically designed playhouse. In 1930, the name was changed to the Paramount Theater. On the far side of the theater is the entrance to Izzy's, an eatery and saloon favored by university coeds and cadets during the 1930s. (EBRPL.)

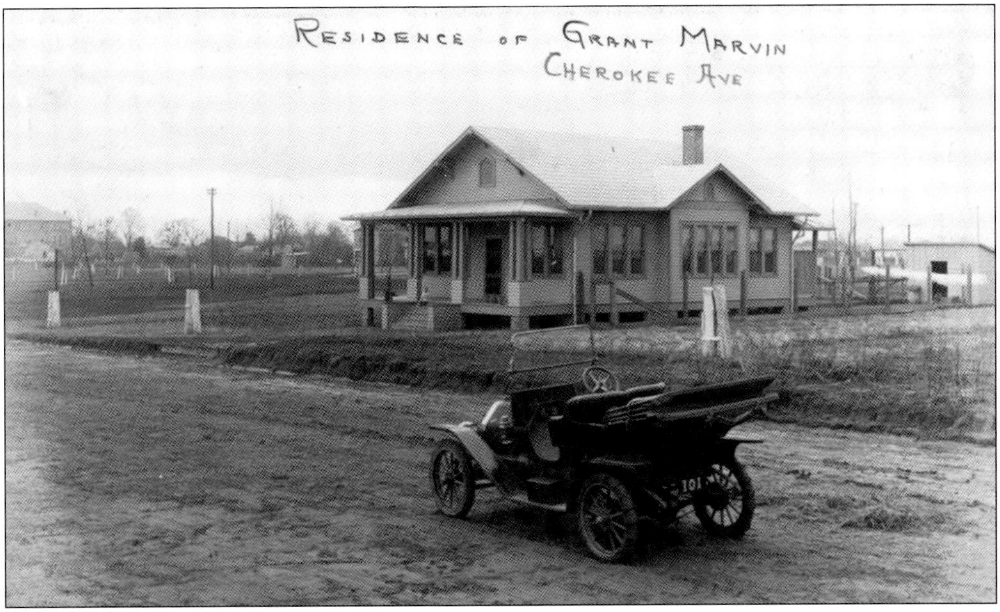

On Cherokee Street in Roseland Terrace, the residence of Grant Marvin was one of the first built homes among many unsold plots in the new subdivision. The image of the photographer's automobile, perhaps Jasper Ewing's, displays a necessity for mud chains on the wheels, which chronicles the poor conditions of many unpaved streets. (EBRPL.)

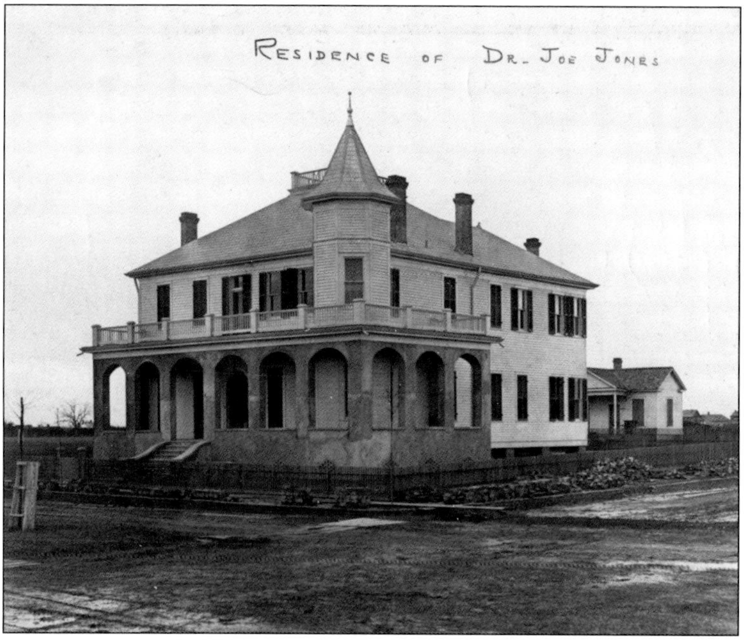

The home of Dr. Joseph Jones was built on the southwest corner of Goldenrod (later Park Boulevard) and Cherokee Streets. Roseland Terrace was promoted as one of the most advanced subdivisions in the South. The home was built in 1912 and is still standing as of this writing. (EBRPL.)

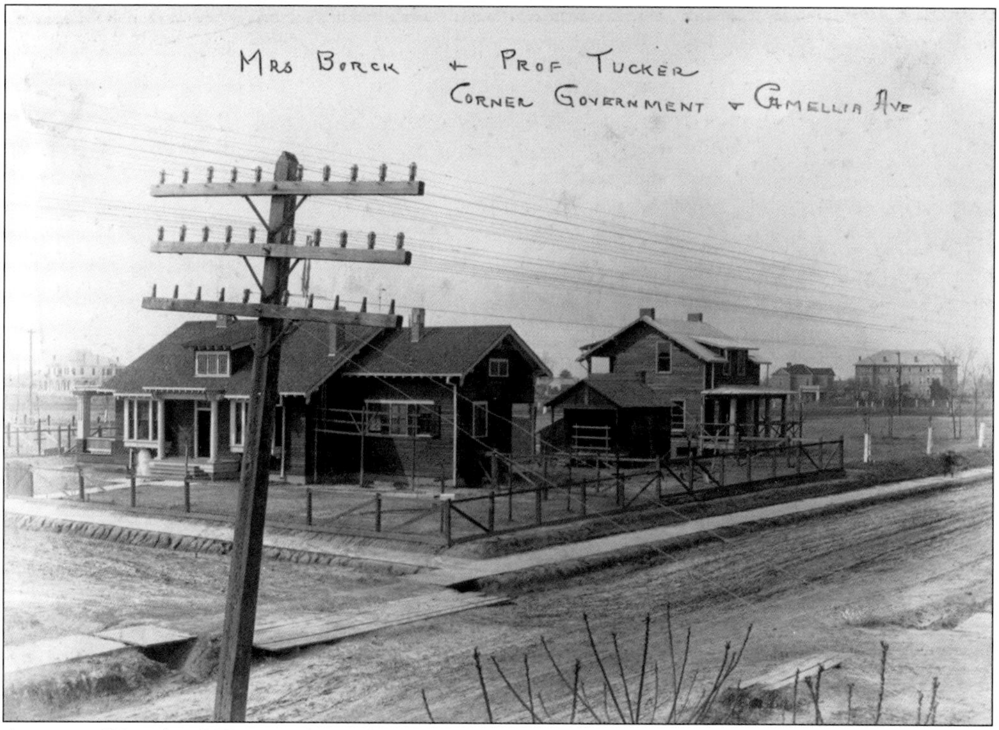

A view of Roseland Terrace from the corner of Government and Camellia Streets depicts the developer's interest in providing amenities such as electric lights, well-drained streets, sidewalks, rear-lot alleyways, and tree planting for every lot. In the foreground are the homes of Mrs. Borck and Professor Tucker, with the homes of Dr. Joseph Jones and Louis Wax visible in the background. The Baton Rouge Academy African American School was located west of the subdivision, seen in the far right background. (EBRPL.)

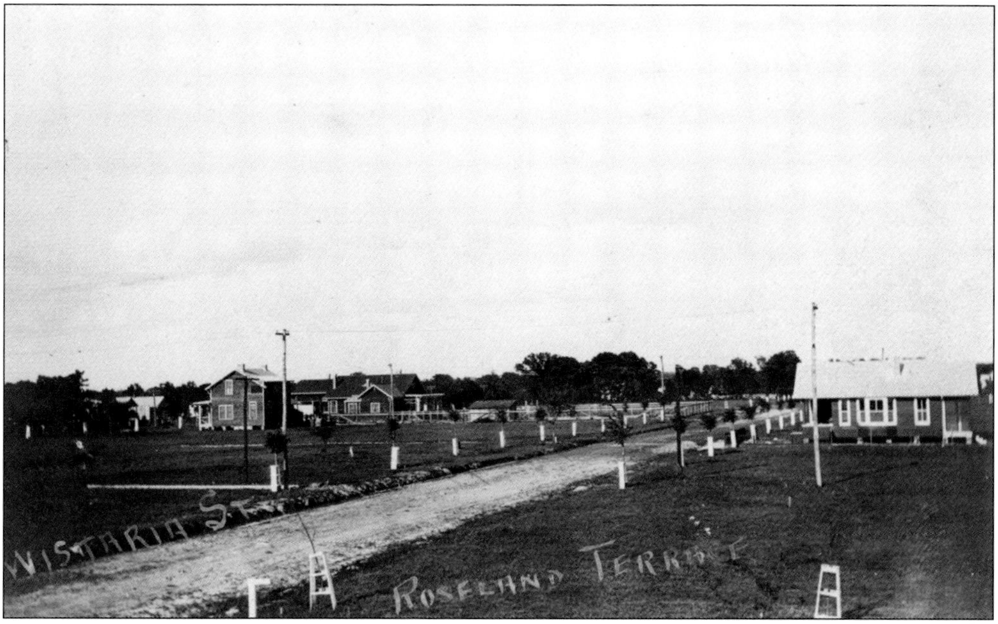

Roseland Terrace was one of the most advanced residential subdivisions in the South. Perfectly graded streets, a tree on each lot, sidewalks, sewer, water, and electricity were provided to every residence. This 1912 postcard advertisement by Zodak Realty depicts Wisteria Street in its completed form. (EBRPL.)

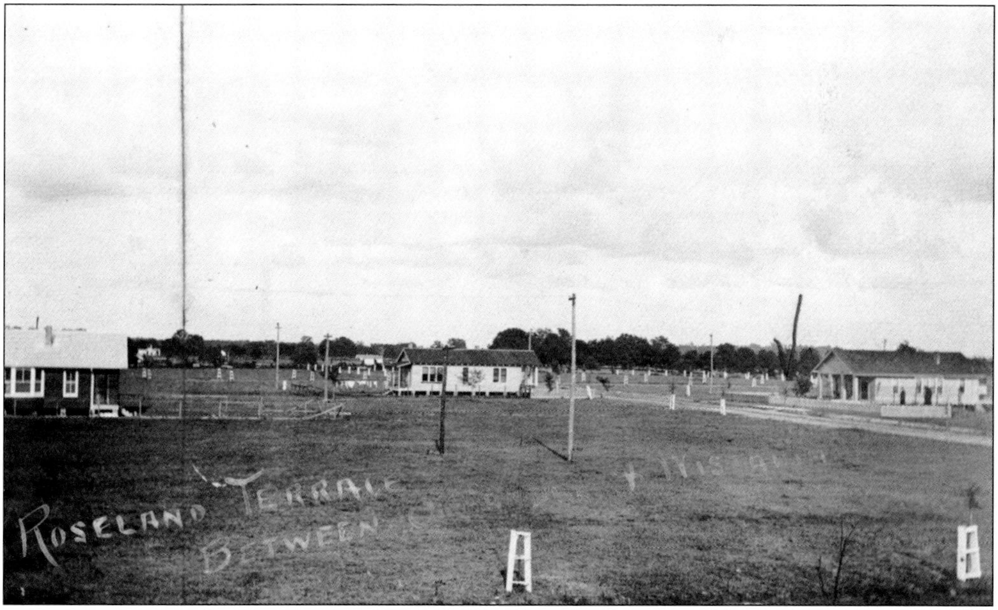

In 1910, A.F. Cazedessus set out with a detailed plan for creating a residential subdivision on a 70-acre tract in the heart of Baton Rouge. This view of Roseland Terrace provides a detailed scene of rear-lot utilities between Oleander and Wisteria Streets. Lot prices ranged from $200 to $550, with restrictions that barred "cabins, business houses and Negroes." (EBRPL.)

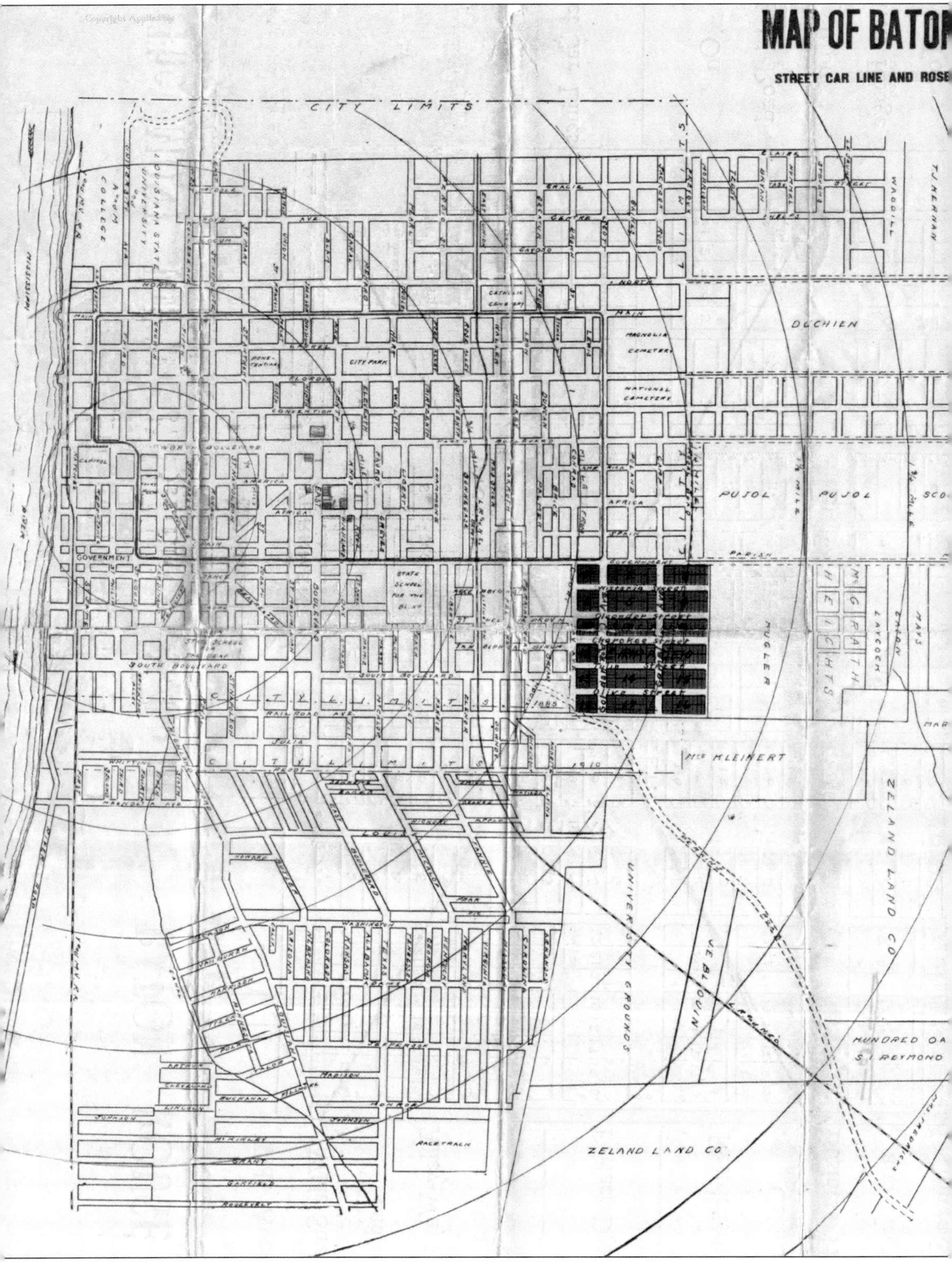
MAP OF
STREET CAR LINE AND
CITY LIMITS
MISSISSIPPI RIVER
LOUISIANA STATE UNIVERSITY
MAGNOLIA CEMETERY
NATIONAL CEMETERY
CITY PARK
DUCHIEN
PUJOL
STATE SCHOOL FOR THE BLIND
SOUTH BOULEVARD
GOVERNMENT
UNIVERSITY GROUNDS
ZELAND LAND CO.
RACETRACK
HUNDRED OA

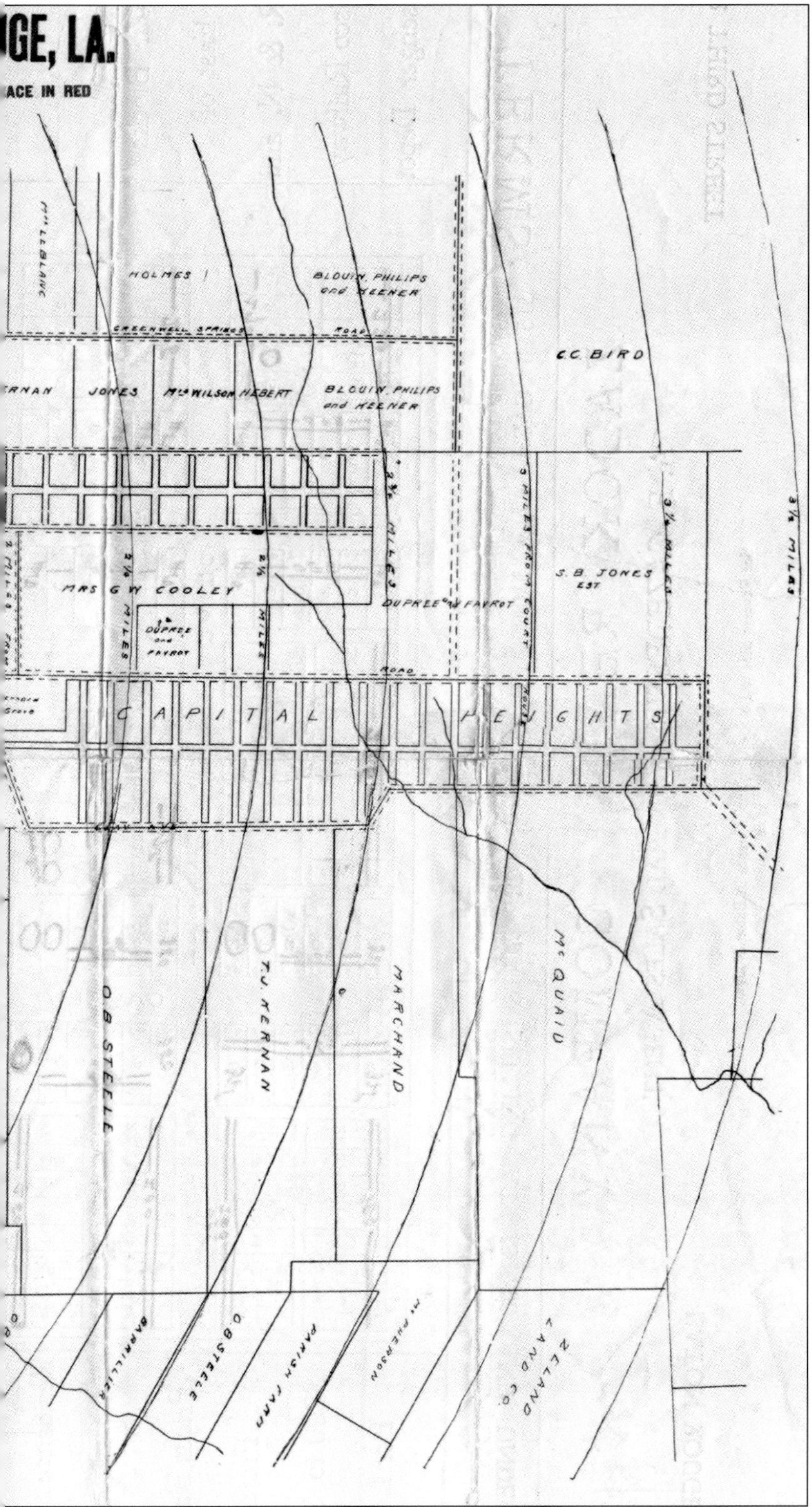

Around 1910, the incorporated area of Baton Rouge spanned slightly more than two square miles. It encompassed the area from the Mississippi River to Twenty-second Street and from Julia and Kleinert Streets to an east-west line running from present-day Memorial Stadium to the river. This descriptive map, showing the Roseland Terrace subdivision (shaded dark), was part of a marketing strategy by Zodak Realty. Concentric circles represent quarter-mile distances from city hall radiating outward to the east. (TABR.)

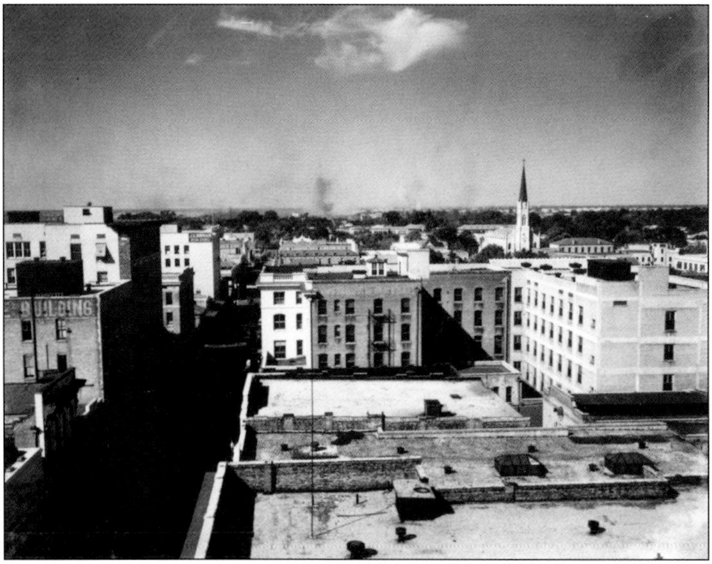

This 1930 view looking north from the rooftop of Louisiana National Bank depicts a skyline absent of the new Louisiana State Capitol, which was under construction. The spire of St. Joseph's Catholic Church towers above all other buildings. On the horizon are visible signs of the vast expansion of Standard Oil Company's refinery and tank farm. (SLL.)

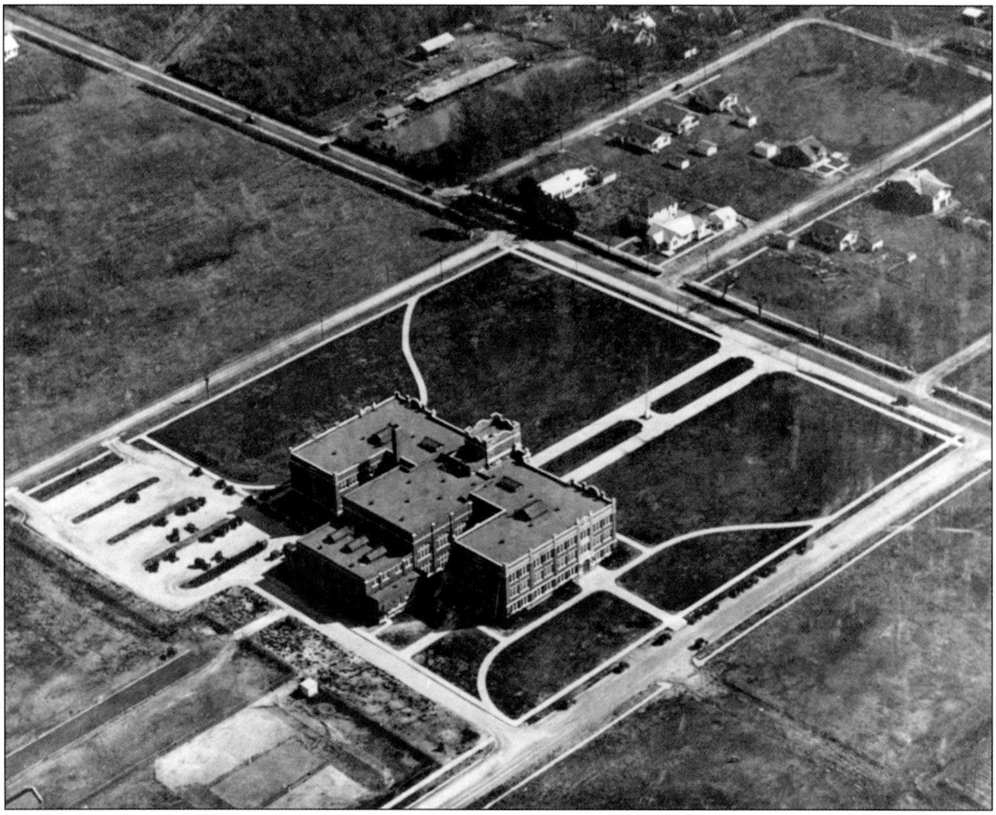

In 1926, Baton Rouge High School moved from its old building at the corner of Florida and Tenth Streets. This aerial view of the new high school at the corner of Government and Eugene Streets illustrates the immense size of the new campus. Government Street runs diagonally, from left to right, across the top of the photograph. (EBRPL.)

The Louisiana Legislature was extremely slow to allocate funds for a new state capitol in 1930 but finally passed a constitutional amendment in a special session that year. By December 16, construction of the mammoth skyscraper had begun. A special rail spur was constructed up to the site for delivery of more than 2,500 carloads of sand, gravel, bricks, cement, limestone, bronze, and granite. Photographer Joe Rogers captured the first of many concrete batches poured for this project. (SLL.)

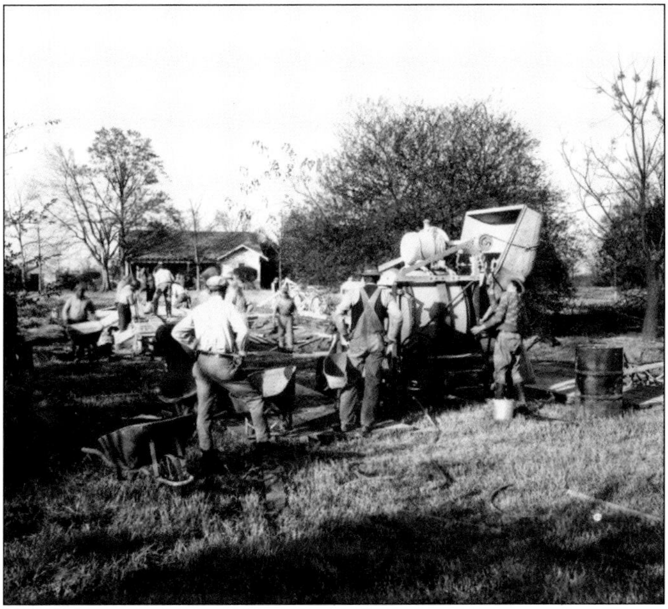

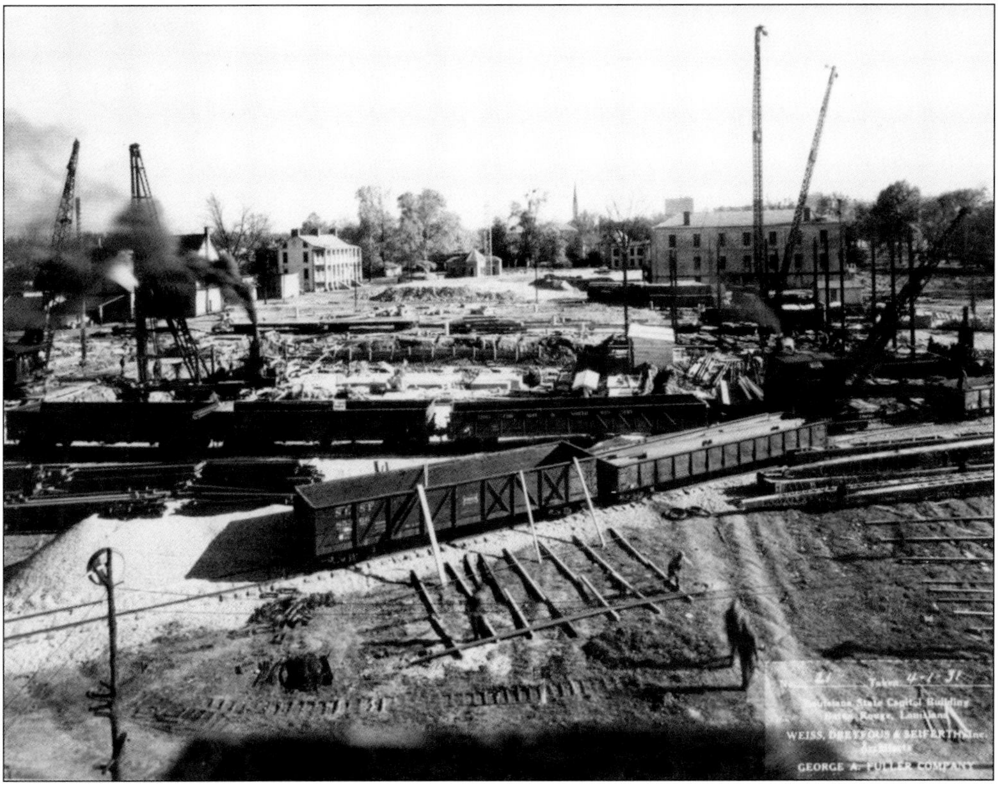

The construction site of the new Louisiana State Capitol was in its early stages when this photograph was taken in April 1931. A dedicated railroad spur from the Yazoo and Mississippi Valley Railroad was constructed to the site for delivery of heavy building materials. The spire of St. Joseph's Church and upper floors of Louisiana National Bank are visible in the background and soon would become dwarfed by the mammoth new state capitol. (SLL.)

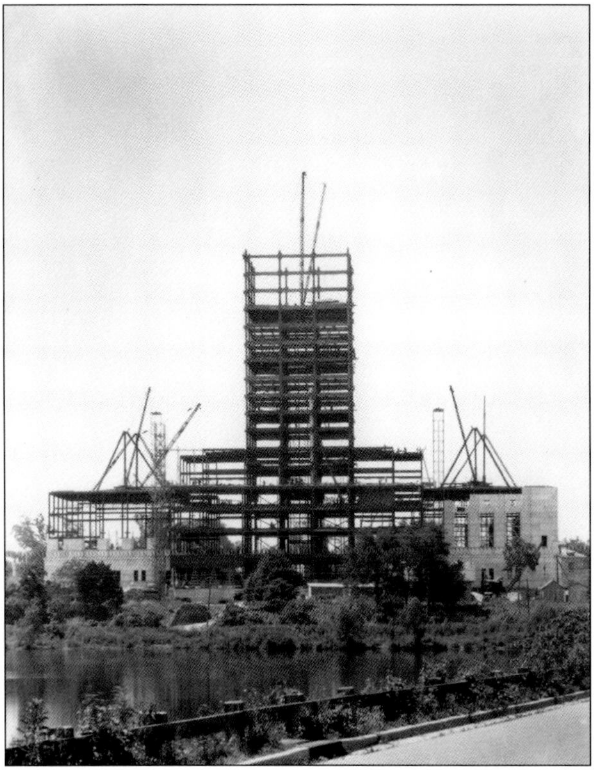

This 1931 photograph of the new state capitol was taken from a vantage point on North Third Street and north of University Lake (later renamed Capitol Lake). The steel superstructure of the state house and senate chambers, as well as the tower of the proposed 450-foot-high building, are beginning to take shape. In 1932, the building was completed, 14 months after constructed began. (SLL.)

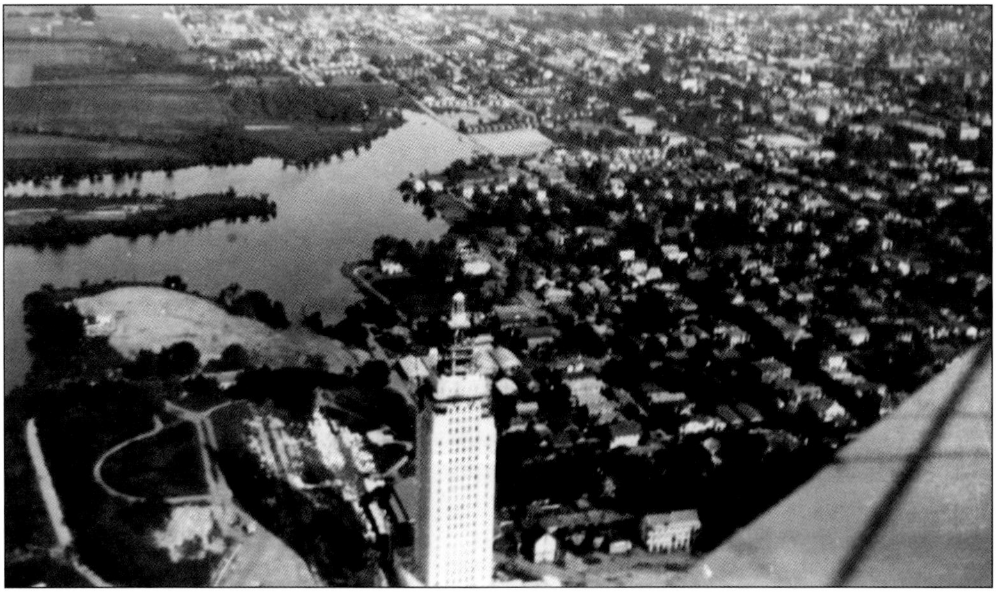

The exterior of the state capitol was nearly complete when this late-1931 aerial photograph was taken. A close look at the image reminds one of the city's rapid growth after Standard Oil arrived. The residential areas nearest the capitol in this image include Aubert Town, Spanish Town, Tivolier Town, Grass Town, University Park, and Jackson Park. A new roadway, Interstate 110, would eventually separate these neighborhoods and the lake from neighborhoods such as Suburb Gracie and Suburb Abramson, located farther to the east. (SLL.)

Five

Civic and Social Events

The cultural foundation of Baton Rouge was influenced by many nationalities. French, Acadian, Spanish, British, Italian, and German compose the short list for this multicultural milieu. The enrichment by that diversity brought about a preponderance of events to this community.

Baton Rouge has always been a magnet for gatherings of people. So too were the organizations, clubs, and societies within the community that gave cause for social events. Since the early 1800s, the volunteer fire department had become essentially a society of active men belonging to each fire engine, hose company, or hook-and-ladder company. Their business was to attend all fires in town. Their clubs provided a social connection for all members. Banquets, balls, parades, and barbeques were frequent annual events, and festivities involved more than just the firemen. Events were supported and drew interest from the entire community. Among the most popular in the city were the President's Day, Firemen's Day, and Christmas parades.

The city, the political hub of Louisiana, frequently witnessed gatherings precipitated by statehouse politicians. Especially during election years, Baton Rouge saw more than its fair share of campaign events and a grand finale of the inaugural celebrations. Between inauguration years, downtown streets were frequently closed to traffic near the governor's mansion when incumbents such as J.Y. Sanders, L.E. Hall, J.M. Parker, and Huey P. Long entertained guests along the broad promenade of North Boulevard, or the Boulevard as it was commonly called.

The women's suffrage movement spawned campaigns to enfranchise women and lobby Congress to pass a constitutional amendment allowing women the right to vote. Women of Baton Rouge participated in picketing and marching for the cause, which was finally ratified as the 19th Amendment. The victory was a significant achievement for women during this era.

This chapter depicts only a fragment of the community's early social life, which consisted of an exhaustive list of clubs, lodges, secret societies, and theatrical organizations. Between the 1890s and 1930s, an increasingly strong economy fostered greater attendance at social balls, athletic events, and theaters. There were no less than 15 private lodges and fraternal organizations and as many as 25 ladies' organizations in the 1910s alone.

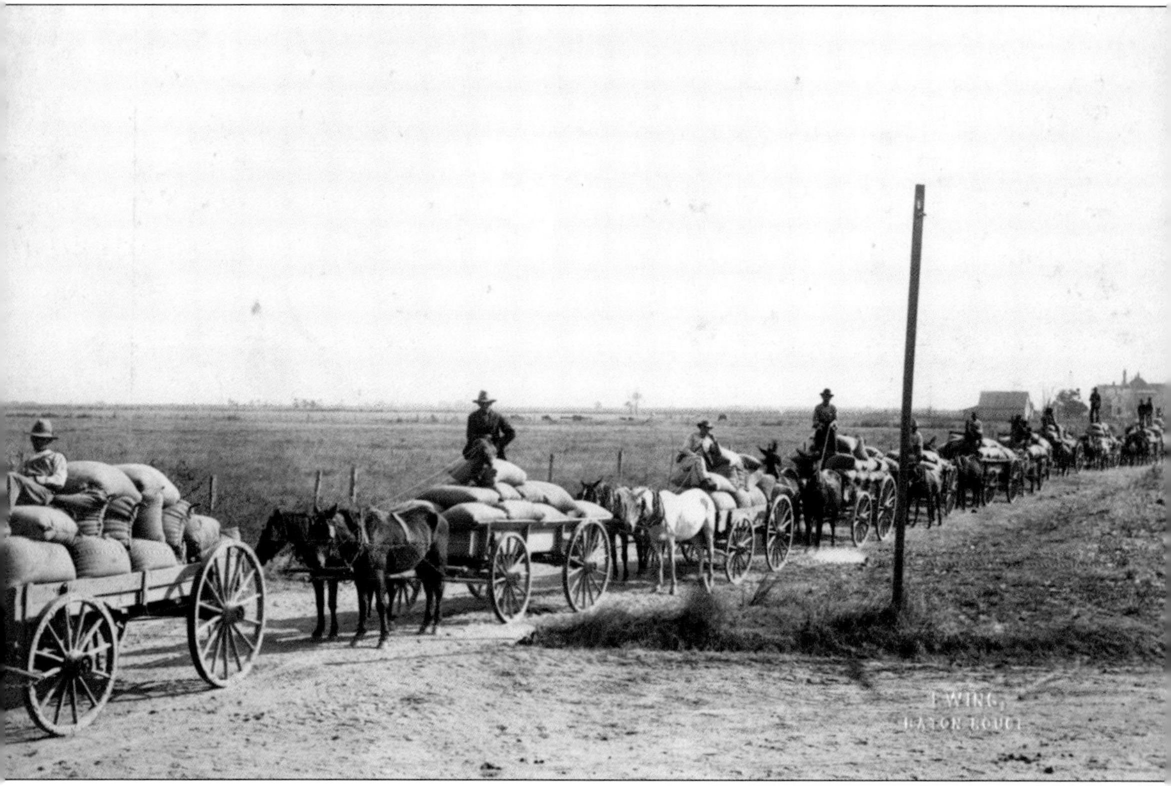

A federal law, the Smith-Lever Act of 1914, established a system of cooperative extension services. The services were attached to land-grant colleges, whereby the latest research in agriculture was shared with farmers and affiliates in the business of agriculture. In this 1915 photograph, a wagon train of grain and supplies for area farmers was provided by Louisiana State University Cooperative Extension Service. (LSUSC.)

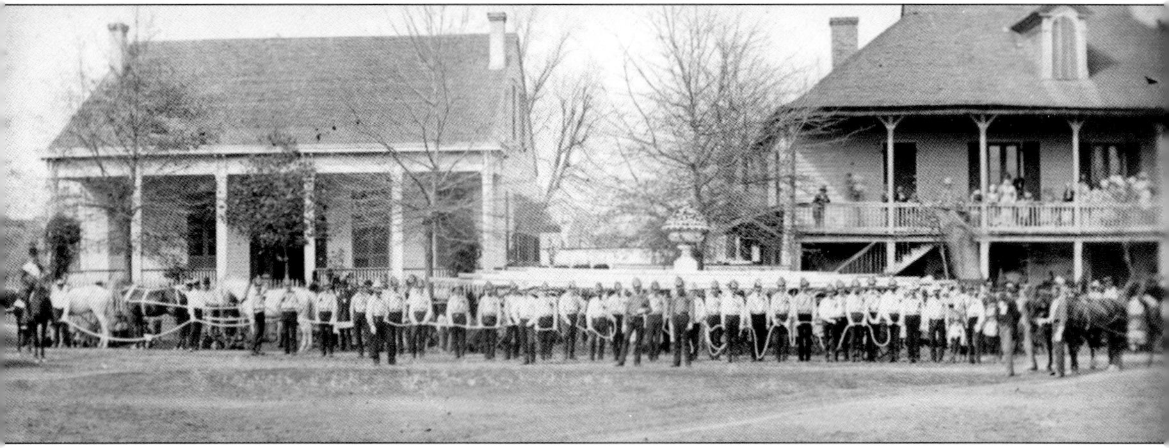

In this 1890s photograph of the Pelican Hook and Ladder Company No. 1, a host of company members in full dress uniforms with their firefighting equipment pose for the camera of Andrew Lytle. The gathering was possibly for the annual Firemen's Day parade that typically coincided with President's Day, or as some people referred to it, Washington's Day. (LSUSC.)

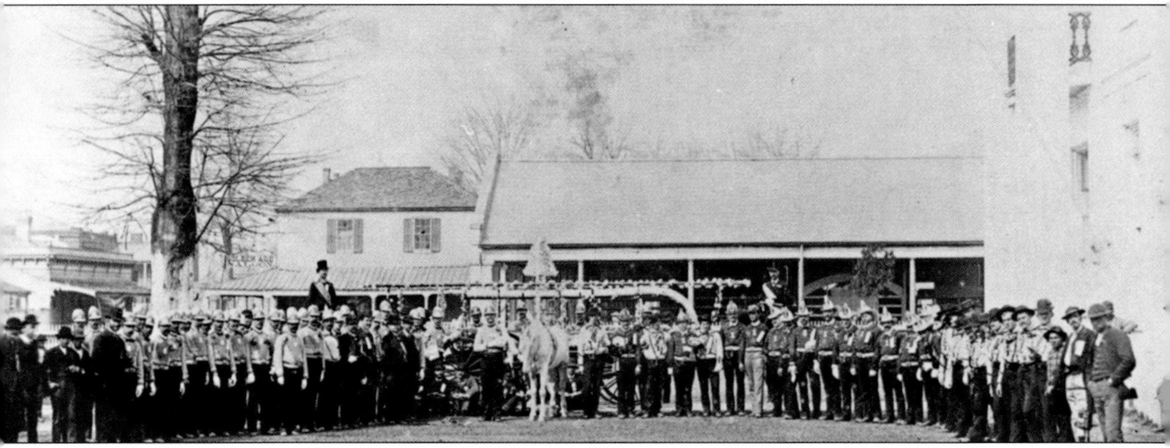

Dressed in company uniforms, Washington Fire Company No. 1 and Independence Fire Company No. 2 pose for the camera around 1900. The occasion may have been for the Firemen's Day parade and festivities as the group gathered in the public space adjacent to the courthouse and city market. (EBRPL.)

The first organized firefighting bucket brigade in Baton Rouge was formed in 1825. Pelican Hook and Ladder Company organized in 1873, and the charter was certified six years later on March 10, 1879. Here, members of the Pelican Hook and Ladder Company No.1 pose with fellow citizens before their new horse-drawn aerial ladder truck. (LSUSC.)

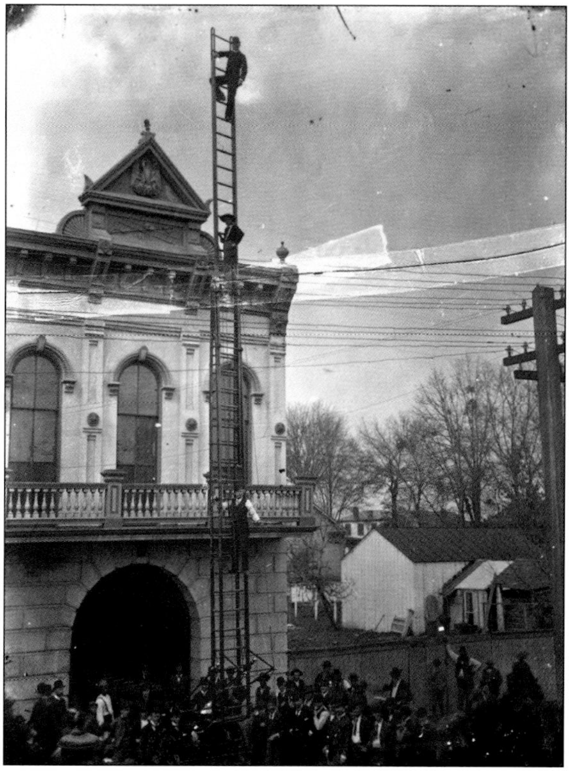

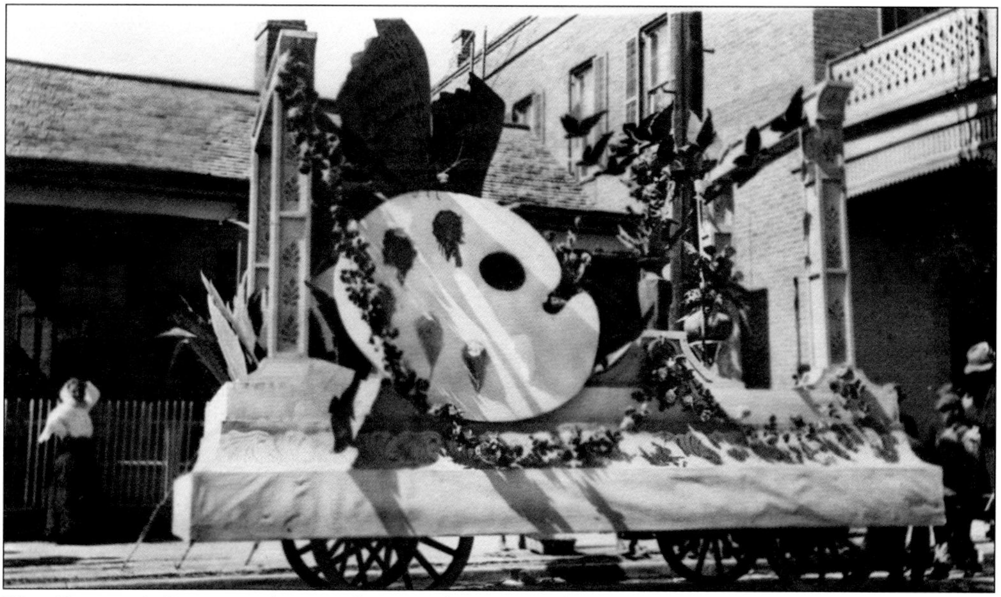

The Firemen's Day parade was the grandest city celebration of the year. The annual event commemorated the establishment of the city's first volunteer fire brigade. Typically, it was family members of the volunteer firemen who decorated the carriages for the parades. This float, from 1912, was decorated by Schloss Hook and Ladder Company No. 5 and was awarded first place. Float entries also included fraternal and social organizations that competed for cash prizes. (POVPC.)

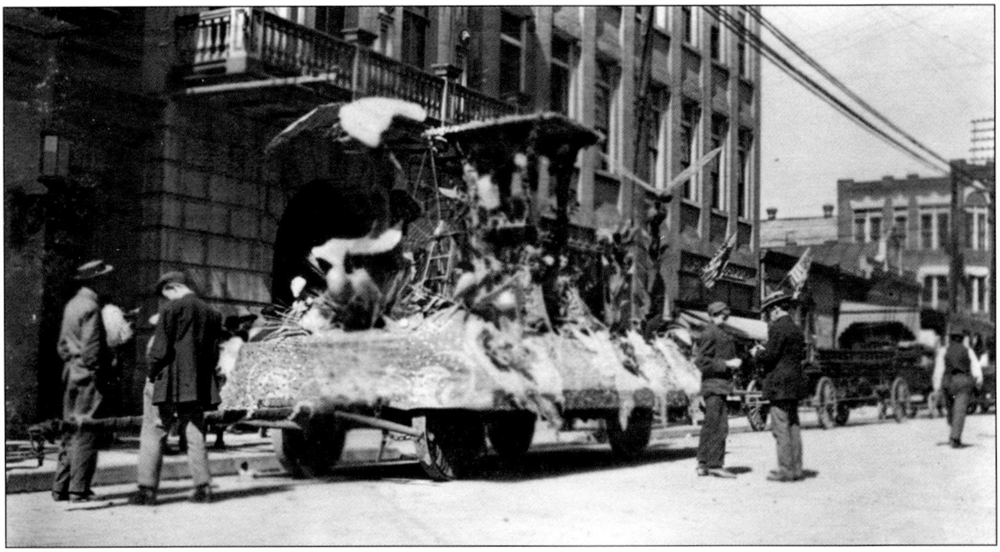

This float, decorated by the Pelican Hook and Ladder Company, took second prize in the Fireman's Day parade. The float is adorned with large garden-variety butterflies. The Firemen's Day parade was usually held in conjunction with George Washington's birthday, or President's Day. The photograph was taken from the west side of Third Street between Convention and Florida Streets. The prized float was parked in front of the Pelican Hook and Ladder Company firehouse. Each volunteer fire company sponsored an annual ball. The ball was one of the many ways separate departments raised money for operational funds. The company's motto was "We Raise to Save." The Elks Theater is visible on the far right. (POVPC.)

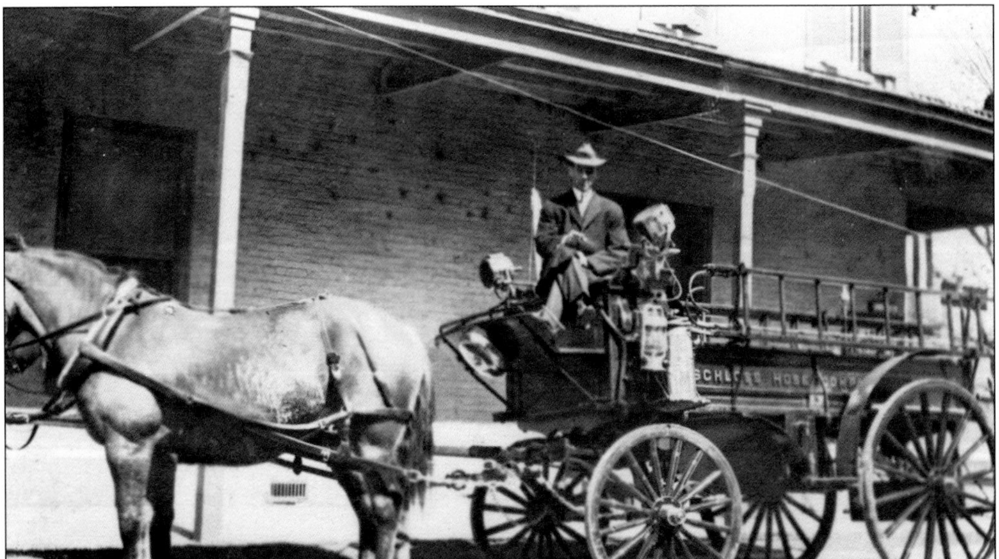

An unknown driver from Schloss Hose Company No. 5 poses for the photographer before the wagon is decorated as a parade float. Each of the fire companies participated in the Firemen's Day parade and entered a contest for the best-decorated float. The companies were carefully positioned throughout downtown for optimal response time in case of fires. In 1908, the list of fire company names included Independence, Washington, Pelican, Schloss, Loucks, and Jackson. (POVPC.)

Children pose for this c. 1900 photograph on a fire company's float before the Firemen's Day parade. Each fire company decorated a unique float for competition between all of the firehouses in the city in hopes of winning cash prizes awarded to the first- and second-place winners. (EBRPL.)

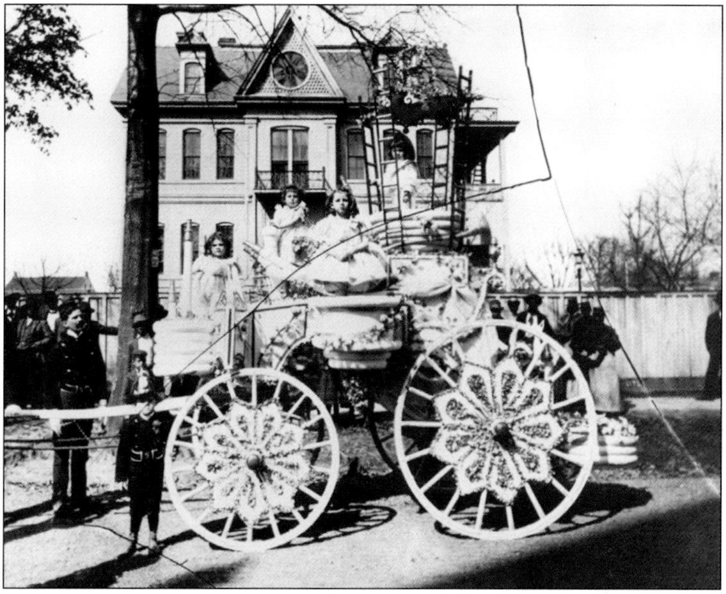

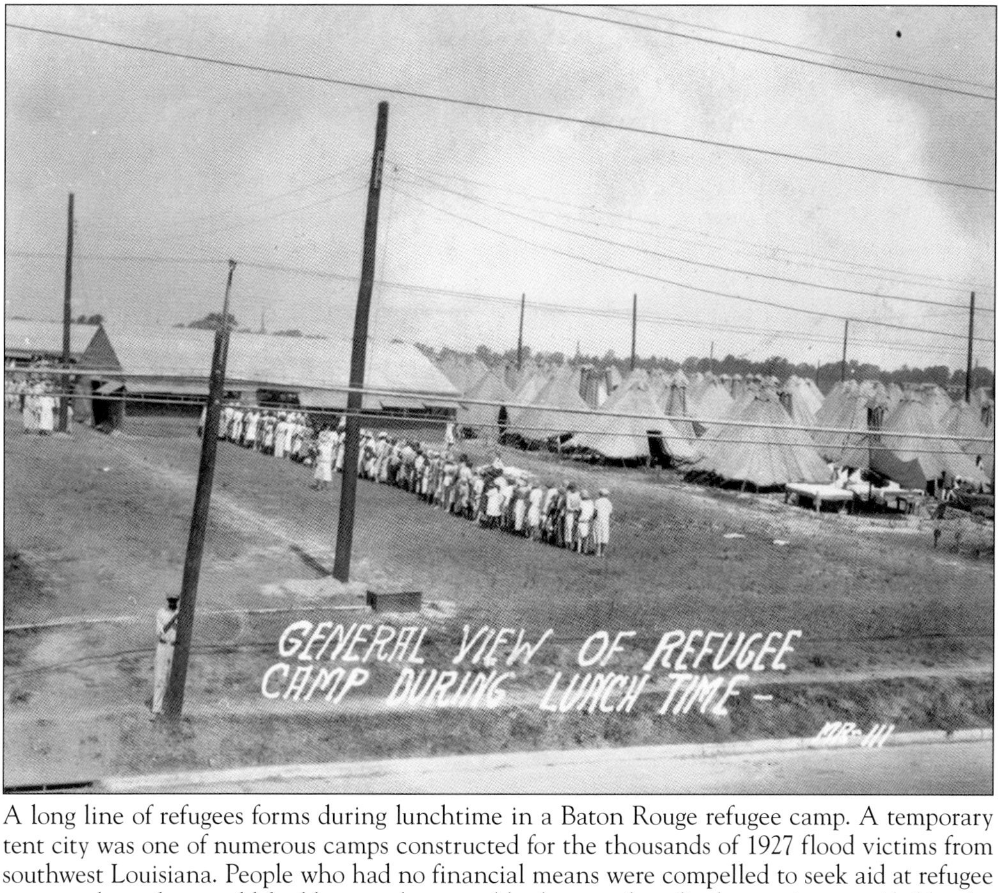

A long line of refugees forms during lunchtime in a Baton Rouge refugee camp. A temporary tent city was one of numerous camps constructed for the thousands of 1927 flood victims from southwest Louisiana. People who had no financial means were compelled to seek aid at refugee camps, where they could find hot meals, warm blankets, and medical attention provided by the American Red Cross. (SLL.)

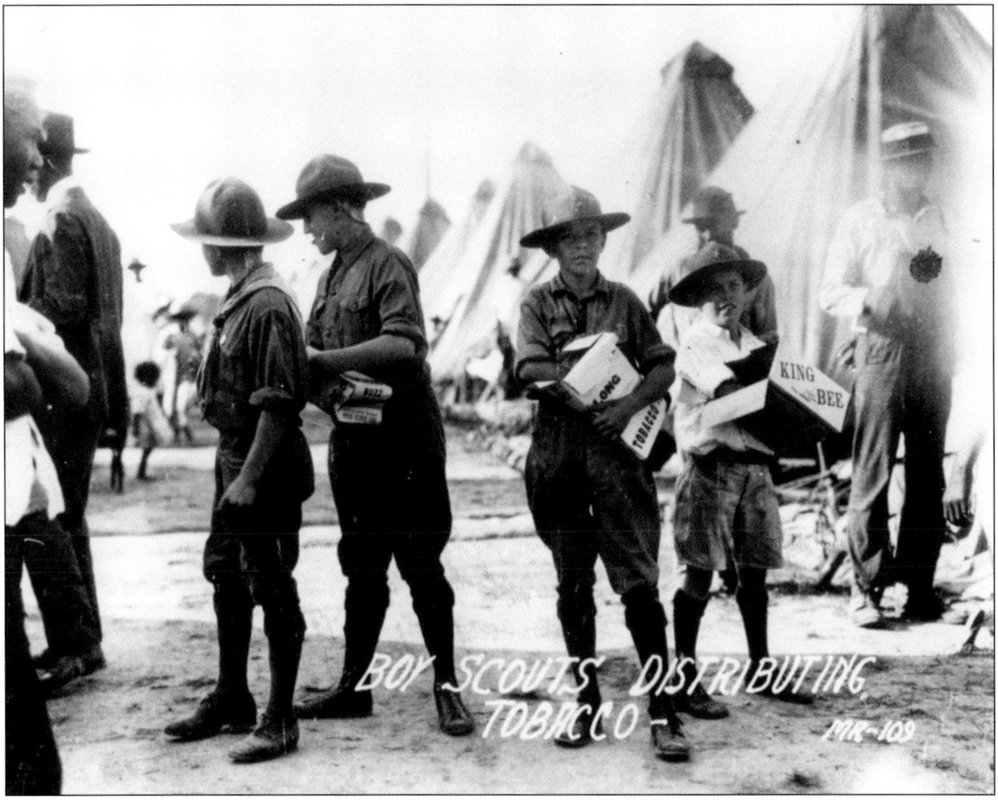

Relief efforts of the American Red Cross recruited volunteer assistance from the Boy Scouts of America in 1927. In this image, local scouts assist with distribution of tobacco products at the Baton Rouge refugee camp. The living conditions in this African American refugee camp were crude and basic, as the local and federal governments were not prepared for a widespread catastrophe. (SLL.)

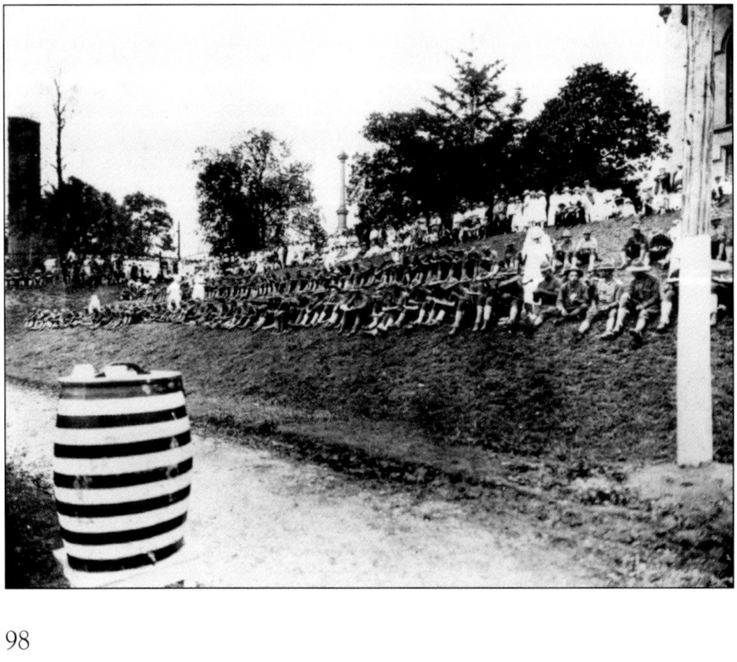

Photographed in 1917 on the grounds of the Old State Capitol, war-bound soldiers wait to board trains at the Yazoo and Mississippi Valley Railroad Depot directly across Natchez Street. Female volunteers for the Red Cross, dressed in white, were called "Blue Veils" and provided food and refreshment to the soldiers. (SLL.)

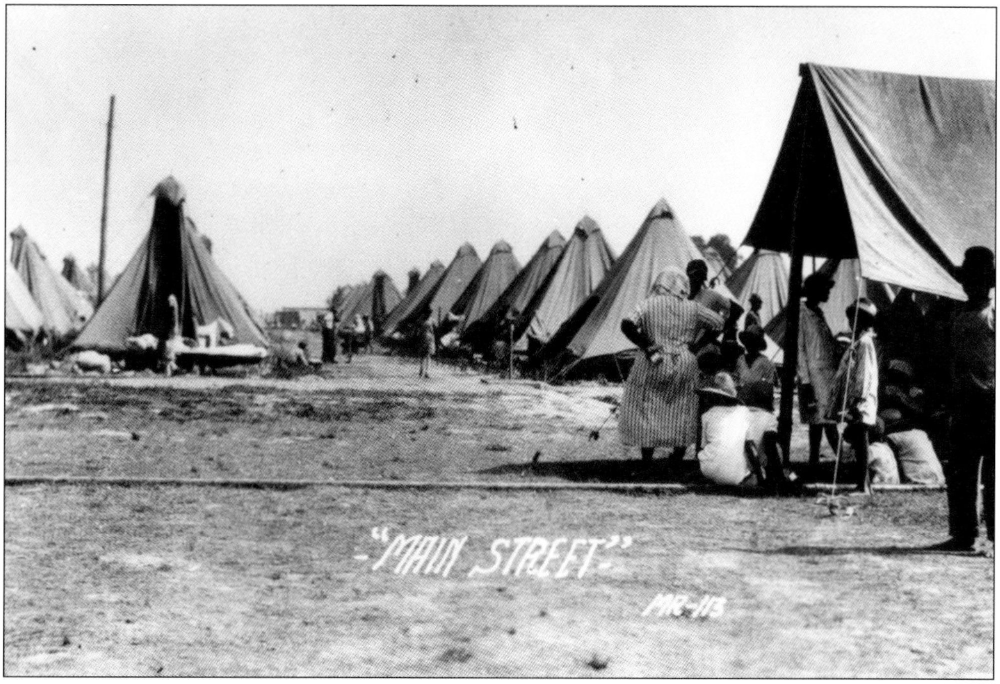

The Great Mississippi River flood of 1927 sent thousands of African Americans into tightly packed and segregated refugee camps throughout the Mississippi Valley. Many migrated to Baton Rouge, as water claimed their source of income in the greatest river flood that America has ever known. (SLL.)

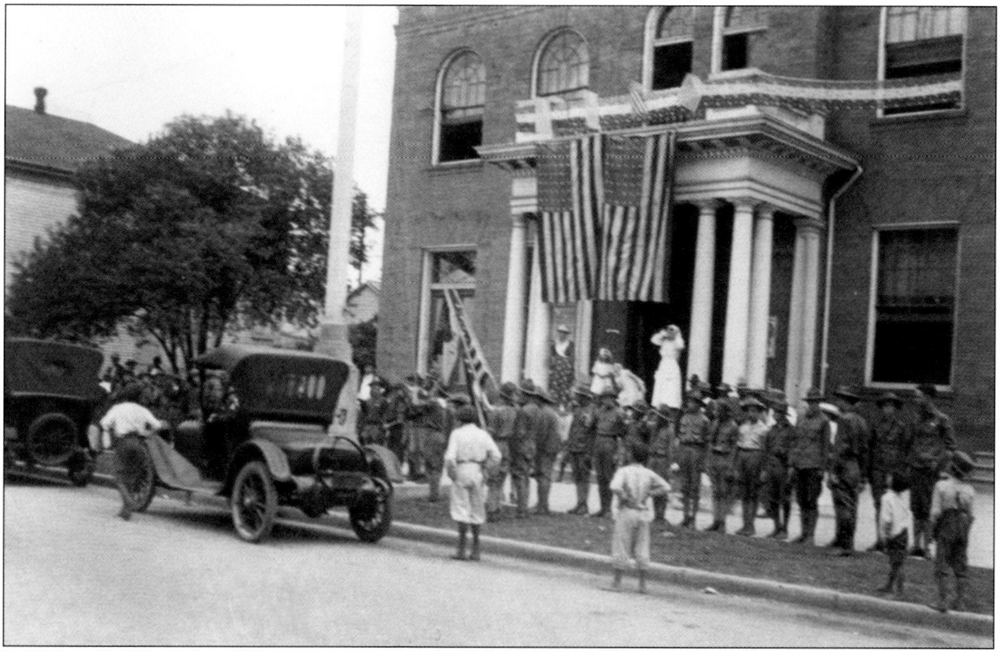

A patriotic special occasion in the 1920s was cause for this gathering of young men in uniform and onlookers in front of Baton Rouge City Hall. The crowd observes as the Boy Scouts raise the flag (not visible) above the municipal building. (SLL.)

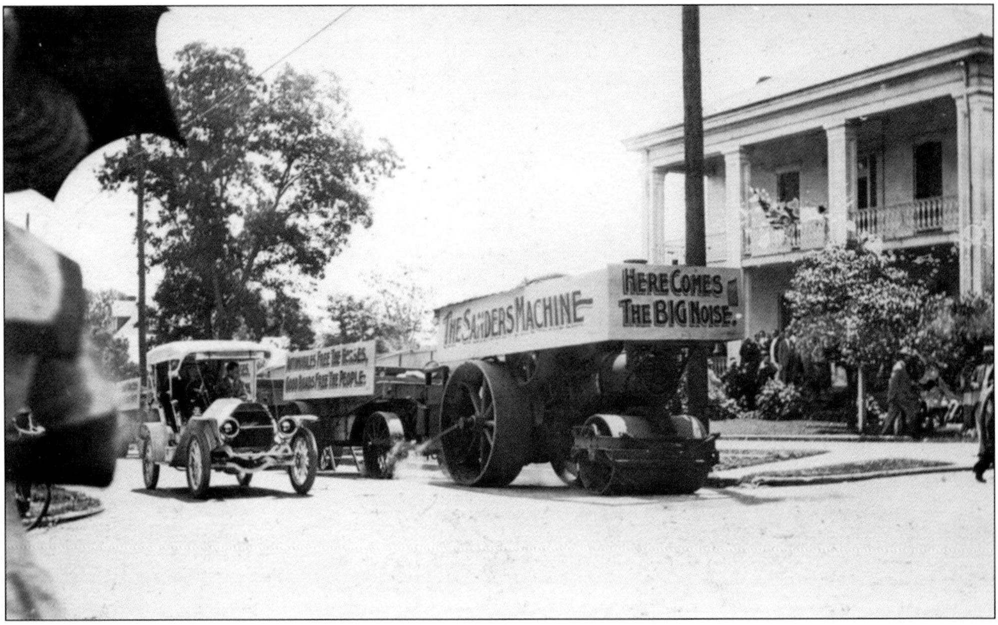

The governor's home was a large, wood-frame mansion originally built by slave labor in 1857 as a private residence for Nathan King Knox and served as the residence for 11 Louisiana governors from 1887 to 1929. The building was located on the corner of North Boulevard and St. Charles Street. Gov. Huey P. Long ordered it razed and replaced with a stucco Georgian mansion built to resemble the White House. In this photograph, a steamroller represents the "Sanders Machine" as it rolls down North Boulevard in front of Gov. Jared Y. Sanders's home. (POVPC.)

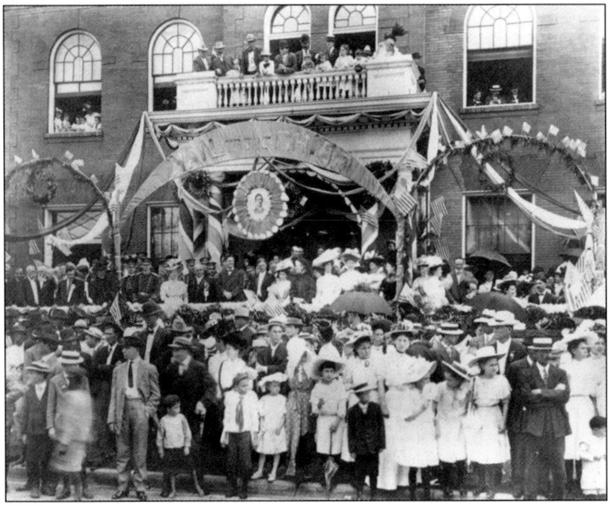

Jared Y. Sanders was a successful businessman, newspaper editor, lawyer, and politician from Morgan City, Louisiana. His career led straight to the governor's mansion after serving as a state representative, speaker of the house of representatives, and lieutenant governor. He served as governor from 1908 to 1912 and eventually won a seat in the US House of Representatives, in which he served from 1917 to 1921. This scene of Sanders's inauguration is on the steps of city hall on North Boulevard in 1908. (SLL.)

Gov. Jared Y. Sanders was a graduate of St. Charles Jesuit College in Grand Coteau, Louisiana, and then graduated from Tulane University's law school in 1893. He first practiced law in Franklin, Louisiana, and eventually climbed his way through state political positions before he was elected governor in 1908. He served from 1908 to 1912, supported Progressive legislation, and became known as the father of the "good roads movement" in Louisiana and as "Gravel Roads Sanders." (LSS.)

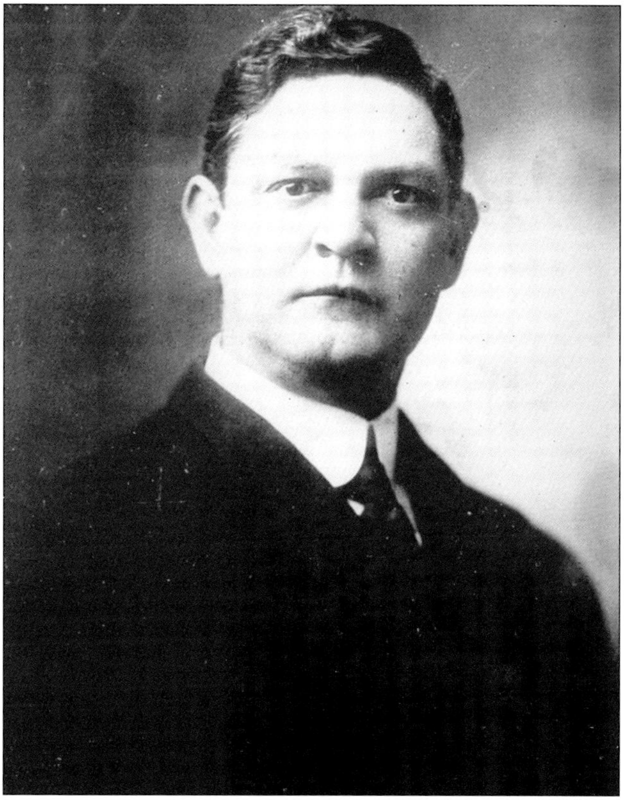

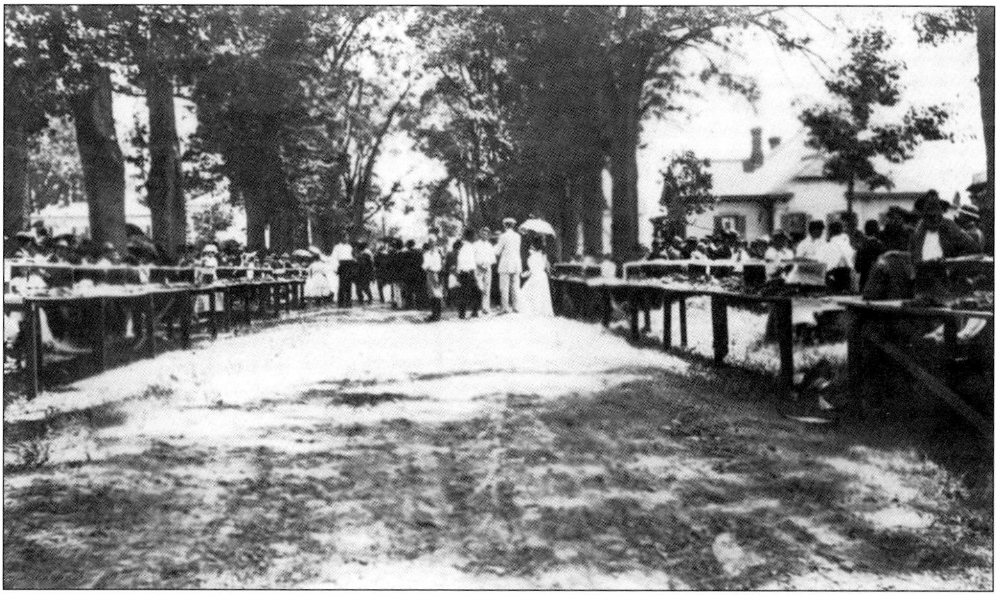

Governor of Louisiana Jared Y. Sanders was noted for regulation of gambling and liquor and the passage of child-labor laws. In this photograph, Governor Sanders is seen sponsoring a barbeque around 1912 that consisted of an elaborate layout of food along one of Beauregard Town's unpaved streets. Governor Sanders was popular for lavish entertainments at the governor's house. Sanders was succeeded as governor in 1912 by Luther E. Hall. (POVPC.)

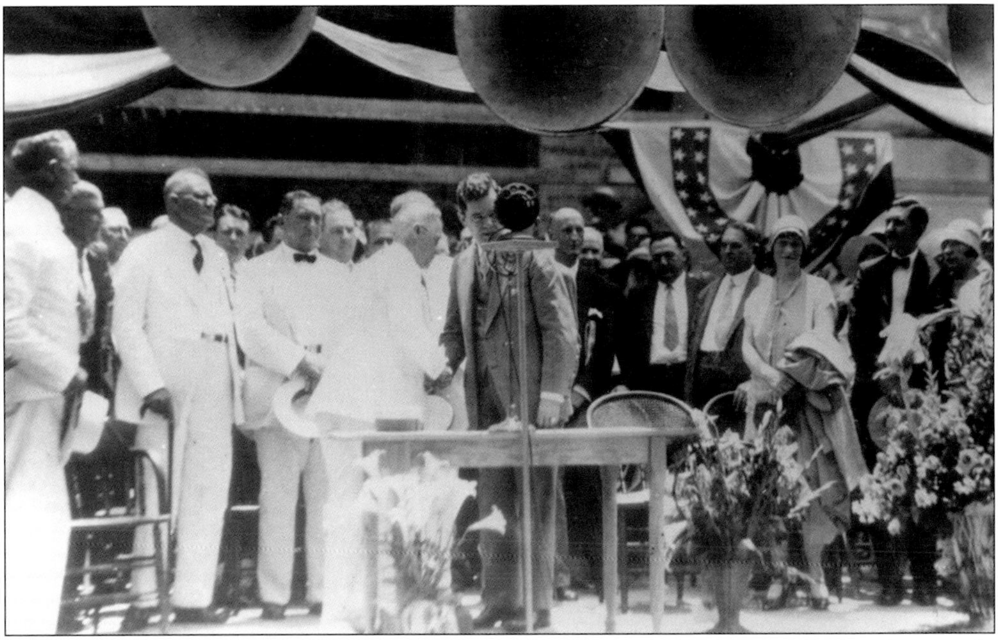

May 21, 1928, was a momentous occasion for the people of the state of Louisiana. In this photograph, Huey P. Long stands on the inauguration platform for the swearing-in ceremony. His address was to a crowd of more than 15,000 people. (LSUSC.)

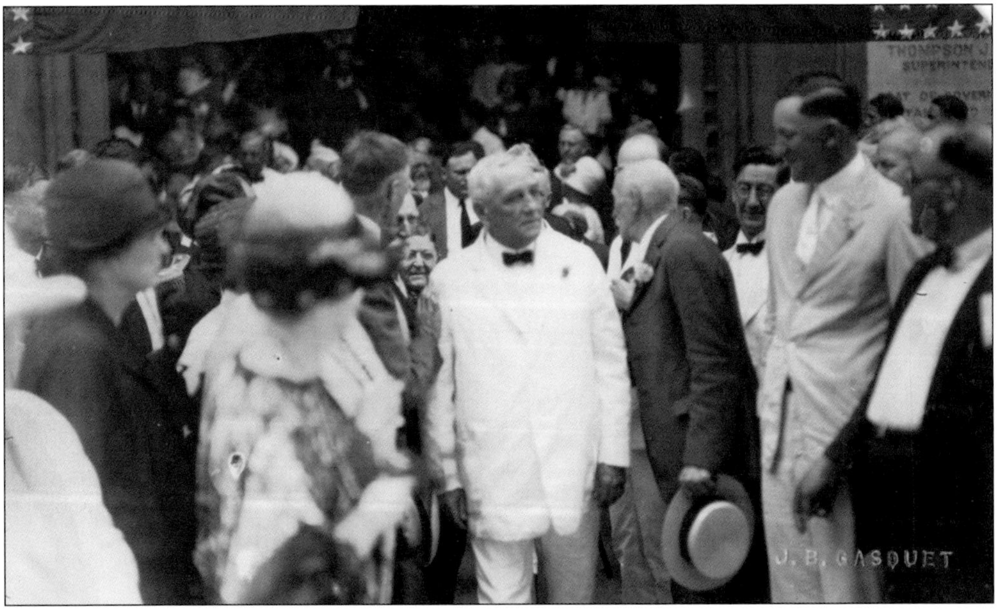

Henry L. Fuqua was a successful Baton Rouge businessman and owner of Fuqua Hardware Company. He was educated at Magruder's Collegiate Institute and Louisiana State University before working for the Yazoo and Mississippi Valley Railroad and later serving as warden of the Louisiana State Penitentiary at Angola. He was elected governor of Louisiana and served only two years, from 1924 to 1926. Governor Fuqua was passionate about constructing more buildings on the new Louisiana State University campus in south Baton Rouge and promoted expansion of Southern University in north Baton Rouge. (SLL.)

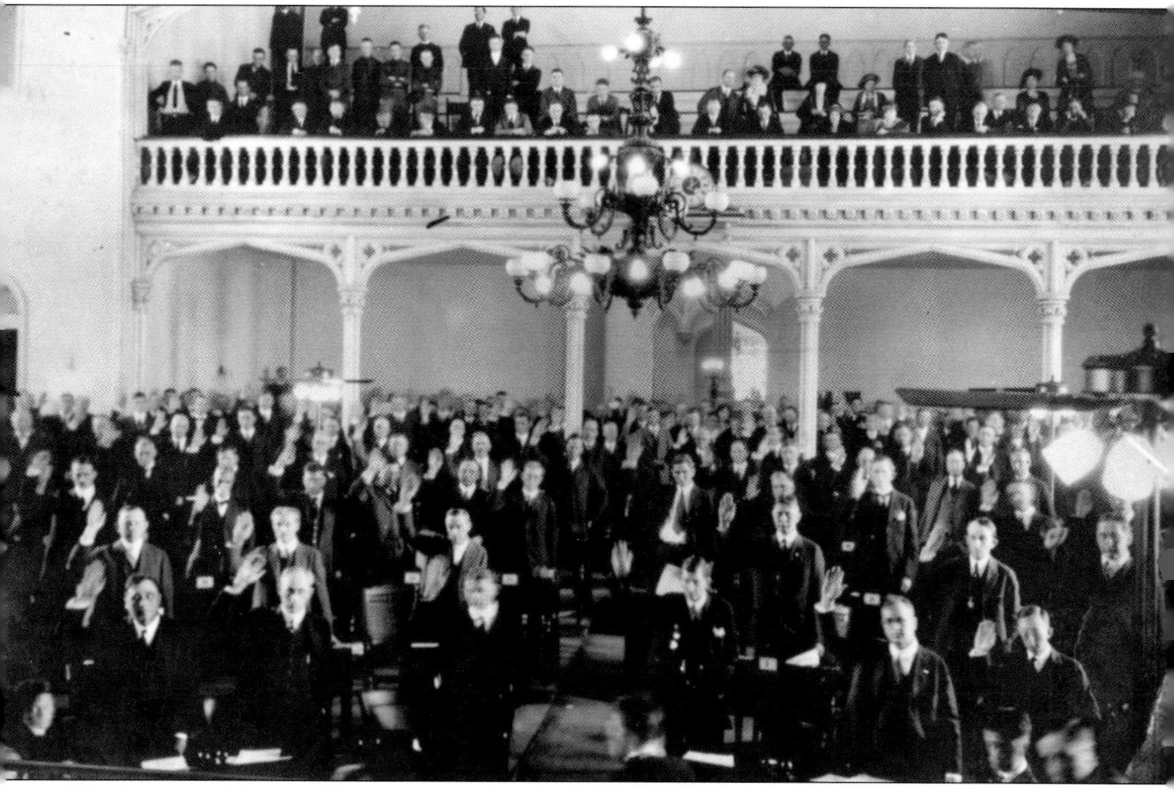

The Louisiana House of Representatives convened for the 1921 Constitutional Convention in order to make changes to numerous articles in the Louisiana constitution. Important changes were made on the topics of forced heirship, the number of Supreme Court justices, and on the Progressive era subjects of minimum wage, regulation of hours, and working conditions for women and girls. This group image of the Louisiana House of Representatives was taken inside the house chambers of the Old State Capitol. (SLL.)

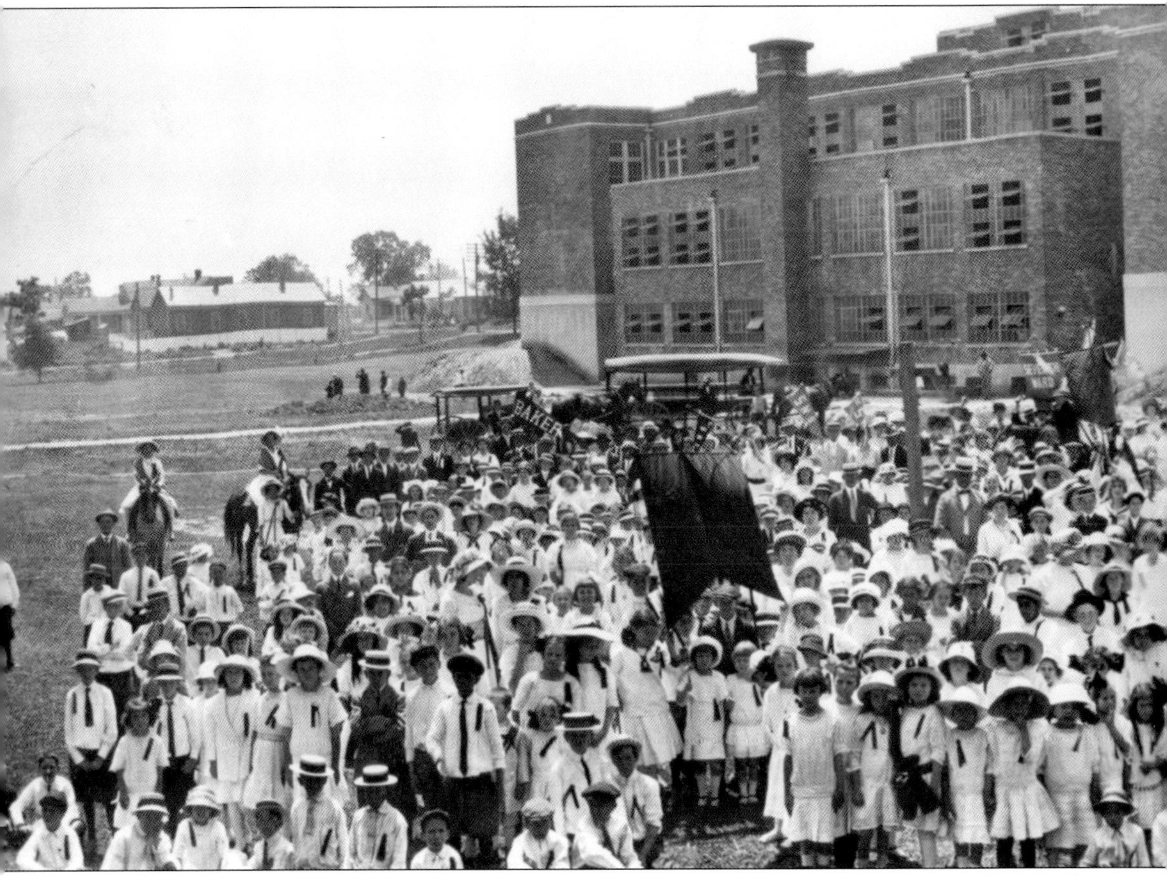

For many years, the biggest event for public schools was Achievement Day. Around 1917, this special occasion involved schools throughout East Baton Rouge Parish and brought students together for the display of schoolwork and competition of curriculum subjects and club projects. In the crowded photograph, school names are displayed on pennants. The event was certainly grand enough for all students to attend in their finest attire. (SLL.)

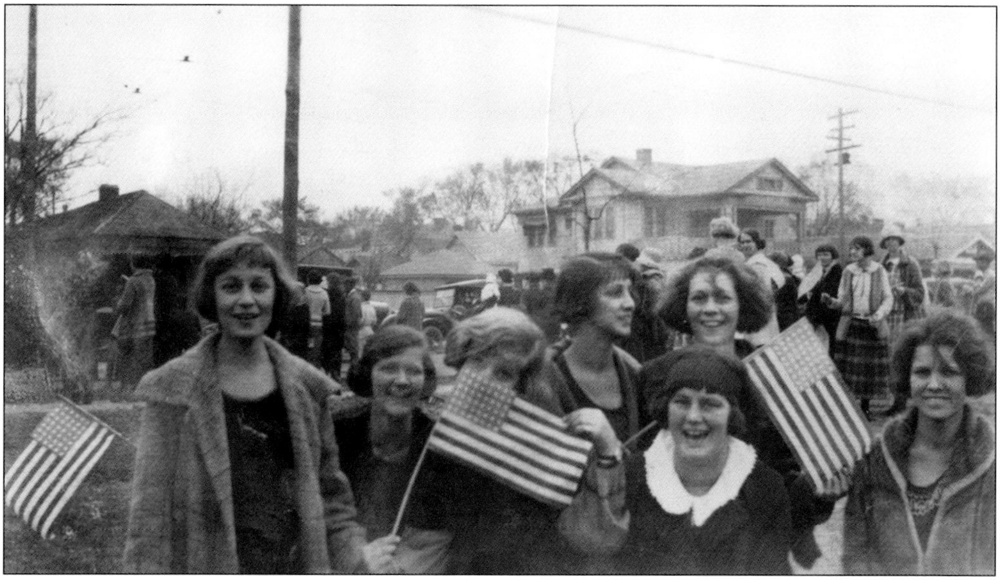

This photograph of Gladys Brechtel's high school friends was taken around 1924 in celebration of Armistice Day. The celebration was a day proclaimed by President Wilson to honor veterans of World War I, which engulfed the civilized world only a few years earlier. (EBRPL.)

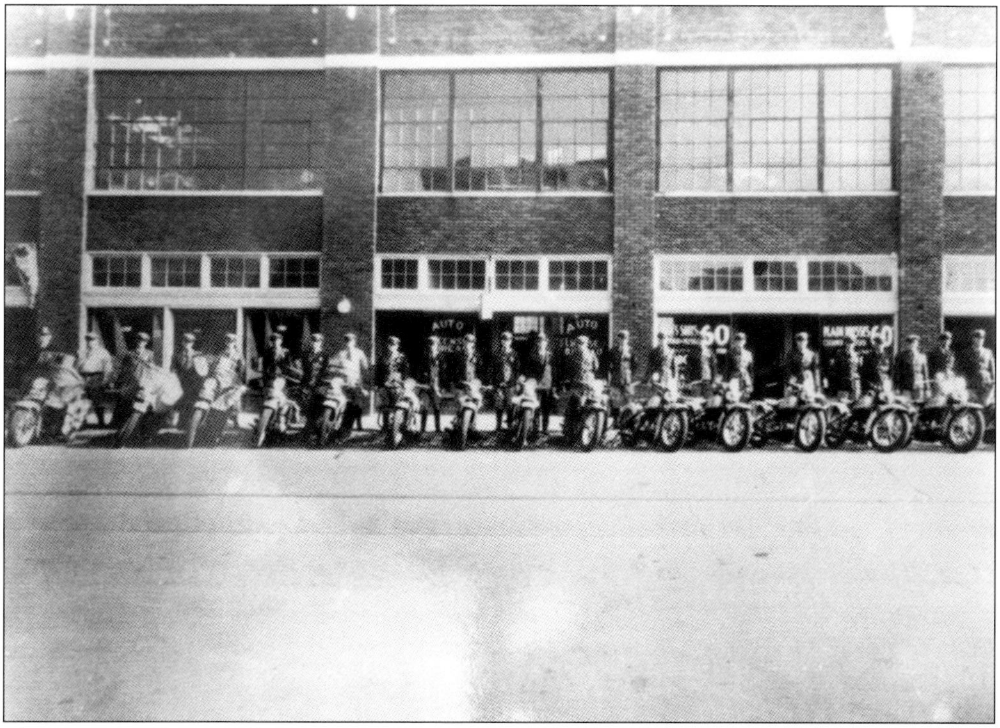

The Louisiana State Highway Commission was formed in 1922 with a motorcycle police force of 16 men who patrolled state-owned roadways. By 1936, the Louisiana Bureau of Criminal Investigation, formed in 1932, was merged with the Highway Commission to form the Louisiana Department of State Police. This photograph of motorcycle state troopers was taken in the 1930s in front of the Auto Hotel on Lafayette Street. The Auto Hotel was the city's first parking garage. (SLL.)

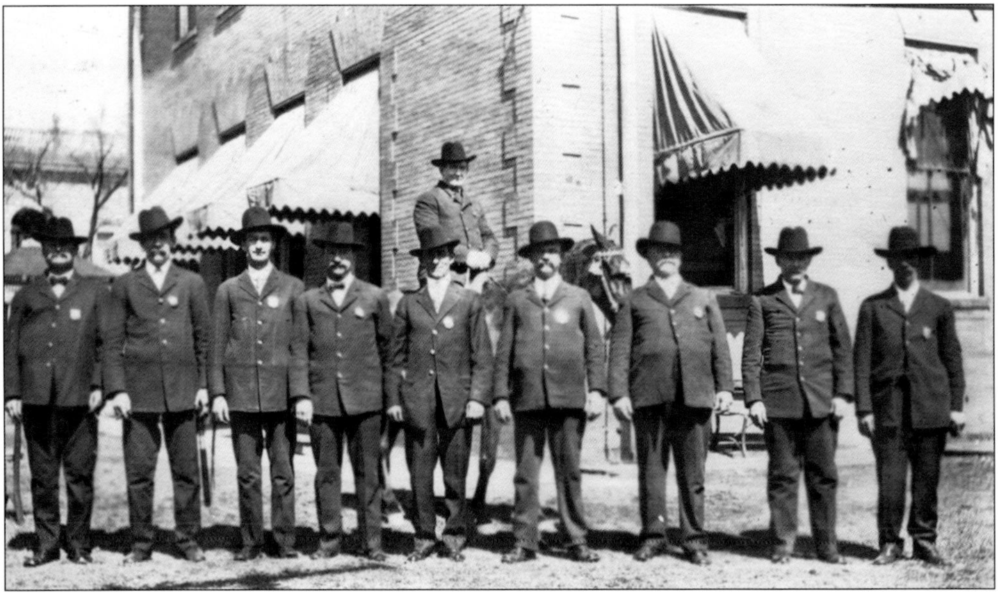

Picture here in 1912, the Baton Rouge police force had dwindled to 10 officers. Two officers died in an incident the year before, and three left the force for unknown reasons. This photograph was taken near the courthouse. A portion of the city market is visible in the left background. Philip Huyck was elected police chief in 1911 and served until 1914. (POVPC.)

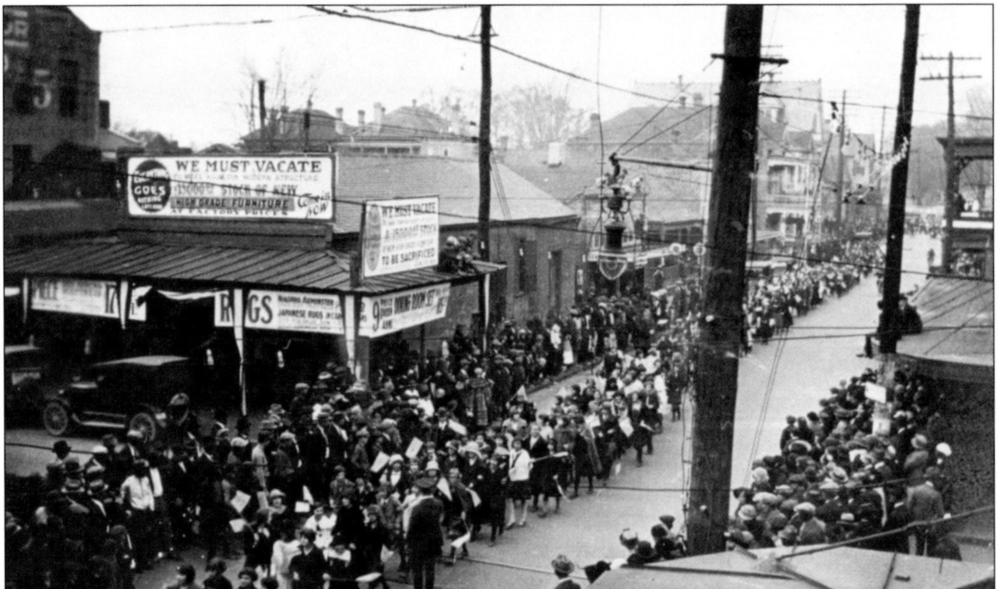

This parade of women marches down Third Street in the 1920s, possibly in celebration of Armistice Day. Armistice Day commemorated the agreement signed between the Allies of World War I and Germany. Perhaps the organizers were members of the Woman's Club of Baton Rouge, which was organized in 1921 by representatives from 10 ladies' organizations. (EBRPL.)

Six

STANDARD OIL COMPANY

Two important occurrences influenced Louisiana in such a profound way that the course of history for Baton Rouge was permanently changed. First came a judgment by Edward Douglass White, chief justice of the United States, the only Louisianan to serve in that position, who conceived and formulated an immensely important judgment labeled Rule of Reason, a standard of antitrust law written in favor of big businesses. Secondly, there was a decision by the board of directors of Standard Oil Company, and particularly from John D. Rockefeller, to build a refinery at Baton Rouge.

Rockefeller established the first refinery in Louisiana nine years after oil discovery in the state. Standard Oil Company of New Jersey, represented by its agent Col. Frederick Weller, for whom Weller Avenue was named, selected a 225-acre cotton field in East Baton Rouge Parish for a refinery because of its strategic location on the Mississippi River as an inland deepwater port and its proximity to the rich oil and gas deposits of south Louisiana. The choice site was ideal for a refinery. The site was free of flooding, fronted the Mississippi River, and was bordered by three rail lines: the Illinois Central, the Frisco, and the Louisiana Railroad and Navigation Company. The site was a natural gateway to inland North America. The oil company broke ground in the bluffs area two miles north of the city of Baton Rouge in April 1909, and by November the plant began processing oil and employed approximately 700 workers.

Standard Oil Company received a warm welcome in Baton Rouge after being shut out of Texas due to unfair business practices. Baton Rouge and the State of Louisiana were pleased with the industrial complex and continued to welcome the industry in the aftermath of the 1912 widespread flooding. The flood and the devastating boll weevil infestation to cotton production had great impact on farms and small towns and consequently forced people to look at Baton Rouge for employment. The arrival of the refinery was perhaps one of the most significant events in the history of Baton Rouge.

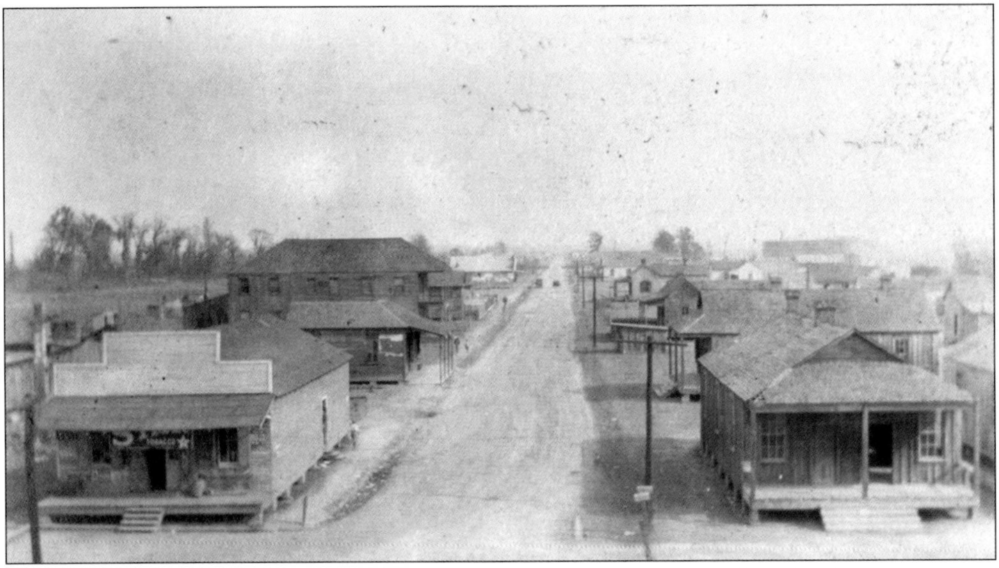

Standard Oil Company of Louisiana executives were very much aware of a lack of housing created by its surge in employment. Standard Oil of Louisiana built one of the first residential subdivisions, Suburb Dixie, platted amidst the cotton fields adjacent to the refinery. The subdivision was laid out in 1929. Dixie Street was the central thoroughfare, and it was aligned later with a street called Weller. Dixie, Cotton, and Cane Streets ran west from Bayou Sarah Road (later Scenic Highway) to Corn Street, which ran parallel to the Louisiana Railway and Navigation Company tracks. (EBRPL.)

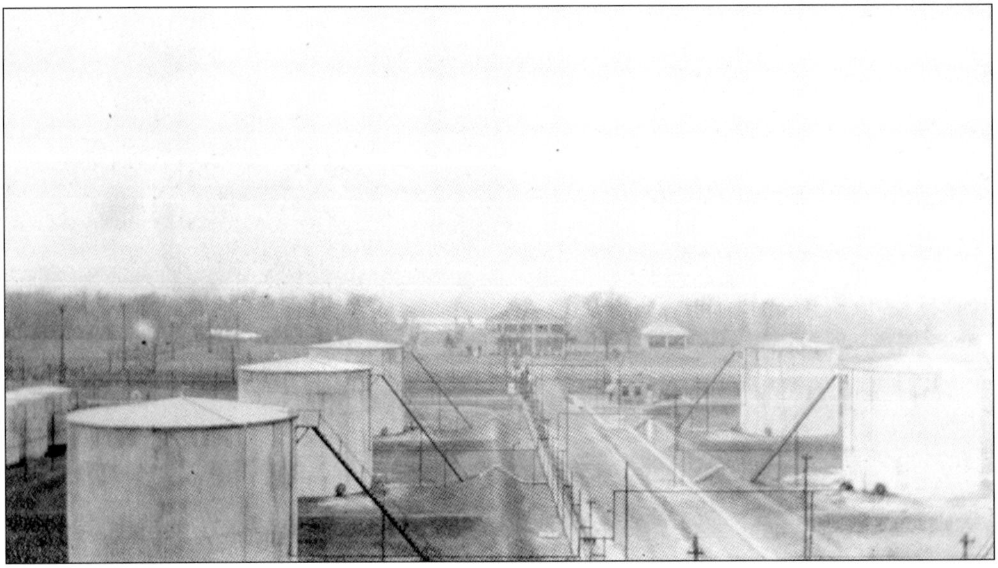

At the end of the main road that ran through Standard Oil's tank farm, company personnel had a superb view of the Mississippi River from the high ground of the bluff on the east bank. Several years after the refinery was established, old farm buildings on the cotton plantation remained, and grazing sheep were kept at the refinery to keep the grass under control. (EBRPL.)

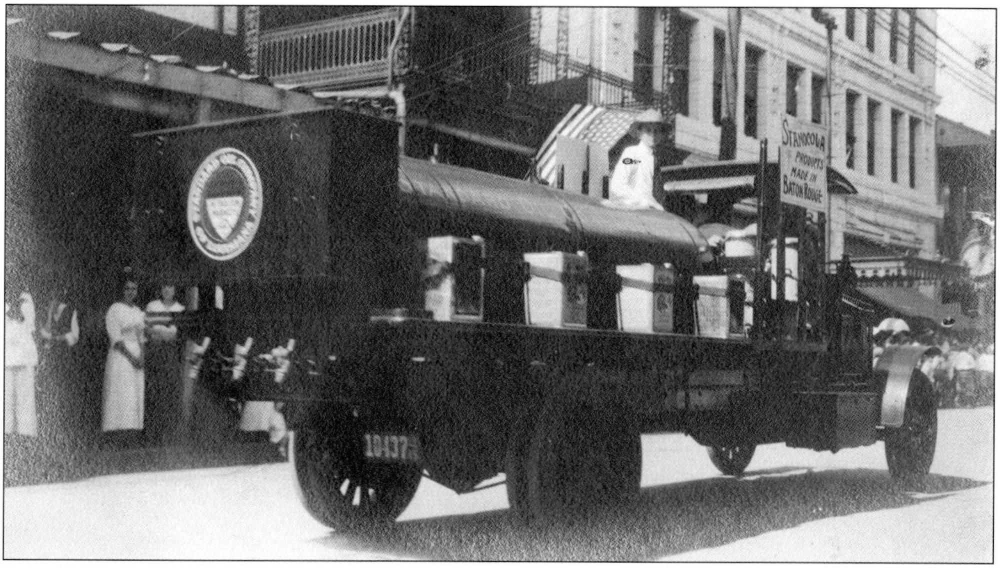

Standard Oil Company of Louisiana, or Stanocola, participated in community events like annual parades. The company's vehicles, as well as its marching band, were regular participants in civic events. In this 1914 photograph taken on Third Street, a Stanocola oil truck represents the giant corporation in a holiday parade. Visible in the background is the Roumain Building and its sidewalk clock. (EBRPL.)

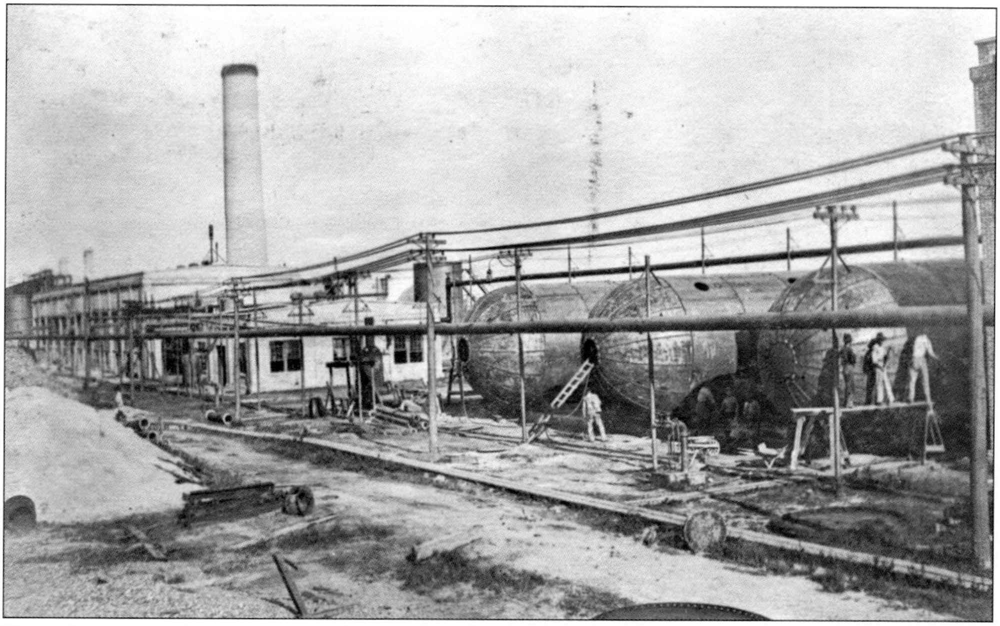

From the outset, the processing plant at Standard Oil continued to expand exponentially. In this photograph, rows of distillation stills are under construction for the much simpler refining process than what is used today. By 1915, the plant employed more than 1,000 people. The industrial site, by act of the legislature, could not be incorporated into the city of Baton Rouge, so the industrial complex established its own police, fire, and health divisions. By 1924, Stanocola Medical and Hospital Association had formed the first of what is now known as an HMO (health maintenance organization) in Louisiana. (POVPC.)

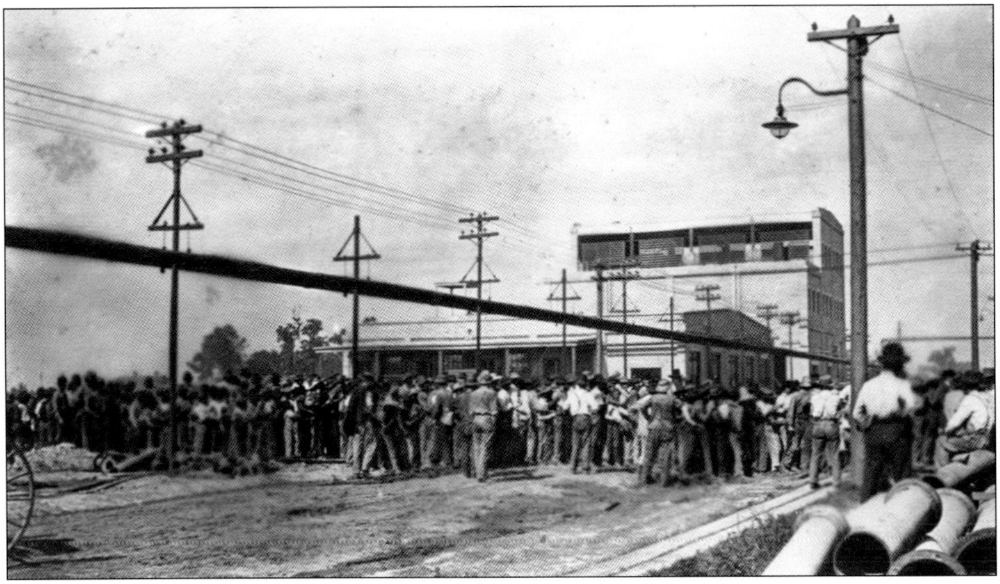

This scene was a familiar sight to photographer William B. Hart, as he spent most of his life working at Standard Oil. The refinery began operations in 1909 with approximately 700 employees. Within a few short years, the number of workers multiplied to more than 1,000. In this photograph near the paraffin plant, workers gather at the pay office for their weekly wages. (POVPC.)

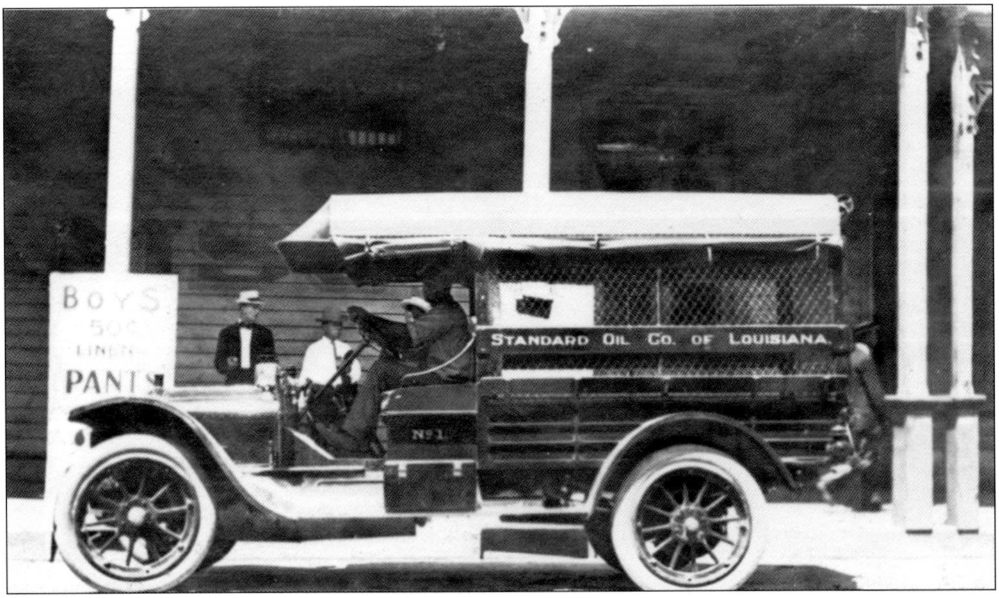

Standard Oil Company's refinery was not without occasional accidents during the early days of construction and processing of crude oil. Such events gave cause for the company to purchase and maintain their own fleet of vehicles for emergency medical needs. In this scene, the Standard Oil Company ambulance driver poses for a photograph in front of Abe Abramson's dry goods store on the corner of Third Street and North Boulevard in 1911. (POVPC.)

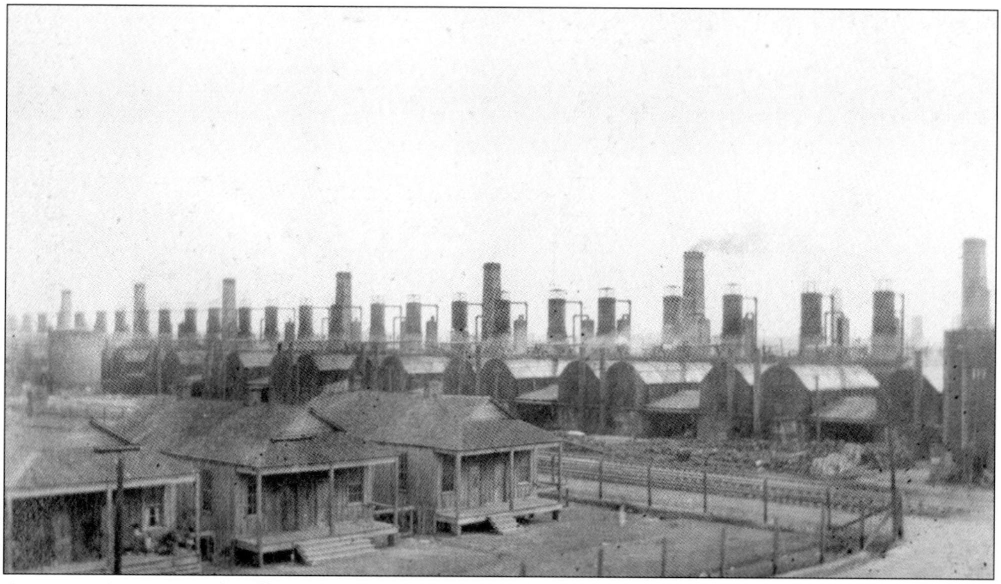

A series of immense distillation stills the size of railroad cars and smokestacks that rose above the rooftops of homes in the adjacent Suburb Dixie were a sign of progress. Dixie would be termed a walkable neighborhood in the 21st century, as there were no accommodations for parking private automobiles in this subdivision. (EBRPL.)

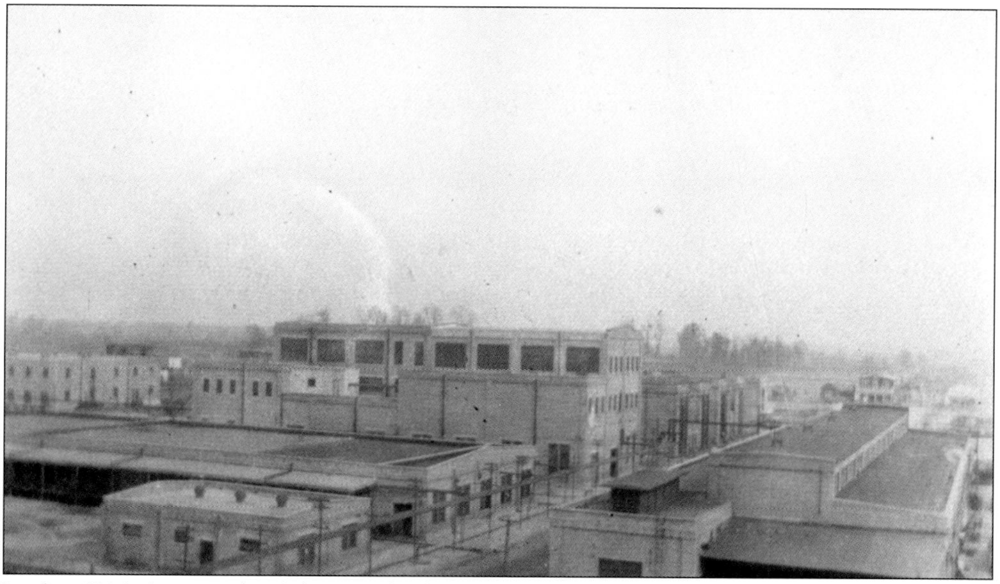

In this 1914 photograph of the Standard Oil refinery, the paraffin plant is on the left and the machine shop on the right. Among basic fractions like gasoline, kerosene, and gas oil, wax distillate was a valuable source of lubricating stock and paraffin. Paraffin is a product that sees daily use, now and then, in candles, cosmetics, paper coating, inks, fabrics, and foods. (EBRPL.)

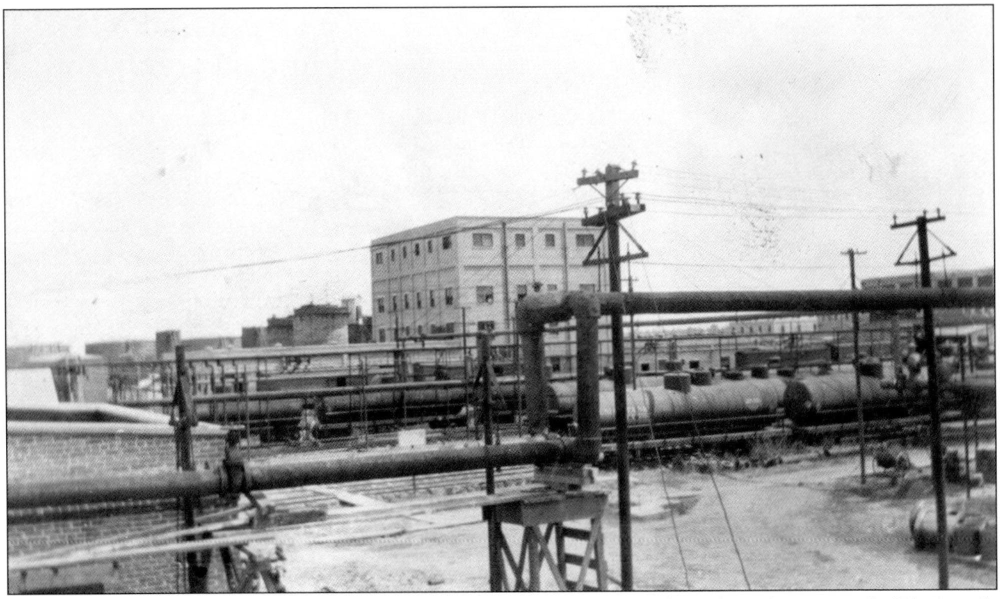

In the heart of Standard Oil Company's refinery, the all-riveted steel tank cars each filled with crude oil wait for unloading into large holding tanks shown in the background. The tank cars came not only from Louisiana but also from distant origins and varied in length, capacity, and age when they rolled into the refinery, seen here around 1914. (EBRPL.)

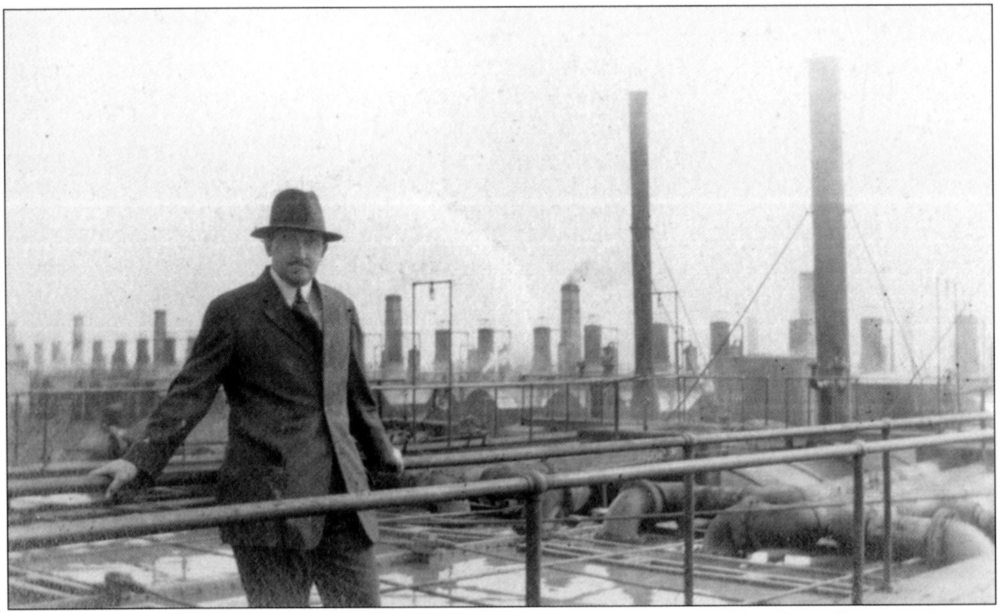

Five years after Standard Oil Company broke ground in the cotton fields of north Baton Rouge, the refinery and its immense mix of tanks, rails, and piping had expanded from Bayou Sarah Road to the banks of the Mississippi River. Chief chemist for Standard Oil Company, Frank C. Read, poses for this memorable 1914 photograph. (EBRPL.)

Seven

The River

Since the first settlers colonized Baton Rouge, the Mississippi River had been the transportation backbone and economic lifeline to this city. Until the proliferation of railroads, the river was the most efficient method of transport. By the turn of the 20th century, Congress enacted legislation that made the city a port of entry for foreign trade, partially because of Standard Oil Company's deepwater port. Though railroads took a toll on the river's robust economy, the port remained one of the largest in the United States.

In this chapter, photographs relating to the mighty river feature vivid scenes that bring to mind the forgotten everyday business along its banks. Steamboats, ferryboats, and tugboats that traversed the river from sunrise to sunset prominently played a key role in the life of the city.

Passenger steamboats of prominence from the postbellum era continued to dock in numbers at Baton Rouge but tapered dramatically after railroads connected major cities. The absence of the paddle-wheel boats was hardly noticed because of other river activity. Daily activity consisted of boats ferrying wagons, pedestrians, railcars, and motorized vehicles. Occasionally, Baton Rouge witnessed US Navy warships and Coast Guard vessels conducting training or humanitarian services during major floods.

At the water's edge, many of Baton Rouge's manufacturing and warehousing concerns found the location to be convenient and efficient. A bountiful list of enterprises had filled the three-mile length of shoreline from the Standard Oil Refinery to the municipal dock. However, proximity to the river had its disadvantages when annual high water lapped at entrances to those business concerns. In this era were also the floods of 1912 and 1927, when the hinterland was also affected. The aftermath, particularly of the 1927 event, had a profound effect on the people and economy of southern Louisiana. Baton Rouge served as an immense staging area and focal point in the rescue operations.

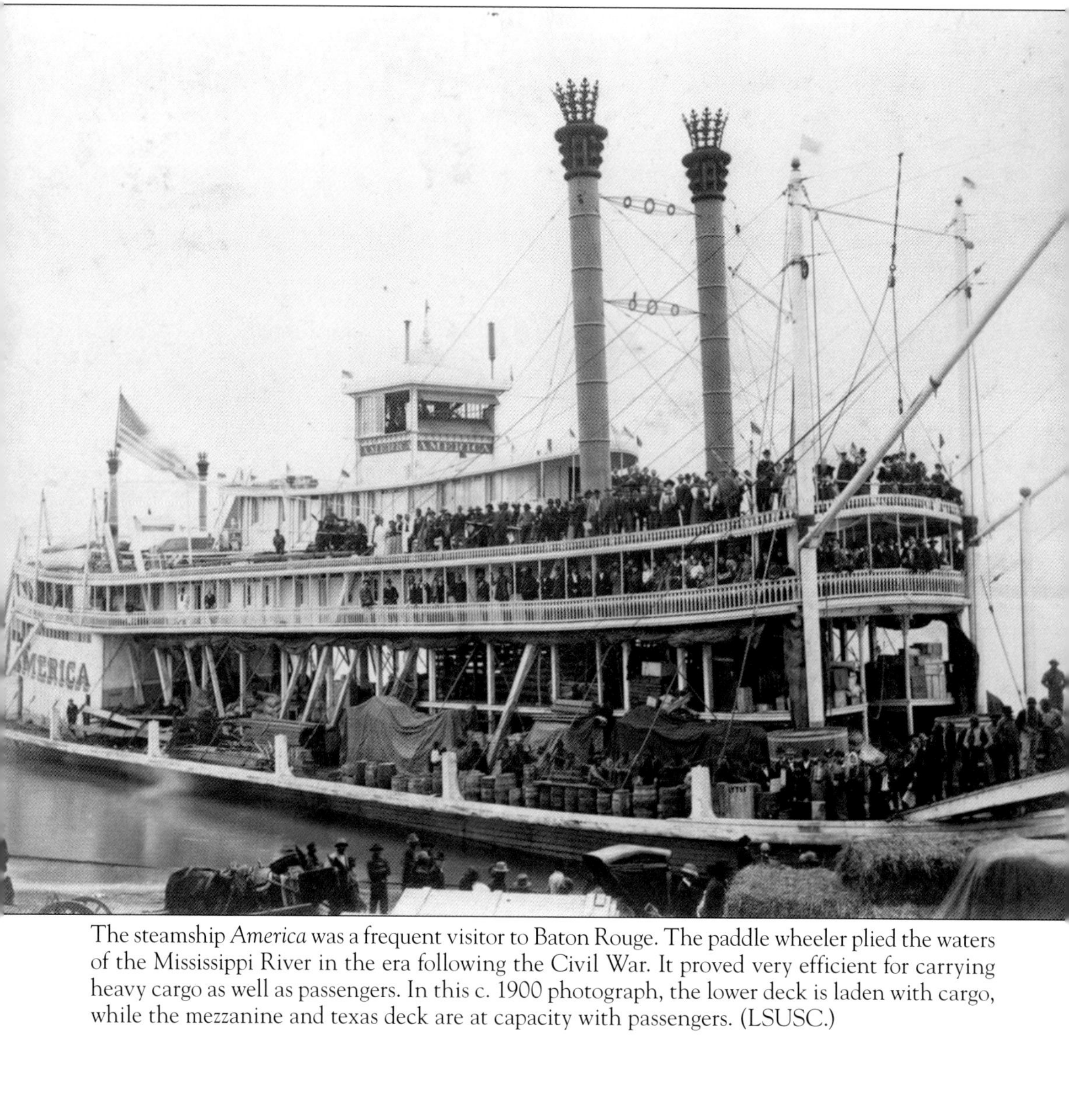

The steamship *America* was a frequent visitor to Baton Rouge. The paddle wheeler plied the waters of the Mississippi River in the era following the Civil War. It proved very efficient for carrying heavy cargo as well as passengers. In this c. 1900 photograph, the lower deck is laden with cargo, while the mezzanine and texas deck are at capacity with passengers. (LSUSC.)

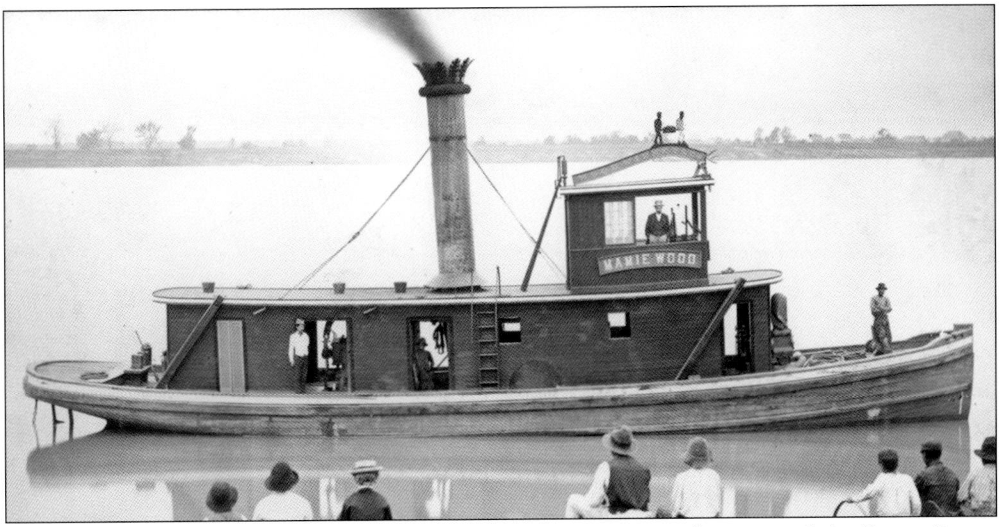

The *Mamie Wood*, a tugboat of the Wood, Widney & Company fleet, served the Baton Rouge area and port around 1890 to 1910. The service company was located on Front Street between Convention Street and North Boulevard, where the boats conveyed coal from barges to railroad cars. (LSUSC.)

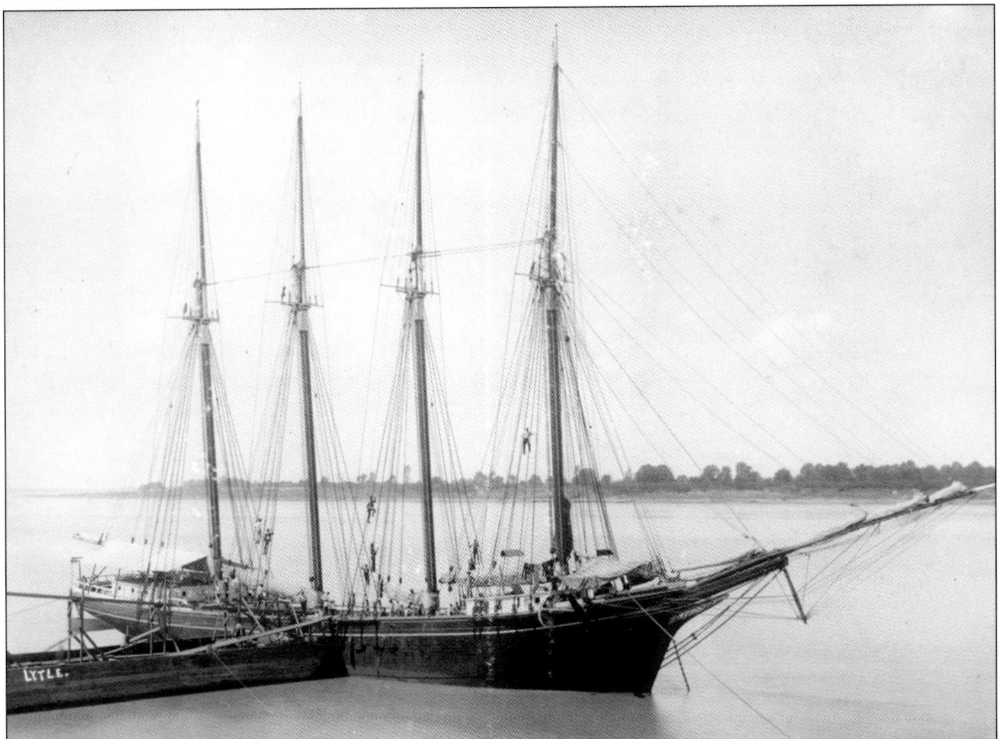

The four-mast schooner *Fanny Arthur* was moored at the docks of one of Baton Rouge's saw mills. The 171-foot-long, American-built vessel was laid down at Camden, Maine, in 1891, for Peter B. Reed. The ship was abandoned by its crew on December 14, 1898, after departing Turk's Island on its journey to Philadelphia, Pennsylvania. (LSUSC.)

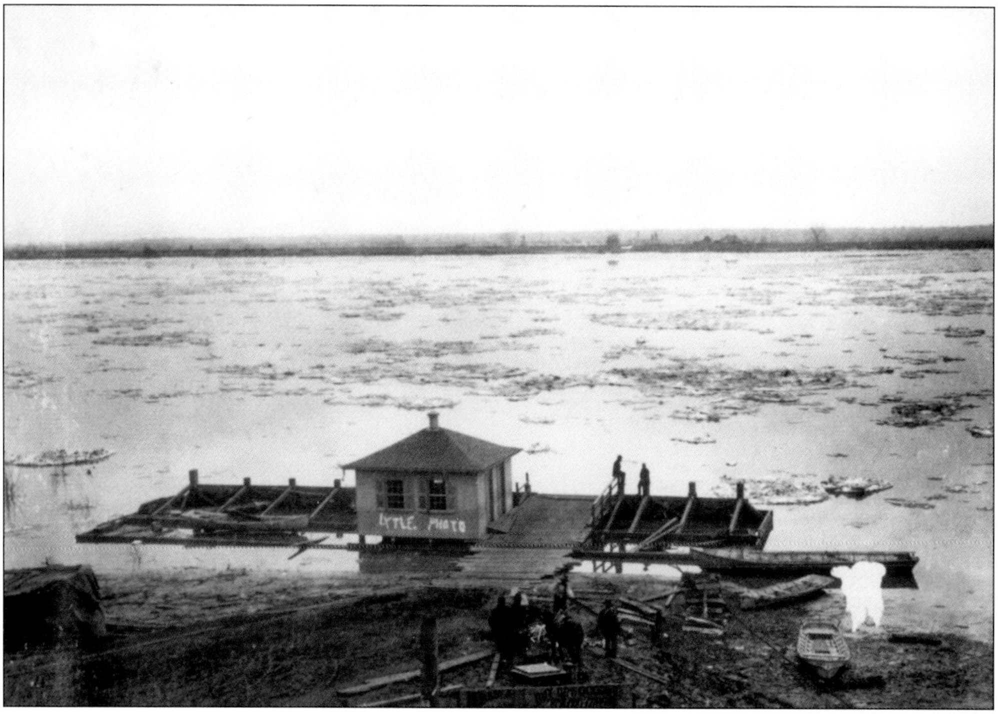

This photograph, taken by Andrew Lytle, features a rare occurrence of ice floating down the Mississippi River at Baton Rouge following a harsh winter. Large chunks of ice were particularly hazardous to riverboats with paddle wheels and wooden hulls. (LSUSC.)

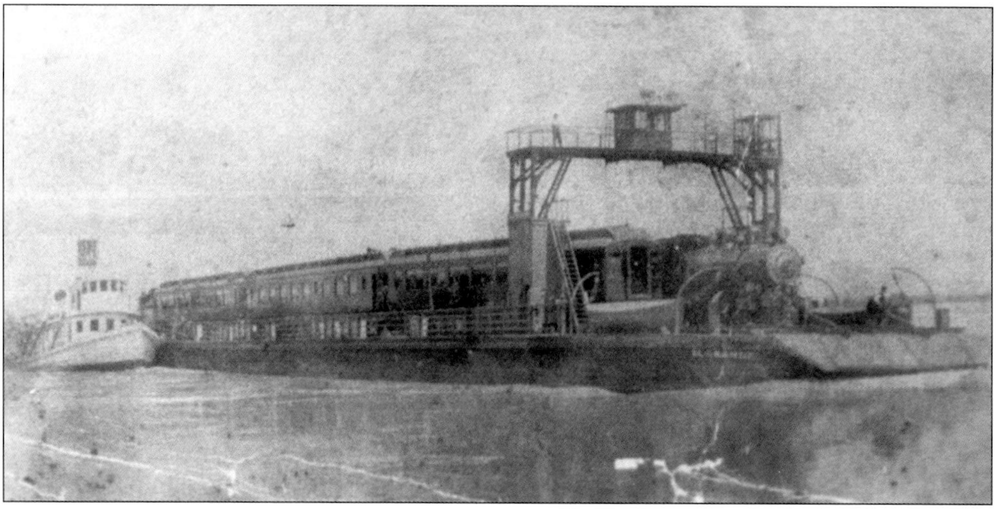

Railroad passengers had to disembark at a railroad depot on the Port Allen side of the river, board a ferryboat in order to cross the Mississippi River, and again board a train at the depot on the Baton Rouge side of the river. Missouri Pacific locomotives, passenger cars, and boxcars crossed the Mississippi River by a specially constructed ferry boat or train ferry from 1909 to 1947. This photograph of a train ferry was taken around 1909. The Huey P. Long Bridge at Baton Rouge was later built and completed in August 1940. The bridge was constructed to carry automobiles and trains. (SLL.)

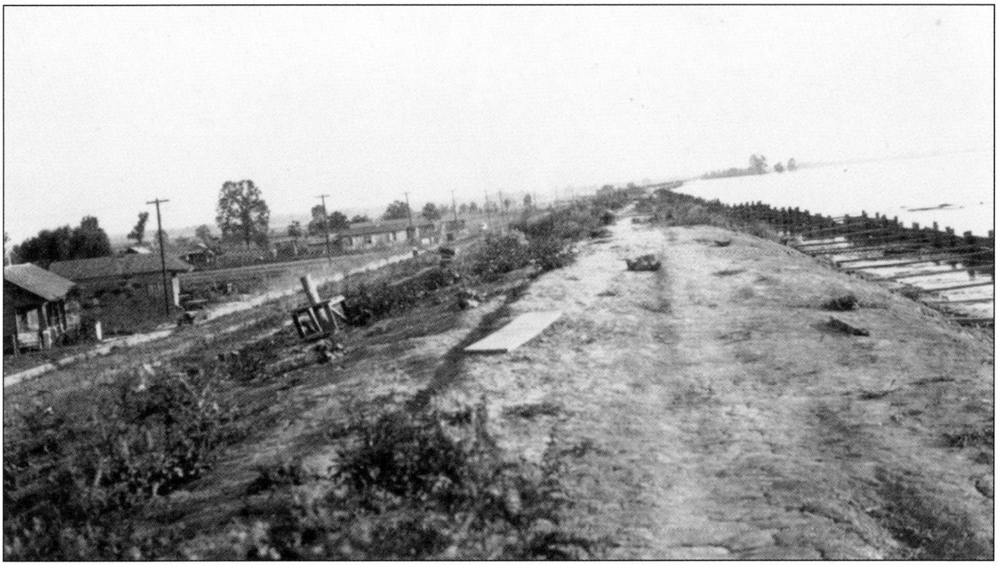

When water began rising on the Mississippi River in 1927, every available method was attempted to impede the forces placed on the man-made levee. Prison labor was employed to raise the levee or build wooden revetments to prevent damage to the fragile earthen levee. (SLL.)

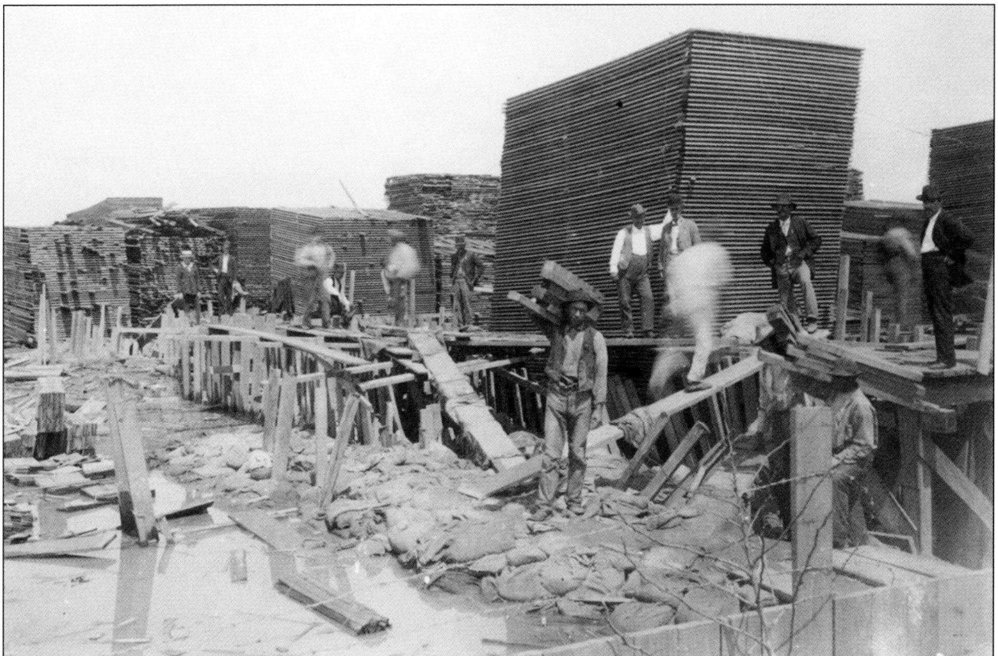

The Burton Lumber Company was established around 1885 with mills in Baton Rouge and Burtville. The owner, Capt. William L. Burton, was a pioneer in lumbering cypress throughout the South. The company was located on the 700 block of Natchez Street, now River Road, and nestled between the railroad and the riverbank. The mill extended from South Boulevard to near France Street. In this photograph, employees of the company are shown sandbagging areas near the sawmill in an effort to prevent the 1912 floodwaters from carrying valuable lumber downriver. (LSUSC.)

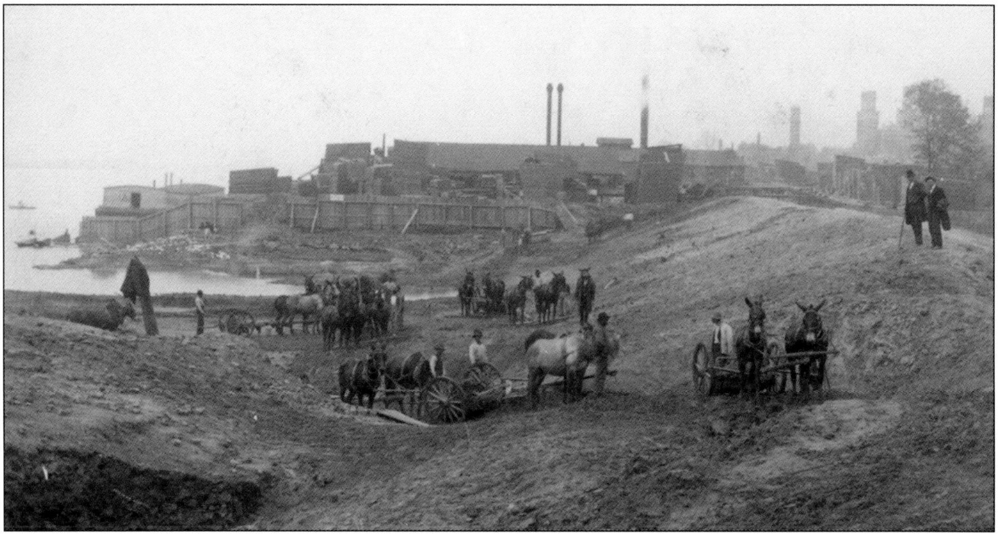

Around the turn of the 20th century, meaningful attempts were made in raising levees well in advance of annual high-water levels on the Mississippi River. The levee under construction in this photograph is in south Baton Rouge in the vicinity of Europe and France Streets. (LSUSC.)

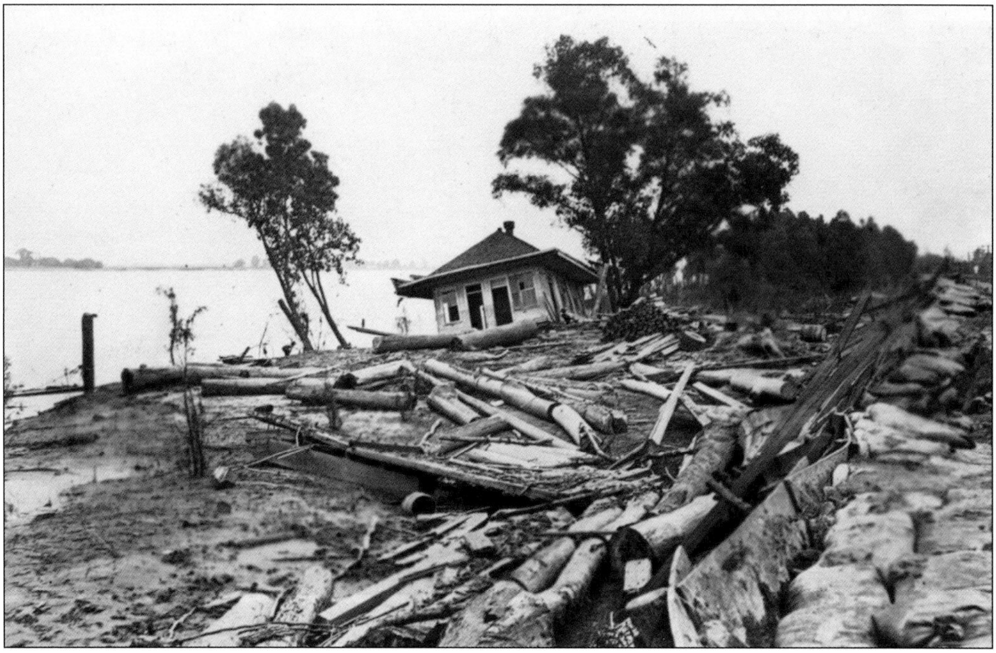

A combination of high water on the Mississippi, Ohio, Cumberland, and Tennessee Rivers was the culprit of the 1912 flood. The high water of 1912 placed great force on meager levees at Baton Rouge, but they held. The waters only topped the levees, allowing the city to escape extensive damage. Baton Rouge suffered its greatest damage along the riverfront. Waters rose on University Lake (later Capitol Lake) and impeded the City Belt Line trolley cars from passage on rails near Main and Tenth Streets. In this photograph, floodwaters have receded, leaving tangled debris and destruction. Visible on the right is the Yazoo and Mississippi Valley Railroad adjacent to the poorly constructed levee running along the riverfront in Baton Rouge. Holmes & Barnes, Ltd. Wholesalers was located adjacent to the railroad to the right and out of the frame. (POVPC.)

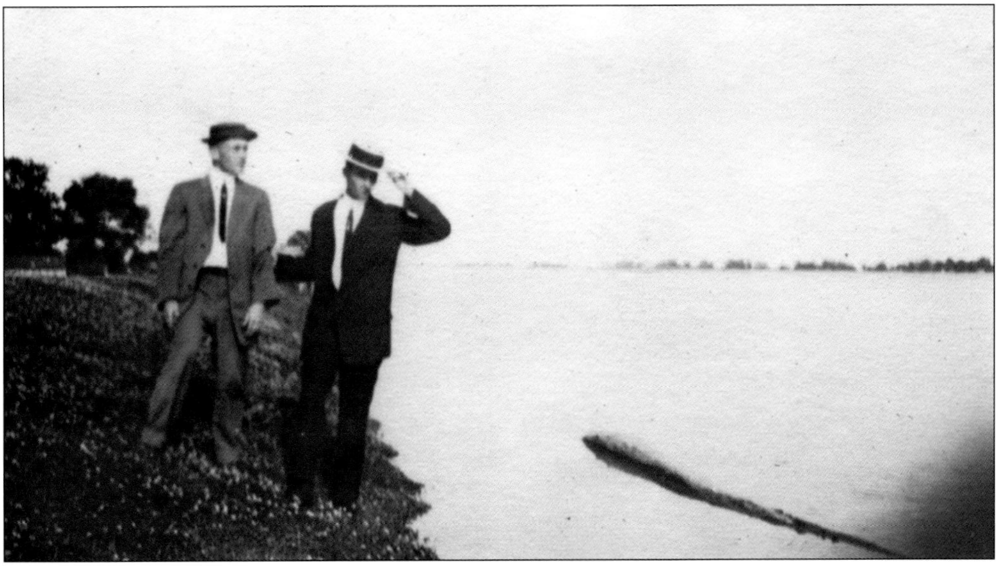

Hart brothers Jesse A. (left) and William B. closely examine the rising Mississippi River in the spring of 1912. The river topped the levee in some areas and was approximately one mile wide downriver from Baton Rouge. The flood caused widespread devastation in Louisiana and displaced more than 60,000 people. Approximately half of the refugees evacuated to Baton Rouge. (POVPC.)

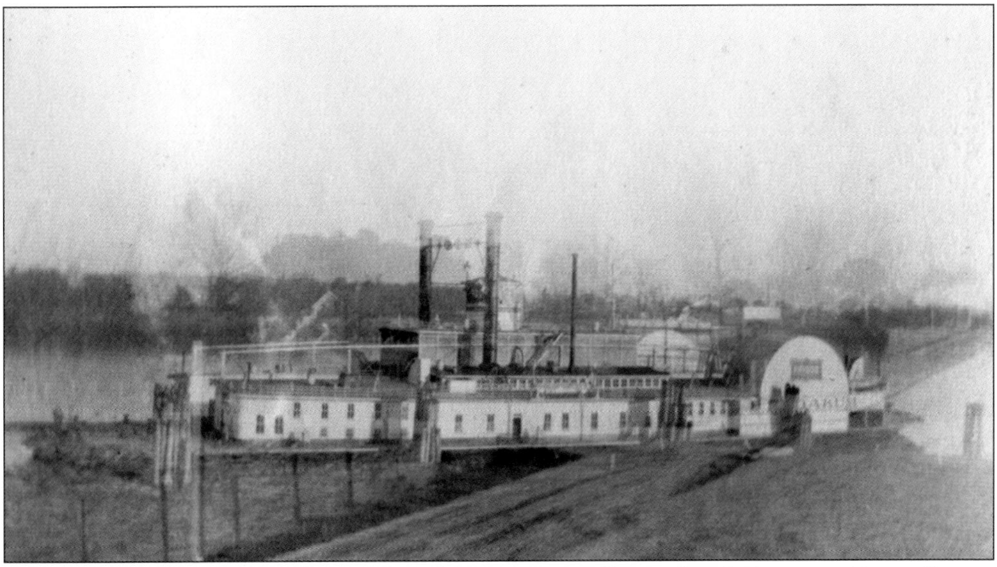

Baton Rouge was served by the Yazoo and Mississippi Valley Railroad Company; Baton Rouge, Hammond and Eastern Railroad; Southern Pacific Railroad; and the Frisco Railroad. The Grosse Tete–Opelousas Railroad, Southern Pacific Railroad, and Frisco Railroad also operated transfers for passenger and freight trains between North Baton Rouge and Anchorage, Louisiana. Anchorage was the place name for a community north of Port Allen where the steamboat landing and railroad terminal connected. (EBRPL.)

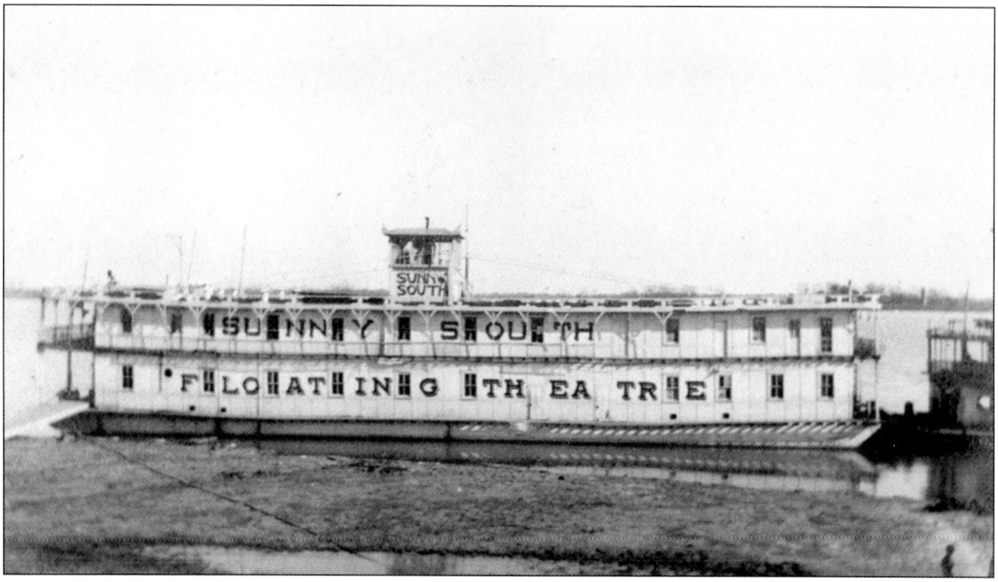

By the 1910s, popularity of the automobile and motion pictures had nearly pushed showboats to extinction. However, a surge in showboat entertainment came when entrepreneurs brought larger, decorative, and elaborately designed boats that had everything that could be found in land-based theatres. In this 1914 image, the *Sunny South Floating Theatre* is shown moored at Baton Rouge. Other showboats of the era included the *Golden Rod*, *Cotton Blossom*, and the *New Showboat*. (EBRPL.)

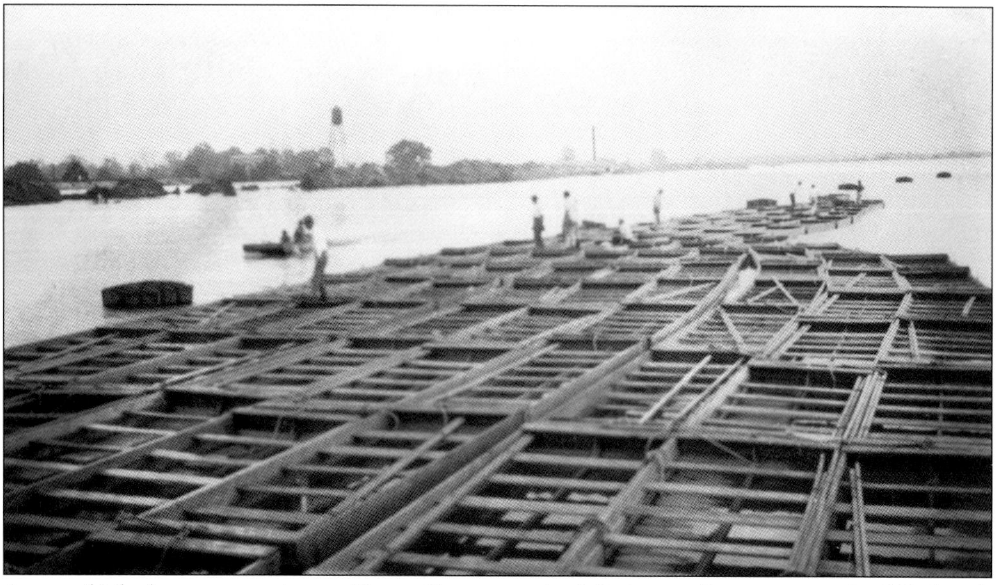

A sea of johnboats moored near Baton Rouge on the Mississippi River wait to be filled with emergency supplies during the 1927 flood. The American Red Cross coordinated efforts with the US Coast Guard to deliver emergency supplies to devastated communities throughout southwest Louisiana. (SLL.)

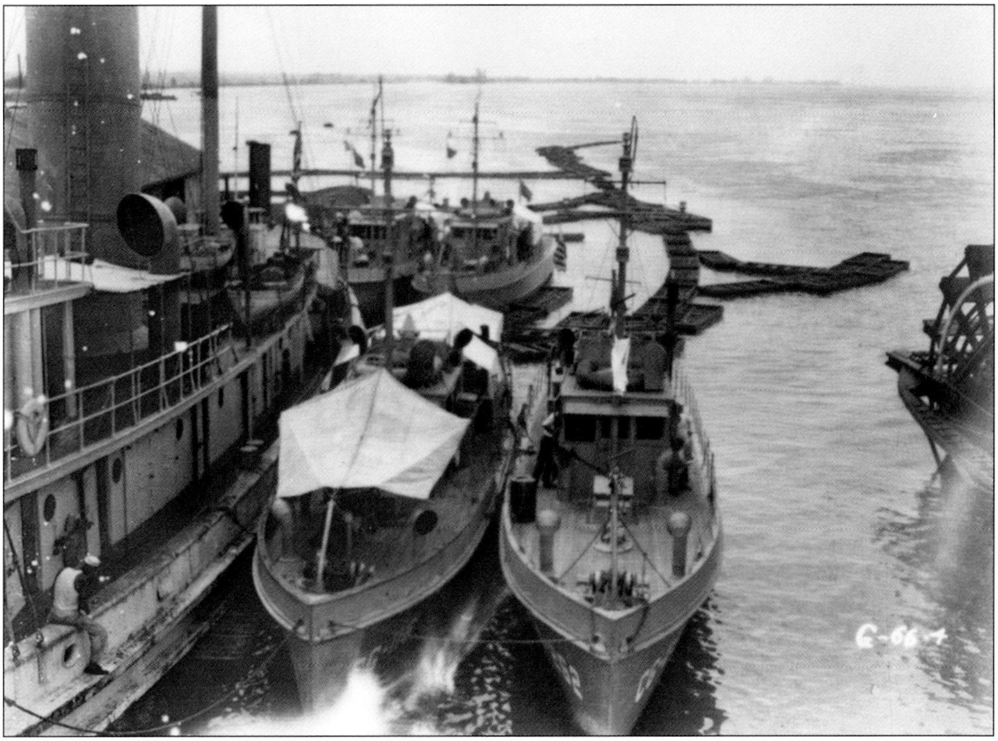

Practically every type of boat imaginable was employed to assist in relief work during the flood of 1927. In this photograph, US Coast Guard vessels tow dozens of johnboats to distribution points up and down the river for reloading of emergency supplies. (SLL.)

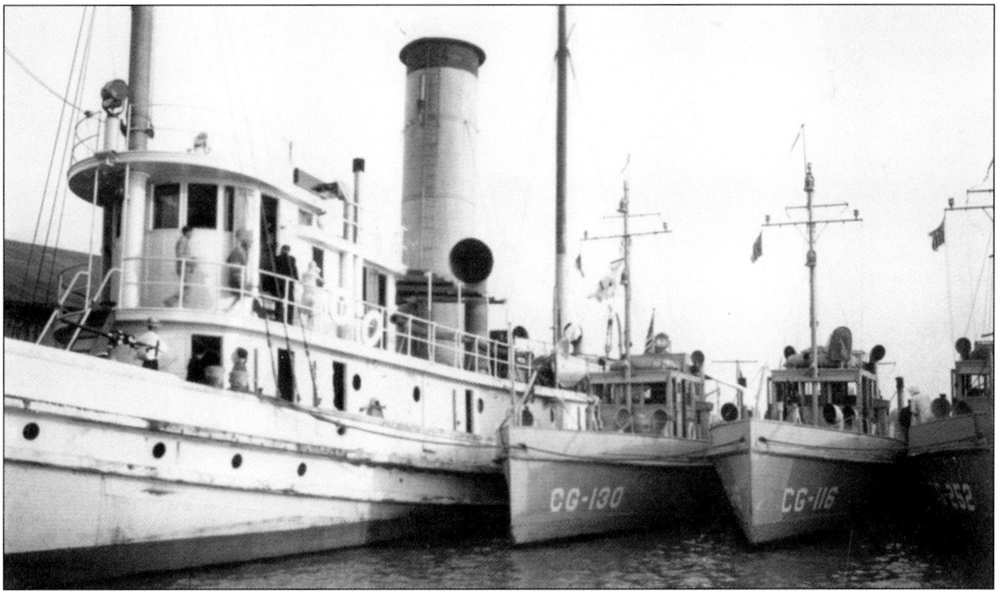

The Coast Guard brought every available craft to the region during the 1927 flood. The Coast Guard tenders, cutters, and patrol boats shown here are being readied for the next mission on the Mississippi River. The Coast Guard deployed 128 vessels in relief operations and removed thousands of persons and livestock from perilous positions to places of safety. (SLL.)

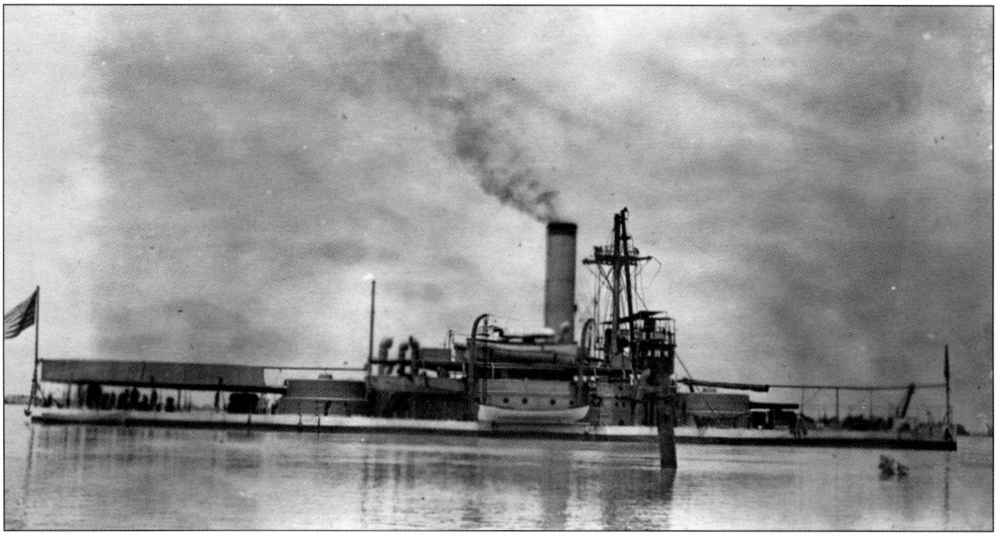

In 1912, the USS *Amphitrite*, an iron-hulled, light-draft, coastal-defense monitor of the US Navy, temporarily moored at Baton Rouge. She was commissioned in 1895, mainly for training. Later assigned to duty in 1897, she saw limited action near Cuba, Puerto Rico, and Key West during the Spanish-American War. She participated in the bombardment of San Juan on May 12, 1898. Between 1901 and 1919, she served as a training ship for reservists at various ports, including St. Louis. She was reassigned to train gun captains at New Orleans. The ship was eventually sold into private ownership in 1920 and used as a floating hotel and gambling casino, a government barracks in North Carolina, and a restaurant and hotel in Maryland in 1950. It was sold for scrap in 1952. (POVPC.)

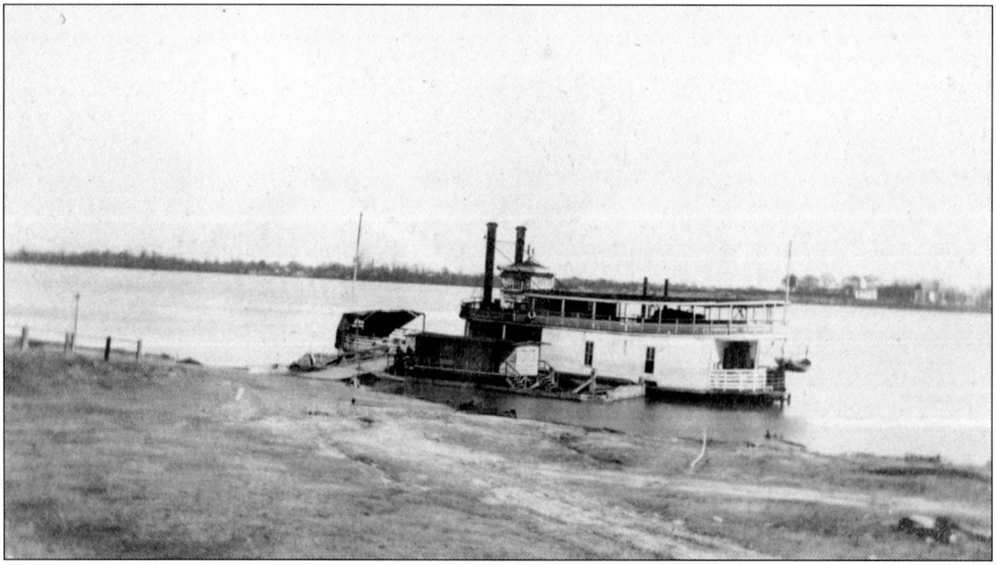

This photograph of an unidentified boat at Baton Rouge shows one of many ferry conveyances that provided transportation to people traveling across the Mississippi River between the 1820s and 1960s. The only way a person could cross the river before 1940 was by ferryboat, which transported automobiles, train cars, and pedestrians from Baton Rouge to Port Allen. The Huey P. Long Bridge was the first bridge in Baton Rouge. It was opened in 1940 and allowed crossing of automobiles and locomotives concurrently. (EBRPL.)

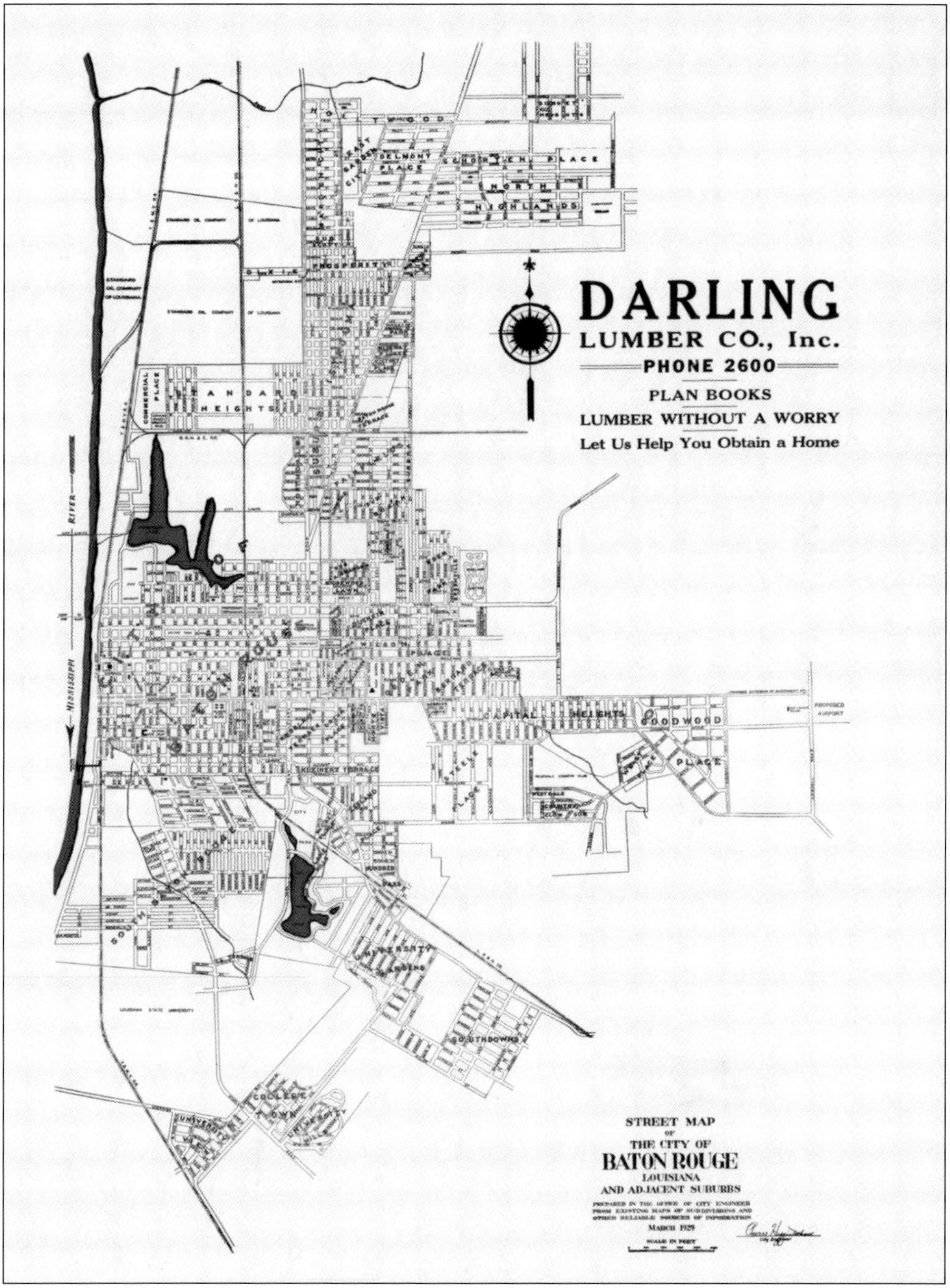

The population of Baton Rouge grew from approximately 10,400 in 1890 to 30,700 in 1930. This 1929 city map of Baton Rouge convincingly depicts Standard Oil Company and Louisiana State University's influence on the city's north and south residential growth. (CBR.)

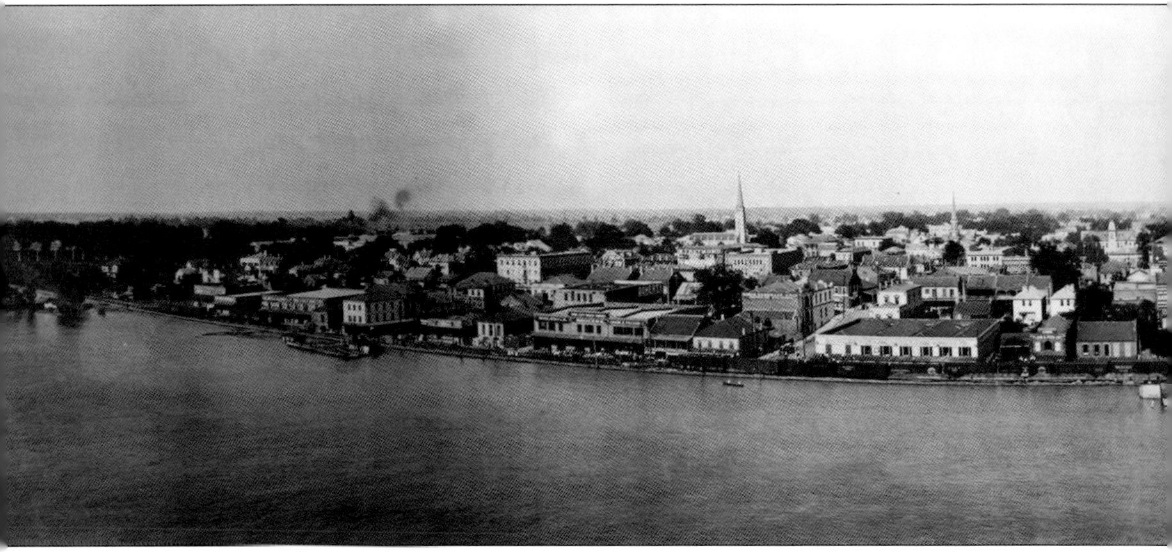

In 1912, the population of Baton Rouge was approaching 14,000. The early 20th century was marked by dramatic improvements, as Mayor Robert A. Hart pushed for approval of bond issues securing brick-and-mortar projects. His ambition to improve health and living conditions included expansion of an existing sewer system, waterworks, electrical services, a school system, hard-surface

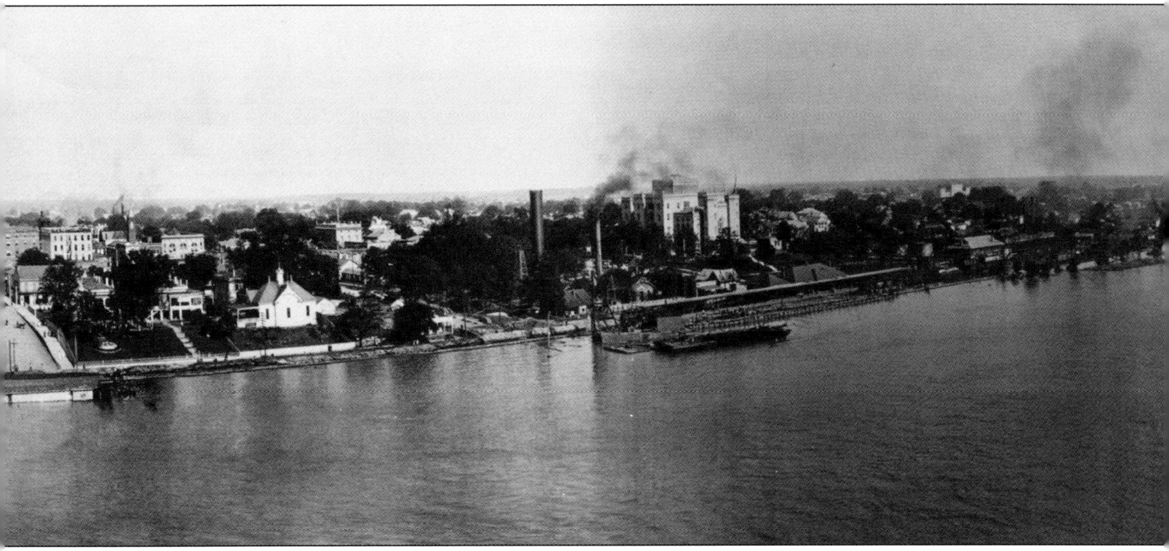

streets, and public buildings. Jasper Ewing snapped this photograph of the busy city from the highest point on the USS *Nebraska* with an objective of capturing high water levels of the 1912 flood but also chronicling the immense progress of the city of Baton Rouge. (JES.)

Bibliography

Carleton, Mark T. *River Capital: An Illustrated History of Baton Rouge*. Revised ed. Tarzana, CA: American Historical Press, 1996.
Cowen, Barry. *Louisiana State University*. Charleston, SC: Arcadia Publishing, 2013.
Martin, Mark E. *Historic Photos of Baton Rouge*. Nashville, TN: Turner Publishing Company, 2008.
Martin, Mark E., ed. *Andrew D. Lytle's Baton Rouge: Photographs, 1863–1910*. Baton Rouge: Louisiana State University Press, 2008.
Rodrigue, Sylvia Frank, and Faye Phillips. *Baton Rouge*. Charleston, SC: Arcadia Publishing, 2008.
Ruffin, Thomas F. *Under Stately Oaks: A Pictorial History of LSU*. Baton Rouge: Louisiana State University Press, 2002.
Insurance Maps of Baton Rouge, Louisiana. Sanborn Maps Company, 1908, 1911.
Muse, E.M., ed., *Elks' Souvenir of Baton Rouge*. Baton Rouge: self-published, 1901.
The Gumbo, 1900–1930, Louisiana State Archives.
The Reveille, Baton Rouge, 1912.

INDEX

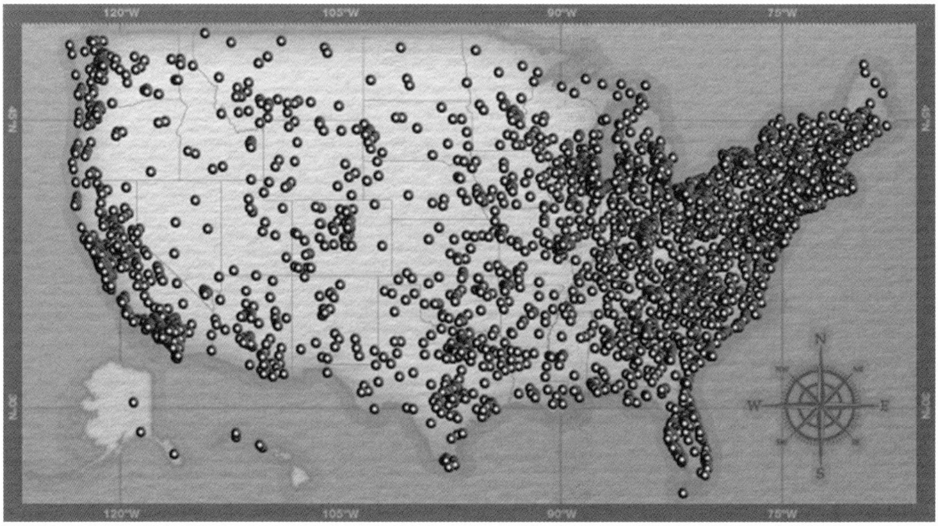